Creating Value for Customers

Creating Value for
Customers

*Designing and Implementing a Total
Corporate Strategy*

William A. Band

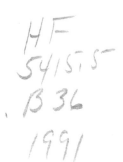

John Wiley & Sons, Inc.

New York • Chichester • Brisbane • Toronto • Singapore

Published by John Wiley & Sons, Inc.

Library of Congress Cataloging-in-Publication Data

Band, William.
    Creating value for customers : designing and implementing a total corporate strategy / by William A. Band.
       p.   cm.
    Includes index.
    ISBN 0-471-52593-6 (cloth)
    1. Customer service. 2. Customer satisfaction. 3. Quality assurance.   I. Title.
HF5415.5.B36   1991
658.8'12—dc20   90-48557

Preface

I wrote this book because I have become convinced that North American businesses face challenges that will require radical new ways for managing successfully in the 1990s. A management revolution is gathering momentum across the North American continent. Those who join the revolution will be swept to success. Those who cling to old ways will be swept aside. The slogans that have become the rallying cries for the revolution are reaching a crescendo—"customer satisfaction," "customer service excellence," "customer focus," and "total quality management." Common to all these management approaches is an emerging consensus among leading organizations that they must put one strategy ahead of all other priorities—*to continuously increase value to customers.*

Without customers there is no business. Without value there is no sustainable reason for customers to choose your organization over the increasingly large number of competitors that crowd into every sector of the marketplace. This book will tell why customer value creation is vital for business success and teach you how to transform your organization into a high-value-delivering enterprise. You will learn from case study examples of industry leaders who are now pioneering the new approaches for becoming increasingly valued by their customers.

Hardly a week goes by without a new book, seminar, or article preaching the need for today's business (and, indeed, government and other not-for-profit) organizations to become more "customer-focused." Seasoned observers of the business scene have argued that this requirement has always been critical to competitive success. In the early 1960s, Theodore Levitt, a leading professor at the Harvard Business School, was reminding business executives that they must "view an industry as a customer-satisfying process, not a goods-producing process. An industry begins with a customer and his needs, not with a patent, a raw material or a selling skill."

"So what's new?" you may ask. "Our company has always taken pride in its quality, service, and concern for customers." What's new is that a new philosophy of management is emerging, a new paradigm for coping with the increasingly bruising competition for scarce and demanding customers in the globalizing world marketplace. We are moving from an era of functional specialization to an era of integration. From individual management "heroes" to high performing teams. From managing tasks to managing business processes. From trying to find "breakthrough" solutions to focusing on continuous improvement achieved through many small steps. The purpose of this book is to help your organization make the transition from the "vision" of being a more customer-driven organization to the "reality" of continuous customer value improvement.

Why is this way of thinking only now becoming recognized as the engine of business success? Mostly because of economic change. In the early 1970s, new factors began to appear in the healthy markets that had been fueling the profits of North American business since the end of World War II. Among the new challenges were globalizing competition, more demanding customers, deregulation, rapid technological change, and a work force insisting on greater involvement in, and meaning from, their work and careers.

In the 1980s, business executives started to wake up to the fact that they would have to change their ways in order to stay competitive in the new environment. "We must become more customer-driven," they said. Business leaders discovered (or perhaps rediscovered) the need for "total customer satisfaction," "customer service excellence," and, more recently, "total quality management." However, by focusing on quality and service, businesses did not always take into account exactly what kinds of quality and service represented true value to their customers. Executives who got "customer religion" during the 1980s sometimes failed to remember that quality and service are the means, but *value for the customer* is the end.

Early initiatives for improving customer satisfaction were also usually taken in isolation. There was no common "quality and service management language" and this often acted as a barrier to integrated change. This is still the case in most companies today. Different parts of the firm have the skills and understanding needed to make improvements, but each filters the problem through its own experience and biases. By taking a close look at the different quality management techniques, customer satisfaction and service approaches that have been evolving in the specialty areas of marketing, operations, and human resources functions, I hope to break down the "language barrier" by providing managers with an overview of what is happening in other functional areas.

I have written this book not so much to introduce new ideas about quality and service management as to draw together in one place the main tools and approaches for value creation and to give senior executives and top-level managers a reliable road map for strategic change.

Value creation is not going to happen overnight. Like any creation, it is a process and a journey. It will take inspiration, hard work, and time to change the way your organization goes about its business. Change requires leadership. It is a personal challenge for everyone reading this book. But, as John F. Kennedy once said, "If not us, who? If not now, when?"

WILLIAM A. BAND

Toronto, Ontario
March 1991

Acknowledgments

The first lesson I quickly learned while writing this book is that it was going to be impossible to finish alone. It takes the time, and talent, of many people to successfully complete a book. I am indebted to numerous friends and business acquaintances for their unselfish support of my efforts.

The idea for the book began as a result of the urgings of John Dill, president of John Wiley & Sons Canada Limited. He immediately put me in touch with his company's able and enthusiastic vice-president of the Professional, Reference, and Trade Division, Julia Woods. John and Julia, in turn, introduced me to John Mahaney, a senior editor at Wiley, who professionally guided me through the manuscript development process. Many thanks to these three for their unflagging support.

This book builds upon and synthesizes many ideas of other writers, consultants, and practitioners in the fields of quality management, service, and customer satisfaction. I have tried to acknowledge my sources clearly throughout the text, and in the endnotes. Credit is due to these many leaders in their respective disciplines. Errors and omissions are my own.

I am also, of course, grateful to my clients, who have helped me shape and refine my ideas about customer value creation. Coopers & Lybrand's policy of confidential client relationships prevents me from identifying many of the most important contributors. In no case does this book contain data that have not been obtained from public sources, or that have not been modified to prevent the identification of a Coopers & Lybrand client.

Many of my colleagues within Coopers & Lybrand, both in the United States and in Canada, have contributed to the ideas presented in the book. Several were generous enough to review early drafts of specific chapters and to offer their suggestions for improvement. Thanks to

Doug Cudlip, Jim Keyser, Don Irwin, and Richard Huot. As well, the support staff at Coopers & Lybrand in Toronto suffered cheerfully through typing endless drafts of the manuscript, which proceeded under the able direction of our editor, David McClellan.

The real "heart" of the book writing team included Anita McCallum and Susan Lipsey, who did much of the research work. I am also indebted to the editorial support provided by Rhonda Malomet, and especially Kathryn Dean, who labored mightily to give my dull prose a style that is much more readable and engaging.

To finish a project of this nature also requires emotional support from important friends who believe in your ideas. I have already mentioned Anita McCallum, who not only did research, but also was my personal "cheerleader" from start to finish. I would also like to acknowledge John Farrow, the partner responsible for Coopers & Lybrand's consulting practice in Toronto, who has unselfishly supported my professional and personal development during the last decade.

Last, but most important, for her tolerance and understanding when I was writing instead of attending to her needs, I thank my wife, Charlene.

Contents

1

Value Creation: The State of the Art

The key to long-term success in business is what it has always been: to invest, to innovate, to lead, to create value where none existed before.

William J. Abernathy and Robert Hayes

"Total quality management," "customer service excellence," "customer satisfaction"—these were the rallying cries of leading companies in the late 1980s, and they promise to transform the way we do business in the 1990s. Today, more than ever before, enterprises must create value for their customers in a way that is demonstrably superior to that of their competitors if they hope to survive the sweeping upheavals now shaking the foundations of business management.

Since the Japanese conquest of many North American markets, companies all over the continent have been looking for ways to regain their former positions of strength. Customer-driven strategy, employee empowerment, and product and service excellence have become boardroom bywords, and advertisers have been quick to get in on the act. Slogans such as Canadian Airlines' "You're Looking at the Leading Edge of a Service Revolution" are shifting the spotlight onto customers and their demand for excellence in products and services. To the extent that their publicity reflects reality, hotels are turning themselves inside out to give their customers the royal treatment, airlines never have a late flight, and quality is a way of life at all kinds of enterprises—from hamburger chains to car dealerships.

Service and product quality also get top billing among senior executives in some of the most prominent and successful companies in North America. In a recent *Fortune* article, John Yasinsky, executive vice-president for World Resources and Technology at Westinghouse Electric Corp., was quoted as saying, "In any major business that we're involved in, we're probably closer to our customers than any of our competitors." And Carl Arendt, marketing m nager for the Productivity and Quality Center at Westinghouse adds that, "By definition, bad quality is a waste of time." Quality, service, the customer comes first— these themes are echoed by executives in all kinds of businesses. Here's Mike Wright, CEO of Super Value Stores (the Minnesota-based grocery retailer that made it to number 3 in *Fortune*'s list of the largest diversified service companies): "You always put the interests of the customers first. You provide the services they want, then you find a way to manage the business to do it efficiently." And in a recent survey conducted by *Canadian Business* to discover the best-managed private companies in Canada, high-level executives from the firms that made it to the top 50 mentioned high-quality customer service more often than anything else as the key to their success.

BRAVE NEW WORLD OR IDIOT'S TALE?

In the increasingly globalized and uncertain markets of the coming years, this kind of commitment to service and quality is not just a nice frill; it is a necessity. As trade barriers fall and world financial markets remain uncertain, companies will be navigating on heavier seas than they have ever known before. Deregulation of industries such as banking—in Canada and the United States—has already resulted in hotter competition; and as more and more financial institutions start offering the same kinds of services, paying scrupulous attention to the needs of customers will be the only way for an individual company to gain a competitive edge.

To add to the stormy environment, aging and sometimes saturated markets, along with a decline in population growth, have resulted in lower demand. This will further intensify competition and push companies to seek the easy way out by opting for price cuts to hang on to increasingly scarce numbers of customers. However, this strategy, in the words of R.C. Inglis, president of the Toronto company Technalysis Inc.,

is nearly always a costly, futile exercise. A company may achieve short-term gains, but most of the time market shares are about the same after a price war as they were before. [Consequently,] if consumers think of products as "all about the same" and price is useful only as a short-term weapon, then customer service [along with product quality, we would add] is likely to be the main factor in deciding who gets the order.

At the same time, markets have become fragmented, and the demand for unique, customized products has increased. Global competitors are seeking ways to better meet the finely tuned needs of ever more specialized customer groups.

In the rapidly changing world of technology, product life cycles have become shorter and shorter, and companies will continue to have difficulty retaining their competitive advantage: Today's innovation will be tomorrow's clone. Furthermore, sophisticated consumers, who have suffered from planned obsolescence strategies and shoddy service for many years, are beginning to demand excellence before they put their money down. As William Davidow and Bro Uttal have pointed out in *Total Customer Service*, North American consumers are now richer and better educated than ever before, so they demand better treatment than consumers did in the past. Industrial customers are also more demanding because of global competition and greater rivalry among suppliers. Rushed two-career couples and baby boomers at the peak of their earning power are willing to pay good money for goods and services—but they want value in return. One analyst points out that this desire for "real, intrinsic" value, as opposed to the appearance of quality, may increase in the 1990s as baby boomers turn away from the yuppie excesses of the 1980s—the "badge value" of designer products and fast-lane living—and turn back to more conservative life-styles.

Laurel Cutler, vice-chairman of the New York advertising agency FCB/Leber Katz, writes that the consumer is going to "insist on making her own trade-offs, and what she's going to reject are manufacturers' compromises. . . . The consumer will want either the best, if it's in a category important to that consumer, or the cheapest of the good-enoughs. Pure value."

This all adds up to a business environment that may look more like a tale told by an idiot, full of sound and fury, than a brave new world. However, as RJR Nabisco's chairman Louis Gerstner has said, ". . . more than anything else . . . the world is going to become more competitive in an industrial, commercial sense. More competitive perhaps than we've seen in the history of modern economic society." Some enterprises will run aground as they try to navigate through the unfamiliar waters; others will find the channel markers and sail through; still others will find temporary haven in a market niche while the storm rages on. To come out on top, businesses will have to operate from strategies based on organizational flexibility, an unrelenting drive to create and deliver true value, and constant attention to the details of the customer's demands.

WHAT'S THE RECORD?

The need for creating and delivering superior value to customers is acute, and businesses across North America are at least beginning to pay lip service to the concept. But to what extent does the rhetoric match the reality? Well, here's one dose of reality (the name of the company is disguised, but the details are true):

It all began one Monday morning when an international trader ordered a sample of frozen shrimp from Brazil for a major Canadian supermarket chain. Since the shrimp was perishable, she took great pains to give instructions to the shipper in Brazil and the clearing agent in Canada to ensure that the shrimp was properly packed on dry ice and that it would not be shipped on the weekend (for fear that the shrimp might sit in the airport for two days and go bad). The shipment was due to arrive the next Thursday.

Thursday came, and the trader (let's call her Josephine) phoned the supermarket contact. "Did you get your shrimp shipment?" No, there was no shrimp in sight.

Friday, 9 A.M. There's still no sign of the shrimp at the supermarket, so Josephine phones the shipping company. "So what's the matter, lady?" says the man on the other end. "Your squid's going to come in any day now."

"Any day now? It was supposed to be delivered yesterday! You'd better trace it starting now! And it's shrimp, not squid!"

The shipper reluctantly does the tracing, but the shrimp cannot be found at any of the various points along the distribution route. "Maybe it'll show up later this afternoon," says the shipper, helpfully.

Friday, 1 P.M. Still no shrimp.

Friday, 3 P.M. *Still* no shrimp.

Friday, 5 P.M. Josephine calls the supervisor at the shipping company, who shows a modicum of concern but is at loss for a solution. Since the trader's office is about to close for the weekend, Josephine gives the supervisor her boss's address, so the shrimp can be sent there if it does show up on Saturday. She goes home assuming the case is solved.

Friday, 8 P.M. Josephine receives a phone call from her boss's wife, who is livid. "What are you doing to me?" she says. "I've got an airplane alternator sitting in a wooden crate on my living room floor packed in dry ice."

"What are you doing with an airplane alternator?" asks Josephine. The next day Josephine phones the shipping company again.

"Oh, yeah, the squid lady," the supervisor says when he comes to consciousness. "You got your squid, eh?"

"It's not squid. It's *shrimp*, and I *got* an airplane alternator packed in dry ice."

"Where'd you get that from?"

"You tell me."

"How come they packed it in dry ice?"

"You tell *me*," says Josephine. "All I want to know is where's my shrimp?"

"It was delivered yesterday."

"No it wasn't. You delivered an airplane alternator and it's sitting on my boss's living room floor."

The supervisor makes some less-than-sincere apology, and says he can't have the alternator picked up and taken away because it's Saturday.

Monday, 5 P.M. The alternator has still not been picked up . . . and so on for the rest of the week.

Wednesday, 7 P.M. Josephine drops by her boss's house to look at the alternator and try to find out who it was supposed to be for. She looks through the packing slip and finds the name of the airline that ordered it.

Thursday, 9 A.M. Josephine phones the airline and tells them she has their alternator.

"What are you doing with our alternator?"

"I don't know," says Josephine. "I ordered shrimp!"

"Well, you'd better call the shipping company and get them to send it over to us on the double. Do you realize how much it costs us to wait for a missing part?"

Josephine phones the courier again: "I've got this $15,000 alternator sitting in my boss's living room, and we're going to put it in the garbage if you don't come and pick it up."

"Why don't you give it back? It doesn't belong to you."

"What do you mean? We've been asking you to pick it up for a week. And we want to be reimbursed for our shrimp shipment."

"Lady, we delivered your squid; we've got the receipt."

Friday. *Mirabile dictu*, the shipper goes to the boss's house and picks up the alternator. "How come they packed it in dry ice?" he asks when he sees the crate in the middle of the living-room floor.

The trading company never *was* reimbursed for the missing shipment; and, as for the shrimp, it was neither seen nor heard of, though the trader thinks it may have been eaten somewhere along the distribution route. Needless to say, the trader never used the services of that shipper again.

This is only a single case, of course, but we have all had such experiences; and whenever we recount them, there are groans of recognition all round. Episodes such as this are not isolated occurrences; they are symptomatic of a wide gap between value *rhetoric* and real-life value *delivery*.

Studies in both the United States and Canada would seem to suggest that North American businesses have a long way to go before they are perceived as consistent value deliverers. In the United States, 15 percent of the respondents to a 1988 survey conducted jointly by Gallup and the American Society for Quality Control (ASQC) "could not think of a single company whose name they associate[d] with high quality." According to the same survey, 61 percent of American customers reported having experience with exceptionally poor quality (as opposed to 51 percent in a similar survey in 1985). Just over half of these disgruntled customers complained to the offending companies; and of these, 28 percent were not satisfied with the result.

In Canada, the Better Business Bureau reported in 1989 that "customers are just as dissatisfied as they ever were, and often just as badly treated." From 1981 to 1989, consumer complaints at the Toronto bureau increased 50 percent, and complaint cases that ended in arbitration or mediation increased over 300 percent. Reflecting the shift from a manufacturing-based economy to one dominated by services, 26 percent of the complaints received by the BBB were about defective merchandise, while 74 percent were about "defective services." The relatively low percentage of product complaints may not reflect higher-quality manufacture: Many machine parts that were repaired in the past are now simply thrown away and replaced—in spite of the obvious environmental damage this causes. The fact remains, however, that there were more BBB customer complaints about service than about products.

These were the kinds of things Toronto customers complained about:

- Not fulfilling the contract
- Nondelivery or slow delivery
- Ineffective guarantee
- Misrepresentation
- Products or services not as advertised
- Rude, evasive, and unconscientious behavior

Poor service has become such a phenomenon in North America that it has been the subject of many a newspaper article. In a 1988 issue of the *Toronto Star,* one reporter lamented the passing of the days of "real" service:

> [A]n overwhelming number of Canadians believe the real disappearing act these days has been pulled by an old stalwart of our consumer society—service.
>
> It left for lunch one day 10 or 15 years ago and hasn't been seen since.
>
> "Sales people are generally less courteous, less concerned than they once were," says [Sally] Hall, president of the Consumers' Association of Canada.
>
> "Something that really bothers people is having a 'customer service' person tell them they'll call them back, and then never calling," said Marilyn Anderson, who runs Star Probe, the *Star's* consumer help column. "People feel they're getting the runaround."
>
> One frustrated consumer notes that most businesses won't take a personal check any longer. It's either cash or credit card.
>
> That personal touch is gone, laments another, recalling how she got a call not from a person, but a computer, telling her that her . . . [department store] account was past due.
>
> All of this makes people, especially those of the older generation, long for the days when . . . [t]he milkman would deliver milk and eggs and maybe even a hearty "good morning." The breadman would drop off a loaf of your choice; the butcher would stop by with a fresh cut of beef; and to keep it all cold, the iceman would come with huge blocks of ice.

"People were so polite. . . . My mother remembers when [the Canadian department store] Eaton's would even park your car," says Hall.

This longing for the consideration and courtesy of bygone years comes through just as clearly in the results of the 1988 ASQC/Gallup survey of American consumers. When respondents were asked what they considered to represent high quality in services, the characteristics most frequently mentioned were: "courtesy, promptness, a basic sense that one's needs [were] being satisfied, and the attitude of the service provider." In other words, "American consumers are not expecting accuracy and convenience so much as they are saying, 'treat us nicely.'"

WHY THE GAP?

If North American companies are so aware of the need to deliver high-quality products and service, why are most of them failing so miserably at the task? The problem is largely strategic. Here is a breakdown of some of the most common company practices and realities that have eroded the delivery of true value for customers:

1. *Internal focus.* In recent years, executives have been most concerned about being the "right size" or having the "right technology" or becoming the "lowest-cost producer," all too often overlooking their most important competitive weapon—their customers. In other words, companies have been looking *in* instead of *out*.

2. *Technology fever.* There has also been a preoccupation with inventing new products and services—especially in the area of new technology—going on the assumption that "if you make a better mousetrap, the world will beat a path to your door." Although this philosophy held true in the past, the rapid pace of technological change has reduced the ability to create long-term competitive advantage through new-product development alone.

3. *Government protection.* Firms faced with hot competition have often lobbied for government protection rather than looking for ways to change their organizations in the light of customer demands. But, as management consultant Milind Lele has pointed out, if there is a market worth having, competitors will find a way around the regulations.

4. *Cutting back for profits in a deregulated environment.* In the wake of deregulation in the financial sector and other industries, some companies have cut back on service to increase profits, either by charging fees for services that did not formerly have charges or by eliminating standard services. In other cases, companies faced with stiffer competition have cut back on employee orientation and training programs—with predictable results for the delivery of quality service.

5. *Short-term economics.* William Davidow and Bro Uttal comment that the inflation of the late 1970s, foreign competition in the 1980s, and the constant threat of takeovers meant that managers are trying, even more than before, to cut costs and make sure short-term results look good. Activities that could lead to great customer satisfaction are often cut out, since the profit value of these activities is difficult to judge except in the long term.

6. *Misapplied technology.* The introduction of time- and labor-saving technology to cut costs has resulted in an increasingly impersonal environment, in the service industries at least. Just as customers have begun to demand high levels of personal services, their desires are being thwarted by well intentioned, but misguided, applications of technology.

7. *Overzealous portfolio management and expansion.* The senior managers of some enterprises have concentrated on manipulating their firms' investment portfolios rather than personally taking charge of reorganizing their businesses to make them more agile competitors.

8. *Management not sold on the idea.* As Karl Albrecht, coauthor of *At America's Service,* has said, "Organizations typically start to turn on only when their senior management groups "grok" (in the words of science fiction writer Robert Heinlein) the idea that there is money to be made in doing right by the customer." Obviously North American businesses still have a lot of grokking to do.

9. *No solution in sight.* Some managers are sold on the idea that companies have to become more customer-focused, but they do not know how to find problem areas in their own operations or they do not know how to solve the problems they have identified.

10. *Change is slow.* Even the best intentioned turnarounds can take a long time in organizations that are weighed down with a slow-moving bureaucratic structure.

11. *Company organization and resource allocation often betray a "lip service" approach to delivering value.* John Goodman, president of the Technical Assistance Research Program (TARP), has estimated that 60 percent of the quality improvement programs in the United States don't go beyond lip service. For a program such as this to succeed, it must embrace the whole organization, and resources must be allocated to reflect top management's commitment to delivering value to customers. Goodman has also pointed out that 80 percent of customer satisfaction depends on "doing it right the first time, which means design, manufacture, and delivery of a product. The other 20 percent is derived from complaint handling and problem solving." Most companies, however, "spend 95% of their customer service time fixing problems and, to be charitable, 5% analyzing why they got into this mess to begin with."

WHY YOU CAN'T AFFORD *NOT* TO CLOSE THE GAP

Having the customer's interests at heart is not a purely altruistic position to take. A customer who is treated well at the time of initial purchase, and after the sale is made, will be a loyal customer. And each loyal customer represents long-term revenue and profit streams accruing from future purchases—especially if their purchasing power increases substantially.

One major credit card company is learning this lesson the hard way. They lost thousands of dollars in potential profits because of insensitive treatment of a customer. The customer wrote this letter to the editor of a leading business newspaper:

> I read with interest your recent column about the unfortunate experience of some executives, who were being sued by ——— for debts of their now-bankrupt company. I too was the recipient [i.e., victim] of ———'s collection techniques in the early 1980s.

> Although I owed only $2,000, which I had covered with a series of post-dated checks, their collection department refused to accept what I was able to pay. They became relentless in their pursuit of payment in full, to the point where I was told to sell my furniture to pay off this debt. They were (and obviously still are) insensitive, uncompromising and destructive in their approach to individuals experiencing problems.

Fortunately, things have gone well for me over the past several years. My yearly travel and entertainment expenses run about $50,000 and not a penny of this is channeled through ———. Although ——— has tried to solicit my business, it will never have me or any of my companies as customers.

This is only one of the stories behind the statistics on the cost of poor-quality products and services. According to one 18-month study cited by Derek Whitely, president of the Forum Corporation, at a conference in Texas, a company with revenues of $240 million can lose $45 million because of poor service and the resulting customer dissatisfaction. According to Whitely, the research indicated that poor service usually results from a bad experience with a company employee. Sixty-eight percent of customers who said they would change suppliers said that their decision was based on the fact that some employee at the supplier was indifferent to them.

Another survey, undertaken by Sandy Corp., a management and staff training firm in Troy, Michigan, estimated the costs of customer dissatisfaction in three major United States industries: banking, hospitality, and transportation. The survey found that 68 percent of the 5,400 senior service-sector executives surveyed felt confident that a majority of their customers were "quite satisfied" to "very satisfied," and 75 percent believed that less than 10 percent of their customers were "dissatisfied but do not complain." Yet 42 percent of all companies performed no customer surveys, and 70 percent had no customer service/public affairs department. In fact, 37 percent of all the companies surveyed did not view customer satisfaction as their number-one priority.

However, the survey estimated that the United States hospitality industry loses customers at an annual rate of 6 percent, or 934,000 customers *per company* surveyed. The survey calculated that it costs $20 to attract a new hospitality client; thus, the average cost to each company is $18.7 million per year. According to the same survey, banks lose an average of 5 percent of their customers each year because of dissatisfaction. At an average cost of $100 to attract a new customer, each bank therefore spends an average of $54.3 million per year just to replace old business. The worst loser, however, is the transportation industry, which sees an annual customer loss of 4 percent, or 169,000 clients per company surveyed. It costs $700 to attract one new customer, which makes for a total customer-replenishing cost of $118.3 million per firm.

Yet another study, this one done by Technical Assistance Research

Program (TARP) for the White House Office of Consumer Affairs, found "that customer service policies had a major impact on brand and line loyalty [and that this] applied equally to the industries that sold to retail or commercial customers." TARP also conducted a survey for an American consumer goods company and found that

> . . . only 17% of those customers who were dissatisfied with a recent customer service experience intended to continue doing business with the offending company. Those . . . who found . . . service . . . to be acceptable reported a brand loyalty of 45% [and] loyalty increased to 73% among [those] satisfied with the company's service." The results were similar in comparisons of line loyalty: ". . . only 17% . . . who were unhappy [with the service] would buy other products or services from that company. Line loyalty increased to 50% when customer service was acceptable and rose to 80% among those completely satisfied . . .

Business lost because of customer dissatisfaction represents a high cost for any organization. Each time a customer is lost, the company forfeits the substantial investment it made to attract him or her in the first place. Major investments in product development, advertising and promotion, distribution network development, and multiple sales calls are frequently required to get the initial trial purchase from a new buyer. According to an often-quoted statistic, it is five times more costly to acquire a new customer than to retain a current one. This is partly because the costs of attracting a new customer easily exceed the gross margin of the initial order, which means that the company is typically "out-of-pocket" at the time of the first purchase. Only with regular repeat purchases from a satisfied customer does the company begin to see a return on its initial effort.

Any customer who slips through a company's fingers because of dissatisfaction also walks away with thousands of dollars of spending potential. According to customer service consultants Karl Albrecht and Ron Zemke, in the automobile industry a loyal customer represents a lifetime revenue of $140,000. Appliance manufacturers calculate that, over a 20-year period, brand-loyal customers are worth $2,800. And local supermarkets count on about $5,000 per year from each regular patron, or $25,000 for the five years an average customer lives in the neighborhood.

John Cleghorn, president of the Royal Bank, Canada's largest, says that the average lifetime customer represents about $80 in profit per year. For the Royal Bank that means that losing a single customer over a service conflict can translate directly into a potential profit loss of about $3,000.

Unhappy customers also become a hidden network spreading negative messages that can undo the efforts of the most costly customer acquisition programs. And the network is a powerful one—as revealed in studies carried out for the United States Office of Consumer Affairs. This is the kind of damage potential they found:

- The average business never hears from 96 percent of its unhappy customers. For every complaint received, the average company in fact has 26 customers with problems, six of which are "serious" problems.
- Out of those customers who are unhappy, 90 percent will not buy again.
- The average customer who has had a problem with an organization tells nine other people about it, and 13 percent of customers who have had a problem discuss it with more than 20 people.

The good news is that the complaint itself is not the greatest problem. It's how the company handles it. Of the customers who register a complaint, between 54 percent and 78 percent will do business with the organization again if their complaint is resolved. The figure goes up to 95 percent if the customer feels the complaint was resolved quickly. Satisfied complainants also tell an average of five people about the good treatment they received.

THE BENEFITS OF CREATING VALUE FOR CUSTOMERS

If losing a customer means losing profits, keeping customers by delivering high-quality products and services is obviously good business. This was borne out in a study conducted by Robert Buzzell and Bradley Gale for their book *The PIMS Principles*. Their database showed that businesses that delivered superior quality (the top quintile of companies researched) earn an average return on investment (ROI) of 32 percent and a return on sales (ROS) of 13 percent. Businesses that delivered inferior quality (the bottom quintile) had an average ROI of only 12 percent and an ROS of 5 percent.

If there is one company in North America that is legendary for the quality of its goods and services, it is the Walt Disney Company--and its dedication to delivering value has paid huge dividends. Walt Disney himself, according to current president Frank Wells, took value creation to an extreme. Before Mickey Mouse made his first appearance (back in 1928) in the animated classic *Steamboat Willie,* Walt had completed another cartoon, *Plane Crazy,* but he shelved it because he wanted his first public effort to be the absolute best. Another famous cartoon character, Pinocchio, went through a similarly rigorous training before he was allowed to hit the theaters in the 1940 film of the same name. At one point, five months' worth of carefully drawn animation was junked and the artists had to start all over again.

The result? *Pinocchio* took in just over $3.5 million at the box office when it opened in 1940, and on its rerelease in 1984, it raked in $26 million. *Cinderella,* which first appeared in 1950, brought in $8 million at the time and more than four times that amount when it was rereleased in 1988. Those are astronomical figures when compared to industry standards: The average gross for a new picture in 1988 was only $8 million and only about one in 20 films ever grosses more than $20 million.

The Land's End mail-order company, another high-profile firm that is famous for delivering superior value to its customers, has seen sales increase 65 percent and earnings more than double to about $30 million since it went public in 1986. Most of the $21 million in capital expenditures the company has made over the past two years was aimed at improving customer service. Among these expenditures has been a computer-aided inseaming system that shortens the time it takes to hem pants and new sorting and packaging equipment to improve efficiency of the company's giant 475,000-square-foot distribution center.

The payoff from this reinvestment in providing superior value for customers is a loyal Land's End shopper—45 percent of the 9 million who receive the catalogs every month have made a purchase within the previous 36 months. Each month a three-inch-thick computer printout of customers' comments from these active and involved buyers lands on managers' desks. Thus, the company is able to quickly perceive changes in customer preferences and expand selectively, offering clothing it knows customers want to buy. And so Land's End's success continues to increase, through its own momentum.

Success stories such as those of the Walt Disney Company and Land's End are not isolated examples of the quality pay-off. When *Fortune* magazine named the Service 500 for 1989, the nine at the top of the list were "imbued with the belief that profits come from providing genuine value. To that end, they hold prices down by keeping costs and systems under rigid control." Stanley Goldstein, chairman of specialty retailer Melville, which was ninth on the exclusive list, said, "Whenever we think about buying a new division, we ask ourselves what value it will provide the customer. The answer may be price; it may be selection. But it's got to be something, or else forget it. The one thing we don't want to do is run after the God of Big Volume." This kind of thinking has brought great rewards. Average return on equity from 1979 to 1988 for the nine companies ranged from Melville's 20.9 percent to ServiceMaster's whopping 63.7 percent.

SO WHAT'S NEW?

When Marie Antoinette's milliner said, "There's nothing new except what's been forgotten," she probably wasn't talking about value creation; but she could have been, since the idea of creating value for customers is not an entirely new one. Those words of French wisdom apply to all the quality and customer satisfaction theories that have been emerging since the early 1980s—and to the more comprehensive concept of value creation.

It has always been important for people to produce high-quality work. People naturally want to take pride in their jobs and to be recognized for excelling at something. Many of us have heard and sometimes followed maxims such as "If it's worth doing, it's worth doing well." By the same token, some manufacturers and service providers have always based their operations on ensuring that their customers received value for their dollar. The guarantee of the Canadian retailer, the T. Eaton Co.—"Goods Satisfactory or Money Refunded"—first appeared around 1884; and L.L. Bean, now the largest United States outdoor specialty catalogue business, has based its business on a credo that puts the customer first: "Sell good merchandise at a reasonable profit and treat customers like human beings and they will always come back for more."

If so many businesses started out with this sort of thinking, why is there a "quality crisis" in North America now? The problem is philosophical, historical, and systemic. First, the philosophical problem. Although North American values have been embodied partly in aphorisms such as the Golden Rule (Do unto others as you would have them do unto you), another, countervailing philosophy has always been just as strong: the gunslinging, rags-to-riches, rugged individualism that has characterized so much of North American business operations. From frontier days to the present, North American entrepreneurs and business people have most often gone on the assumption that someone always has to be on top. If there was any such thing as participation, cooperation, and idea sharing, they were merely means to individual ends.

This kind of thinking also underlies the management systems and practices that began with the industrial revolution and have flourished since World War II: the "continuous 'top-down' control, reinforced [by] strong financial and budgetary considerations," that has been typical of most North American companies. Of course, the "shoot-'em-up" style has not been restricted to internal operations alone; it has also informed the way companies view their markets. In 1953, Charles Erwin Wilson, then president of General Motors, summed up the whole idea when he made his famous boast: "What's good for the country is good for General Motors, and vice versa." Although this kind of "customer-comes-last" thinking would be a recipe for disaster today, for years it did not prevent enterprises such as GM from being phenomenally successful.

This was because, immediately after World War II, there was apparently no special need to think about product and service quality and customer satisfaction. Consultant Tom Peters points out why: (1) There was "pent-up demand for products" after the war, (2) tough international competitors were scarce, and (3) a post-Depression workforce "felt lucky to have a job." And so, the top-down management model flourished. The finance department was considered more important than other company functions, and the market had to buy what business could profitably produce.

High-quality products and service were not extinct, of course, but the industrial and commercial organizations that provided them were more interested in their own bottom lines than the needs of customers, and their structure did not encourage craftsmanship and pride in a job well done. For the moment, the Golden Rule was put on hold.

Meanwhile, the Japanese were struggling to reestablish their war-torn economy. At first, their industrial output was shoddy, but in time they began to take to heart the quality philosophies of consultants such as Dr. Joseph Juran, Armand Feigenbaum, and W. Edwards Deming (Americans whose ideas were not so popular in the United States, but who found an audience among the Japanese). In an effort to live down the stigma attached to the label "Made in Japan," Japanese companies made gradual but continuous improvements to their output, playing the tortoise to the North American hare. Basing their designs on careful analysis of customer requirements, their products got better and better (think of the first Honda automobiles compared to the Hondas of today), and eventually they staged the North American invasion of the early 1970s that everyone remembers.

The North American gunslingers were caught off their guard, and after they had recovered from the initial shock, they started looking to the East to find out where they'd gone wrong. What they discovered was that they'd forgotten about quality and service and that they'd been riding roughshod over their customers for too long. As one analyst put it: A "philosophy and practice [had] evolved which suggested a business could be good at quality but only at the expense of price, or low in price only at the expense of quality." (A few more of the differences they discovered are shown in Figure 1–1.) And so it was that during the 1980s the importance of quality management began to gain prominence. But true to gunslinger form, the improvement efforts started out as scattered, stand-alone initiatives.

Separate parts of the organization, which had always focused on some kind of quality control or customer service, began revising their approaches to delivering quality and value. The *marketing* area began adapting some of its marketing research tools so that they could be used to monitor customer satisfaction in a more sophisticated way. Customer satisfaction research became the marketing department's contribution to the quality movement. Meanwhile, *human resource* specialists began beefing up employee training programs and integrating customer service principles into employee incentive and compensation packages. From the *operations* area came a proliferation of quality management principles—quality assurance (whereby quality improvement techniques focused on uncovering the root causes of quality failures rather than just inspecting goods for quality after they had gone through production); total quality control (TQC) (in which the definition of quality management was broadened to include business functions outside the quality assurance department); the "zero defects" philosophy; and finally corporate-wide quality control, popularly known as CWQC or TQM (total quality management).

In some cases, the efforts at quality management were genuine and effective; in others, they were hamstrung by insincerity or incompleteness. In the "insincere" category were the add-on, band-aid, and lip-

Best Japanese Companies	Typical U.S. Companies
Focus on customer satisfaction	Focus on profit
Market-in (supply demand)	Product-out (create demand)
Manage by means/systems	Manage by objectives
Holistic approach	Linear/segmented approach
Patience	Impatience
Incremental improvement	Breakthrough improvements
Teams	Individuals
Leaders teach	Staff/consultants teach
Continuous education (investment)	Sporadic training (expense)
Top management has technical background	Top management has marketing or financial background
Top management contact with plant/customers	Top management distant from plant/customers
Your subordinates are your customers	Your boss is your customer
Homogeneity (conformity)	Diversity (individuality)
Problems are treasures	Problems are a sign of weakness
Visual communication techniques	Verbal communication techniques
Sequential phases of corporate direction	Independent corporate programs not sustained
Standardization is essential	Standardization is constraining
Focus is clear to everyone	Everything is important
Top down direction is followed	Top down direction is resisted
Everyone is responsible for improvement	"They" are responsible for improvement
Top people working on TQ	Staff working on TQ
Methodical/relentless	Hit and run
Make commitments	Make promises
Engineers/development in plants	Engineers/development away from plants
Management span of support	Management span of control
Continuity	Frequent assignment changes
Crisis mentality	Complacency

Figure 1–1. Comparison of Management Philosophies

Source: From "Leading the Total Quality Effort," speech given by John A. Saxton, Vice President, Noxell, Procter & Gamble Company, USA, April 27, 1990.

service programs, the pep rallies and the lectures from the CEO extolling the virtues of teamwork—with no extra resources devoted to the cause and no examination or revision of company strategies and structures. In the "incomplete" category were the programs that were effective in one area but had little impact on the overall operations and image of the company because they were not communicated to other areas.

Recently, all quality management and customer service efforts are beginning to converge, and the trend is towards cooperative efforts between departments. At the same time, customer satisfaction concerns have extended beyond the limits of the customer service department and have made their way into executive strategic planning sessions. Quality and customer satisfaction principles are also beginning to change the structure of organizations.

Symbolic of this organizational impact is the emergence of the *self-managed work team*. Where, in the recent past, employees may have participated in quality circles that had the authority to investigate a problem but did not disturb the organizational status quo, self-managed teams have the power to arrange schedules, set profit targets, order material and equipment, communicate directly with customers, and sometimes even hire and fire. In other words, they are taking on the middle management function and thus have the potential to eliminate a whole stratum in the corporate hierarchy.

CREATING VALUE: THE ULTIMATE CUSTOMER STRATEGY

In the midst of all this tumultuous change, however, the means has become confused with the end. Executives who got the quality and service "religion" during the 1980s sometimes fail to remember that quality and service are the means, but *value for the customer* is the end.

This is where our approach comes in. Value creation includes all the quality, service, and customer satisfaction tools that have been evolving in different areas of North American business, but it combines them in such a way that the whole is greater than the sum of its parts. A truly integrated philosophy of competition will be required if businesses are to cope successfully with the myriad challenges that business leaders are facing today. Myopic business concepts and strategies will no longer suffice.

When asked the question "What kind of company do I want?" most executives will respond with either a product or market definition of their business, or a financial ratio of success. But, as James Belasco points out in *Teaching the Elephant to Dance*, "... long term successful companies stand for more than just profit or market share. They also stand for people—people who contribute *net value* to society." [Emphasis added.]

Henry Ford understood this idea—it was perhaps the secret of his phenomenal success. Although criticized in his later years for losing touch with his customers, in his heyday he knew exactly what it took to build a successful company. In 1915 he said, "Wealth, like happiness, is never attained when sought after directly. It comes as a by-product of providing useful service."

The idea of creating value may, indeed, be reduced to a concept as simple as striving to become ever more "useful" to customers. But, of course, good intentions must be transformed into practical reality. The businesses that will succeed in the decades ahead are not those with advantages defined in terms of internal functions, but those that can become truly market-focused—that is, able to profitably deliver sustainable superior value to their customers. This means being able to do the following:

- Choose the target customer and the combination of benefits and price that to the customer would constitute superior value, and
- Manage all functions to rigorously reflect this choice of benefits and prices so that the business actually provides and communicates this chosen value and does so at a cost allowing adequate returns.

Looking more closely at the question of user value, we find the following characteristics:

- Quality—expressed in terms of features of products or services that are consistently valued by users
- Cost—the "sacrifice" required of the user (in terms of money, time, risk, or self-esteem)
- Schedule—the delivery of user-valued features in the correct quantity, time, and place

Thus, the manager's fundamental responsibility is to always know what is valued by the user and to create, and continually improve, organizational systems that, when used by the people within the business, result in increased user value.

In a recent article entitled "Management Leadership in the New Economic Age," G. Harlan Carothers, Jr., Richard D. Sanders, and Kenneth E. Kirby gave a good summary of the new management paradigm that must be adopted by companies that want to succeed in the 1990s and beyond:

The creation of value as an organizing principle and as a measuring rod for efficiency can be utilized by management at every level of the organization and at every stage of operation.... Those firms that do not provide value, by inability, inattention, or choice, will be selectively eliminated by the customer at the point of purchase. The implications are clear: The organization's objective in the 21st century will be to become increasingly valued by the user of their products or services, and this principle holds for producers of both industrial and consumer goods.

Creating value and delivering it to customers is more than a passing business fad. It is an approach to strategic management that can be used to transform "rigid organizations into responsive, world-class performers" by examining every corner of the business's operations in light of its contribution to quality and customer satisfaction. According to this way of viewing a business, customers must not just receive quality; they must feel they have received value for their dollar.

Value creation is strategic, systemic, and continuous. It is *strategic* because it is based on the assumption that delivering what customers value is at the center of the company's corporate strategy. It is *systemic* because it often entails organizational change as well as behavioral change. It is *continuous* because the challenge of gaining and keeping customers in a fast-changing world marketplace requires unrelenting attention to achieving constantly higher levels of performance.

If value creation forms the basis of a company's strategy, the desire to meet the customer's expectations will be at the root of all company activities and systems. That is, the company will become more and more market-oriented and customer-driven. In a *production-oriented* company, the starting assumption is: "If only we could reduce the product or service variety to a few core items, then we could produce more efficiently." In the *sales orientation*, the assumption is: "If only our potential market knew more about us, then we could sell more effectively." The final step in the evolution to a *value-creation orientation* takes the company from the question "Why don't customers buy what we make?" to the question "What do our customers want from us?" The difference is simple, yet profound. The company that asks the first question is focusing on its internal concerns; the firm that asks the second question is focusing on its customers and their needs.

Value creation is the ultimate customer strategy because it draws on the multiple perspectives of all the company's functional areas and brings them together to work toward the common goal of creating and delivering value to customers. In the past, the lack of a common "quality and service management language" has often acted as a barrier to integrated change. Different parts of the company have the skills and understanding needed to make improvements, but each filters the problem through its own experience and biases. By taking a close look at the different quality management techniques and customer satisfaction and service approaches that have been evolving in the specialty areas of marketing, operations, and human resources functions, we hope to break down the "language barrier" by providing managers with an overview of what is happening in other functional areas.

Value creation is not going to happen overnight. Like any creation, it is a process and a journey. It takes inspiration, hard work, and time to change the way a company goes about its business.

This book has been written not so much to introduce new ideas about quality and service management (hundreds of books have been written on the topic already) as to draw together in one place the main tools and approaches of value creation and to give senior executives and top-level managers a reliable road map for strategic change.

In the next two chapters, we will look at the roots of value creation— knowing your customer and knowing yourself—and at value creation as a basis for establishing a corporate culture and making strategic decisions. In Chapters 4 to 7, the focus will shift to the individual contributions that marketing, operations, and human resources have made and are making to the value-creation revolution. In the last three chapters, we offer some practical guidelines for implementing value-creation-improvement processes. After all, value cannot exist unless it is created. And it can't be created if you don't know how.

2

Know Your Customers—
Know Yourself

The business of business is getting and keeping customers.

Peter Drucker

Even the biggest players can make obvious mistakes when it comes to delivering value to customers. In a recent interview with *Fortune* magazine, John F. Akers, chairman and CEO of IBM, acknowledged that his company's slow growth in the mid-1980s stemmed largely from getting out of touch with its market. "We took our eye off the ball," he confessed. Companies that had gobbled up IBM's mainframes in the past were moving toward networks of more powerful desktop computers, and instead of changing their product to fit the new need, Big Blue concentrated on protecting the market for its basic product. Akers has broken with tradition and admitted the company's error—and has now launched an initiative to make IBM "the world's champion in meeting the needs of customers."

A big part of IBM's success in meeting this goal will rest on its ability to read the minds of its customers—both the lost and the loyal. In fact, many firms that have aspired to leadership in creating value for customers lose at the starting gate because they don't take the time to learn who their customers are and what makes them satisfied. And this kind of learning is more than doing a few surveys and follow-up phone calls. It means learning customers' needs and expectations, in detail and continually, and using that information as a basis for strategic decision making.

But how do you go about doing that? Later in this book (in Chapters 4 and 5), we will be describing specific market research techniques and ways of building relationships with customers that any company can use to get close to its customers, but for the moment, here is a preview of how three companies learned what their customers wanted and what they did or are planning to do about it. The first two made the list of Canada's 50 best-managed private companies in May 1990.

Emery Apparel Canada Inc.

When CEO Alex Starko bought this Edmonton-based maker of protective workwear in 1975, he went the extra mile to discover what his market needed and wanted. After an order for coveralls came in from an oil firm, he drove out to the oil field and spent three days working with the crew, watching how they did their jobs and listening to their complaints. What he discovered he would never have guessed if he'd stayed behind his desk reading market research reports. He learned that almost no one fit comfortably into any of the three standard sizes of coveralls and that the garments' five-inch pockets were no match for the eight-inch wrenches the workers used. And when he saw workers laying down their tools to pick up two-way radios, he got the idea of adding shoulder loops to hold the radios.

Now Emery's coveralls come in 45 sizes (and 15 colors) and researchers sometimes spend as long as 18 months developing the clothing, getting feedback from workers before approving the final design. This meticulous attention to the demands of the market has paid off: Emery's sales have soared from $3 million in 1985 to $12 million in 1989.

Alderbrook Industries Ltd.

This top Canadian supplier of collectible Christmas ornaments based in Pickering, Ontario, goes to no end of trouble to learn and respond to the needs of its individual customers. When the company's sales agents discovered that some retailers were concerned about being loaded down with unsold ornaments that showed the date, Alderbrook produced and shipped those particular customers undated ornaments— within two weeks. This kind of hair-trigger response is what has increased Alderbrook's sales from $12 million in 1985 to $18.4 million in 1988.

Circuit City Stores

In the coming decade, it will also be important for companies to plan their systems around gaining detailed knowledge of customers. Richard Sharp, CEO of this rapidly growing American home electronics and appliances chain, predicts that his operation will be setting up computerized files containing a complete profile of each customer. In addition to providing basic information about the customer and speeding up service and repair, the system would identify Circuit City's best customers and give them priority service. If the database showed that the customer bought a TV one year and a VCR the next, it might send him a flyer advertising video cameras. As Sharp has put it: "The winners of the 1990s will be those who can boost service and cut prices at the same time." One way of doing that will be to develop efficient systems for describing and targeting customers.

BACK TO BASICS

Emery and Alderbrook found out what *their* customers wanted, but those needs were specific to their own businesses. Can their experience be generalized to all enterprises? The jury appears to be in on this point: If a company is going to survive, it will have to let the market define what value is. A product or service may conform perfectly to specifications— the traditional quality standard—but if the specs don't meet market requirements, it will fail.

What, then, does the market want? How do you get to know your customers? A recent survey conducted on behalf of the American Society for Quality Control (ASQC) asked 1,005 adult consumers what quality factors they considered important when they purchased a product or a service. For manufactured items, the most important items were, in rank order: performance, durability, ease of repair, service availability, warranty, and ease of use. Surprisingly, price was ranked seventh in importance, out of nine factors. Appearance and brand name received the lowest ratings.

The same survey defined service quality as courtesy, promptness, a basic sense that one's needs are being satisfied, and a good attitude on the part of the service provider. Less frequently mentioned were factors such as price, accuracy, convenience, and trouble-free service. In other words, customers will be more forgiving of difficulties if they perceive that they are being treated with personal care and respect.

This principle has been applied by the Mackay Envelope Corporation of Minneapolis, which offers high-quality products and trains its salespeople to cater to the personal needs of buyers. All sales staff fill out a 66-question profile on each of the company's customers, describing what the customer is like as a human being, what he or she feels strongly about, and what he or she is most proud of having achieved, among other things. With such in-depth understandings of their customers' personalities, the sales reps can tailor their marketing approaches appropriately. Company president Harvey Mackay even spends time on weekends reading the profile information on the company's top 10 accounts. Mackay, famous for his best-selling book, *Swim With the Sharks Without Being Eaten Alive,* attributes his company's sales growth and success to the personalized attention given to his customers.

Even in the impersonal mail-order business, the payoffs of the personal touch have been proven. When Gary Comer founded Land's End in 1963 as a catalog supplier of sailboat hardware and other equipment, it was the engaging tone of his catalog copy that first attracted customers. It helped that he personally liked the things he sold: "I picked things that I liked," he has said, "and over the years people interested in the same things sort of gathered around." Since then, Land's End has shifted its focus to casual apparel and has become a huge operation, but it hasn't shifted its attention from the customers. When catalog shoppers phone Land's End's toll-free number in Dodgeville, Wisconsin (near Madison), they don't have to wait in switchboard limbo or fend off aggressive phone-sales tactics. The operators are polite and helpful but not pushy. Noreen, who has been a Land's End operator since 1983, summed up the approach: "Customers expect an awful lot from us, and we have to make each one feel like he is the most important person we talk to today. It's not always easy, but we do it." And the catalog copy? It hasn't lost the panache that Comer wrote into his first efforts. Here's a sample from a recent one: "At $31 we thought last year's Popular Twills were a darned good value. Unfortunately for us, the boss didn't agree. '$31 is a good price but not a great price,' he bellowed. So we rolled up our sleeves. And after several gallons of coffee (and a few broken pencils), we came up with a lower price that would still allow us to keep our jobs: $29.50." This promotional tack works for Land's End because it's backed by high-quality products and an apparently sincere concern for the customers' interests. The combination has worked: Since the firm went public in 1986, its sales have gone up by 65 percent and its earnings have more than doubled, to about $30 million.

In air travel, passengers' perceptions of the quality of service are determined largely by their expectations. People who fly first class will naturally expect more comfortable seats and better menu selections, since these are among the first-class perks the airline has promised to provide. Although economy passengers expect decent service and reasonable comfort, they would not consider the airline unreliable if it did not give them first-class service. They look forward to a quality experience, but within a narrower range of expectations.

In many industries, where the risks and costs of failure to customers are high, warranties are critical to the customer's satisfaction. One research company found that good warranties give truck dealers a competitive edge in serving a commercial customer who, for example, operates a trucking fleet. Down time for a trucking operation means thousands of dollars lost; a warranty that guarantees a replacement vehicle or service within a certain number of hours saves money for customers and can therefore be a critical factor in their decisions to buy.

Car warranties for the general public may or may not be important as a sales tool, says Raymond Richardson of DesRosiers Automotive Research Inc., "But when you get to the medium truck market, it's commercially important because it means that the fleets who are operating these trucks can take them back in to get them fixed. This gives commercial people a fallback, because this is a piece of business equipment. So if this warranty doesn't have a lot of catches in it, it's dollars in their pocket."

An attractive warranty offer can also help reestablish credibility for a company that has lost market share or has otherwise fallen from grace. In late 1989, General Motors of Canada Ltd. announced that it would be offering upgraded warranty coverage for its new line of medium-duty trucks, presumably as a means of gaining an advantage in the extremely competitive market for these vehicles.

One Toronto building company, Bramalea Ltd., made an unusual move in 1987 by offering a 12-month extended warranty on homes it built, in response to problems of material and labor shortages that had begun the year before during a construction boom in southern Ontario. Although the offer was made as a means of reestablishing credibility with customers, it may be the first in a line of many such warranties. At the time, one of Bramalea's senior vice-presidents, David Ptak, predicted that, "As consumers get more sophisticated and demanding, other builders will adopt [the warranty]."

THE BEST-LAID PLANS

No matter how hard a company may try to understand and respond to its customers, life in the real world means that things will go wrong at some time or other. As Ralph Waldo Emerson put it, "Things are in the saddle and ride mankind." Cars break down, hotel reservations get lost, trains come in late, and microwaves go on the fritz. What is critical at times such as these is the way the company responds. Does the customer's contact with the firm solve the problem or does it only make things worse? Once again, the guiding principle is *know your customer*—in this case, know that *what annoys the customer most* is a defensive corporate attitude. One author identified five kinds of defensiveness that really irk customers:

1. Cumbersome or complex complaint procedures
2. A slow and grudging approach to refunds and repairs
3. Numerous exceptions in warranty policies
4. An adversarial approach to dealing with customer complaints
5. Delays in making necessary changes in products or services

Especially in cases where the customer stands to lose significant amounts of revenue as a result of a product breakdown or poor service, a fast, efficient response to problems is mandatory. One analysis revealed that customer dissatisfaction does not just increase in a linear way. After the first period of delay, dissatisfaction increases sharply. If a farmer's combine breaks down in the middle of harvest season, for instance, the farmer will tolerate a repair time of up to four hours. However, if the machine takes more than four to six hours to fix, the farmer will start to get concerned. Down time of eight hours, and the farmer becomes frantic.

John Deere, the agriculture machinery manufacturer, has responded to this problem by opening satellite parts stores, which have eliminated lengthy trips to the dealership for many rural customers. The company has also enhanced its image for reliability by promising parts service within 24 hours anywhere in North America.

Companies that set out to create value for their customer have appropriate warranty policies and streamlined complaint procedures. They also give front-line personnel the authority to solve problems, and they train all employees to view complaints as opportunities to make up for poor value delivery and to gain a loyal customer.

"SEASONS CHANGE AND SO MUST I . . ."

When Henry Ford first produced the Model T, his approach was a textbook example of how to create real value for customers. The car had a high chassis so that it could avoid the bumps that were all too frequent on the unimproved dirt tracks that made up much of the U.S. road network at the time. The Model T was easy to fix, and its price was right for the average buyer. By 1922, Ford's sales had topped $100 million.

But then Henry started concentrating on manufacturing efficiency, and while he was perfecting the production line he got out of touch with his customers. Roads were improved and customers started demanding more speed, comfort, and variety, but Ford refused to change. When a group of dealers asked Ford if he could offer the Model T in a few different colors, he retorted with the now-famous line, "You can have any color you want, boys, as long as it's black." Why? Any changes in the car would have slowed down production and raised the cost. By 1927 Ford had lost its position as market leader to General Motors for the first time, and since 1936 it has not caught up.

Obviously, part of getting to know your customers is understanding their changing needs and values. There seems to be a natural law, however, whereby companies will tend to move in the direction of internal focus unless there's an equal and opposite force pushing them back into the marketplace. And it is the successful firms that may be most tempted to rest on their laurels and focus on internal problems rather than stay in touch with the customers who gave them their success in the first place. Writes one services marketing analyst:

> Unless an ongoing effort is made to connect the organization to the customer, people begin to serve management rather than the customer. . . . It is particularly important to get executives and managers closer to customers. For example, many automotive company executives are given new cars every one to two years, and these cars are serviced at work by a company-operated garage. As a result, the executives never experience the level of service that is provided by the average car dealership, and they are disconnected from the customers' typical experience with their organization. . . . The research and development people also need to have direct contact with customers. Kenichi Ohmae, the managing director of the Japanese division of McKinsey & Company [the giant management consulting firm] says that the average R&D middle manager in Japan spends 50 percent of his time every year on the road talking to customers—a marked

contrast to the average middle manager of R&D in an American organization.

The customer-value-driven company also has to be in touch with changing world opinion. Beginning in the mid-1950s, Fluorocarbon Co. of Laguna Niguel, California, manufactured industrial seals, gaskets, and bearings using materials known as fluorocarbons. Sales had been healthy until the 1980s, when the public's environmental consciousness was raised and some company investors objected, mistaking fluorocarbons for chlorofluorocarbons (CFCs), the chemicals that have been found to be damaging the earth's ozone layer. Unlike Henry Ford, this company acted on the new information immediately and hit upon an innovative scheme to win back and keep its customers. It offered a grand prize of 100 shares of its stock to the customer who submitted the best new name for the company. The solution acknowledged the name problem and involved the customers in the process—a way to increase communication and gain a chance to reposition the products in buyers' minds. Had the company not been in close touch with its customers' attitudes and aware of the concern of the general public, it might have learned about the problem too late.

IBM's hegemony in the computer industry has also been threatened by changing seasons. In the past the key users of computers were specialists who had a high level of technical skill. Today, however, a large part of the computer market—executives—uses the machines as strategic tools. Using a desk-top machine, an executive can scan prices and profit margins on a variety of goods, for instance, and decline to order from vendors where margins are insufficient. The speed of this method is completely canceled out when the computer has byzantine commands, tough-to-decipher screens, and difficult barriers between databases. Users who are bewildered by the masses of incompatible machines on the market are pushing for "open systems," which would allow software to run on many different brands of hardware. But a move such as this would threaten IBM and other companies that have encouraged closed systems. If these players don't change with the times, they may find themselves on the benches.

In the manufacturing sector, companies have to deal not only with changing tastes but also with changing needs as products mature. Early in the development of an industry, buyers will place great value on receiving high levels of technical and applications support. As two analysts have pointed out, "The FUD factor—fear, uncertainty, and doubt—will predispose them to pay a premium price for a product of known reliability coupled with effective support." Then, as customers become more knowledgeable, they focus on the performance characteristics of the product. Customers entering the market at a later stage will tend to be more price-sensitive, as lower-cost competitors begin to offer similar products. Finally, as the market becomes saturated with relatively undifferentiated products, customers will purchase the product that gives them benefits directly related to their greatest buying needs.

LET YOUR CUSTOMERS KNOW YOU

The best-run company with the highest-quality products or services may still come to grief if its customers do not see it in that light. Since customers have nothing but their own perception to go by when choosing where to place their business, it is crucial for any company to know how they are viewed by their customers, and to take measures to change that perception if necessary.

When Corning purchased Revere Ware cookware in 1988, it knew that consumers perceived the brand to be outdated. Convinced that it could change that perception, the company conducted focus groups and research studies on brand awareness and attitudes about the qualities of Revere Ware. As a result, Corning decided not to reposition the Revere Ware brand, but to develop two new, and separate, line extensions, one for the mass market and the other for the high-end market. The Pro-Line brand was developed for the gourmet cooking market, while the Vista brand was created for the mass market, and the original Revere Ware was repackaged with a new look. New advertising campaigns were developed to promote the revived line of cookware using Corning's image as a producer of high-quality consumer cookware, tabletop, and storage products. The strategy has been successful, since Revere Ware is now in a leading position in the industry.

Another household products manufacturer, Rubbermaid, also staged a comeback recently after having problems with customer perception. During the 1980s, the company lost sales to look-alike competitors such as Tupperware and Frig-O-Seal. Rubbermaid Canada president and general manager Martin O'Neill placed the blame for the decline in consumer popularity squarely on the company's shoulders, since it failed to communicate effectively to prospective buyers the superior quality performance of its products.

Under O'Neill's direction, a new company mission statement was formulated using the theme "unbeatable." Rubbermaid's sales have rebounded, and the company has been recognized by *Fortune* magazine as one of the best-run businesses in North America.

To some extent, a company can also determine customers' perceptions of value by managing the customer's expectations. Xerox has a strategy, for instance, of not over-promising on repairs. If a repair person says that the estimated time of arrival is 10:30, the customer contact will promise that the repair person will arrive by 11:00. When the repair person arrives at 10:30, the customer perceives that good service has been delivered.

WHAT YOU HAVE THAT YOUR COMPETITORS DON'T

Reading your customers' minds, producing reliable products, and giving caring, personalized service—these are all important, but they're only part of the story. It is good to know your customers, but you won't be able to act on your knowledge if you don't also know yourself. What are *you* good at? What can you offer that your customers need? What do you have that your competitors don't?

This whole line of thinking comes under the age-old management school topic of assessing your *competitive advantage.* There are many ways of figuring out your company's edge, but one of the most useful ones has been popularized by Michael E. Porter, a professor at the Harvard School of Business. In his book *Competitive Advantage,* Porter suggests that a business can be viewed as a complex "transformation system," with a supply system providing its inputs and a user system taking its outputs. The whole thing is a long *value chain,* made up of two kinds of value activities: primary and support. *Primary activities* are those that are directly involved in the transformation of inputs into outputs and in delivery and support after the sale. *Support activities* underpin the primary ones and include such functions as procuring inputs, controlling inventory, managing human resources, developing technology, marketing, and providing general administrative functions. This all sounds logical, but what does it have to do with competitive advantage? This: As in any chain, a company's value chain has some links that are weak and some that are strong, some that could make or break the company and some that are not so vital. The trick is to determine which links in your chain give you an advantage over your competitors—or which links you must strengthen if you don't want to be beaten out in the market.

The relative importance of different activities within the value chain depends, of course, on the nature of the business you are in. Sellers of pencils, pens, and paper clips, as Porter points out, are not likely to be concerned with service after the sale; but for producers of computers and high-speed photocopiers, customer support is crucial to success. In other words, it's not good enough just to have a strong service department—your customer has to *need* service before that strength becomes a competitive advantage. Only then does service become a vital link in the value chain.

Following are some of the vital links that can be managed:

- Sunfresh Limited, a supplier of unbranded food products, has concentrated on the inputs, production, and delivery links in its value chain to create a competitive advantage. By supplying Ontario's Loblaws stores with all its generic label products, Sunfresh does not have to spend money on advertising or elaborate packaging. This means its costs are lower than those of competitors that must spend heavily to create consumer demand and convince supermarkets to stock their products. As a result, Sunfresh's products are offered at prices substantially lower than those of advertised competitors. Other companies with a low-cost advantage might choose to offer the same prices as competitors and to reinvest their wider profit margins into corporate expansion, new product development, employee training, or other activities that will give them more muscle to compete in the marketplace.

- In the pharmaceutical industry, technology development is often a key factor in gaining a competitive advantage. IAF BioChem International Inc., a Canadian-based pharmaceutical company, invested more than $3 million in the development of an AIDS diagnostic test in 1986. The investment paid off when the firm's team of international scientists developed a test that reduces both risk and cost for potential customers and provides more accurate results. The test allows for the recognition of both strains of the AIDS virus (most procedures use separate tests to ensure that neither strain is present). Of course, this reduces the amount of lab and technician time needed and will help cut health-care costs. The use of synthetic materials in the test has also eliminated the need for dealing with hazardous biological material, and the test can detect recently infected people two to six weeks earlier than was previously possible. Obviously, the product needs to be marketed and distributed effectively before BioChem will start seeing good returns on its investment, but the company set itself on the right path when it provided the financial support needed to gain an advantage in one of its areas of strength—R&D.

- When People Express started operations, it used unique personnel management methods as one of the key links in its value chain. Its early success was credited mostly to its innovative management system, which included extensive employee participation and job rotation and an informal structure. This, along with some shrewd purchasing of used planes, allowed the airline to offer cut-rate fares. It was only when it stopped playing to its strength and started focusing on becoming a national carrier that the strong link became the weak one. After it acquired Frontier Airlines, the operation became too large for the informal structure and the airline ran into financial difficulties.

Every enterprise has to offer a *core product or service*—that is, the minimum qualifiers that allow the company to even enter the market. The next step is the *expected product or service*, which represents benefits that buyers think the company must also provide because "it is in the business." The core service of a bank, for instance, is loanable funds. However, it must provide other benefits if it expects to get customers, including a staff knowledgeable enough to help customers open an account, take out an investment certificate, or get a loan. All of these are basic entrance requirements, features that any self-respecting business will offer. It is only when a company enters the realm of *enhanced product or service* that it starts to get a competitive edge. An enhanced product or service does not merely satisfy customers; it delights them by making their life much easier or simply by making them happy.

In the mature markets of today, anyone who delivers less than the enhanced product or service will likely be out of the running. The exceptional is no longer the exception; it has become the rule. As John Naisbitt has said: "In today's 'Baskin-Robbins' society, everything comes in at least twenty-one flavors. Do you remember when bathtubs were white, telephones were black, and checks green? The diversity of choices available to customers today is exploding. This is being driven by companies around the world by the new-found need to become increasingly customer-driven in order to win buyers in an intensively competitive marketplace."

That's why some business thinkers have started talking about the *future product or service*—that is, the best product that could ever be offered, featuring "everything that might be done to attract and hold customers." The benefits of such a product are restricted only by the budget and the imagination. Of course, the future product may eventually become reality, in which case it might be called a *super-enhanced product or service.*

Austin Trumanns Steel, a British steel distributor, did some futuristic super-enhancement thinking when it borrowed an idea from the pizza business. Like the pizza chains that promise delivery in 30 minutes or the meal is free, Austin Trumanns set up a "touchdown guarantee" that assures the customer of on-time delivery of steel. If that doesn't happen, Austin Trumanns *pays its client* 10 percent of the value of the order.

Of course, a company that decides to provide value-enhancing features that exceed the customers' expectations has to make sure that it can actually deliver the extras before it advertises. Efforts to improve service and quality have to be balanced against the company's operational capabilities. Once operations have been taken into account, however, the sky is the limit for companies that have decided to gain a competitive advantage by offering products and services that are better, faster, more sophisticated—or whatever will make their customers not just satisfied, but ecstatic.

In addition to managing your *own* company's value chain, it is useful to look at your *customers'* value chains. Can their weak but crucial links be strengthened? Can your company do something to strengthen them? A grocery operation, for instance, has to keep its shelves fully stocked without wasting valuable shelf space—that is, the inventory control link in its value chain can have a great effect on its profitability. This means that any supplier of groceries should concentrate on the delivery link in its own value chain. The supplier's goal will be to make delivery run so smoothly and efficiently that it stands head and shoulders above the competition, at least in this crucial area.

Procter & Gamble is managing the link between its own delivery and technology-development areas and the inventory-control function of the Wal-Mart retail chain. The two companies have created a just-in-time ordering and delivery system for the Pampers and Luvs brands of disposable diapers. Because the diaper packages are bulky and two days' stock on hand takes up a lot of storage space, the retailer has the choice of being pressed for space or running out of diapers. To remedy the problem, a computer has been installed to monitor store sales data. When stock runs low, Wal-Mart sends an order by satellite to the P&G factory, which automatically ships the order direct to the outlet. All this means that Wal-Mart can carry smaller inventories and reduce the number of times it runs out of diapers.

Sighting Trends

Although managing vital links and paying attention to customers' individual needs are essential parts of the value delivery process, the company that becomes too infatuated with its own expertise at meeting the demands of its current customers might end up like little Jack Horner who sat in his corner and found one plum in his pie, but (from what we know) didn't feel the need to get up and look for any more. It's easy for an enterprise to lose touch with what is happening outside its little corner of the market, as long as it finds a few plums from time to time. If this goes on for too long, it will start losing sight of the trends in its larger environment that are affecting its customers' thinking; it might even be concentrating on the wrong customers without knowing it.

Dave Nichol, president of Loblaw International Merchants, the Canadian grocery retailer, can never be accused of Jack-Hornerism. On a trip to Europe in 1988, he noticed that shoppers had become extremely environment-conscious in Britain, West Germany, and Sweden, where supermarket shelves were stocked with "green" products. When he returned, Nichol launched his own green line—a list of almost 100 products that had a less harmful effect on the environment than the equivalent items he had been selling previously. And he started up his program in a revolutionary way—by asking the environmental lobby group Pollution Probe to endorse the line. "Colin Isaacs and I had a conspiracy," he said, referring to the then head of the environmental organization. "Colin wanted to help us launch environment-friendly products, help us make them very successful, so that we'd force every manufacturer and every retailer to scramble like mad to make the environment their number one priority." There was strong disagreement at Pollution Probe about whether the products should be endorsed (and in the end Isaacs was pressured to resign for having cooperated with Nichol), but there is no doubt that Loblaws' president had put his finger right on the public nerve—and on a lucrative market. Polls of the time showed that Canadians were more concerned about the environment than regional economic development, job creation, or free trade with the United States, and those who were most anxious tended to be better educated and had higher-than-average incomes. Nichol spotted a megatrend and did something to capitalize on it. And he claims that other retailers have started to plan the introduction of their own green lines.

Managing Market Segments

Trend setting isn't for everyone, however, and there is risk involved in anticipating customers' demands; but no company can afford to miss out on the long view when it comes to identifying key market segments. The goal is to isolate high-potential customers, develop a deeper understanding of what they want, determine how much should be spent to satisfy them, and calculate what the returns will be.

There are many ways to segment markets for the purposes of targeting the customers that a firm can best satisfy. Markets can be segmented according to physical attributes (geographic location, demographic classification, and socioeconomic characteristics) or behavioral characteristics (psychographics, product usage, and benefits segmentation).

Geographic classification is obviously most important if convenience of location is vital to customer satisfaction, as it is in the case of essential services such as banks and dental clinics. *Demographic* data can be used to isolate specific groups (defined by marital status, family size, sex, household income, and ethnic or religious background, for instance), which have similar needs and buying behavior. *Socioeconomic* classifications are determined by measuring such factors as education, occupation, and home ownership.

Psychographic classifications overlap somewhat with socioeconomic groupings, since they are based on life-style analysis. (General Mills' Betty Crocker line of microwaveable products, for instance, is directed mostly toward the working woman with little time to spend in the kitchen.) IKEA, the Swedish home furnishings import company, focuses on another life-style segment: buyers who want to be able to set up housekeeping quickly and then move on easily when circumstances change.

LSI Logic Corporation, a Silicon Valley computer chip maker, is one of many companies that have zeroed in on a specific market segment by using the criterion of *product usage.* LSI Logic solved the problem of worldwide excess capacity and oversupply of commodity chips by meeting the demand for customized chips from customers who want to differentiate *their* products from those of their competitors.

Similarly, Ecusta, a subsidiary of paper maker P.H. Glatfelter Co., has managed to become one of only two U.S. suppliers to the domestic tobacco industry, even though it is a small player in a paper industry dominated by billion-dollar giants such as Weyerhauser and International Paper. It has done so by specializing in serving the needs of a few, very large buyers of unique grades of fine paper.

Glatfelter services different customer groups with the same type of product using a strategy of *benefits segmentation*. The same kind of light-weight paper that it sells to tobacco companies for cigarette manufacturing is also suitable for use as fine paper in such books as Bibles and dictionaries. While the tobacco companies value the fact that Glatfelter papers run well on their high-speed production equipment, printers appreciate the paper's light weight. Although the product is the same, Glatfelter has two separate markets for it, because it has succeeded in emphasizing to each customer the benefits that each values the most.

Customers can also be classified according to their potential degree of loyalty to the firm. In her book *Winning and Keeping Industrial Customers*, Barbara Bund Jackson suggested that enterprises measure their customers against a scale based on the customers' "switching costs"— that is, the degree of risk perceived by the buyer in entering into a relationship with the company and the difficulty of moving to a new supplier if the buyer becomes dissatisfied. At one end of the spectrum are the customers who

> [c]an easily switch products or services (e.g., buyers of commodity chemicals or shipping services). At the other end are those who have an incentive to stay loyal (e.g., customers of costly computer and office-automation systems). In the middle are the majority, who are easily swayed (e.g., fleet buyers of company cars).

When the perceived risk is high, and the changing of vendors is difficult, buyers respond well to strategies that emphasize a closer relationship between buyer and seller. However, when switching costs are low, buyers are less interested in a long-term commitment to vendors, and price carries more weight. Understanding switching costs is important in order to avoid building a costly relationship with a customer who does not need or want such a commitment, and to provide an adequate amount of vendor support to those who are in for the long haul.

Calculate Costs, Benefits

As a company considers the needs of new target markets, it has to take into account the fact that meeting those needs will incur costs for the specialized plans, product line extensions, price schedules, advertising, programs, and sales force activities that will be required. These additional costs must be matched against the type of buying response the company expects to achieve from the target segment. Some of the worst-performing segments may be the most expensive to serve. In the firm's zeal to get close to the customer, it is possible to overserve buyers in a particular segment without seeing commensurate returns in increased sales at attractive profit levels.

In fact, the well-known Pareto Principle usually applies: 80 percent of a company's results comes from 20 percent of its efforts. That is why it's essential to define the *vital few* who *must* be pleased and to give less attention to the *useful many*, each of whom has only a modest impact on the company's profitability.

Opinions differ on the degree of focus a company should have. Some kinds of business might profit from serving a highly diversified market, but only if each market segment is related to the others in a way that brings in profits. General Motors, for example, has a broad scope in automobiles, which gives it a substantial advantage over Chrysler because serving many markets increases production volume, which in the auto industry drives down costs.

In cases where there are significant differences between the special needs of different segments of the market, however, a high degree of focus is better. The company with a proliferation of offerings may not be able to build true superiority with any particular buyer group, because it simply cannot be all things to all people. Worse, the satisfaction strategies for one group may come into direct conflict with the strategies for another group. And without a clear customer target, there is the risk that employees will become confused about the aims of the business.

Edwin (Honest Ed) Mirvish, who runs a famous discount-store operation in Toronto, puts it like this:

1. Fulfill a need.
2. Go against the trend.
3. Keep it simple.

Louis Gerstner, CEO of RJR Nabisco, sees focused strategy as an essential weapon against the worldwide slowdown in demand and resulting overcapacity that will be the biggest challenges facing the global manager of the 1990s. He says,

> Those CEOs who automatically think the answer is that their company should compete around the world are making a mistake. More often

the opportunities are going to be for companies that can dominate a niche, a product niche or a geographic niche. The answer lies in defining a core strategy that is built on your company's competitive strengths.

When Frito-Lay, a leader in the potato chip business, decided to move into the packaged cookie market, they learned this lesson the hard way. Their plan sounded all right. By applying their highly effective customer service strategy of frequent delivery to food stores, they reasoned, they would be able to supply cookies as well as chips. Unfortunately, although the concept worked well for chips, which have a short shelf life, it was a flop for the cookie business, which works on a slower turnaround time. Quick delivery was very expensive and offered no particular advantage. The firm soon abandoned its expansion plans and went back to its specialized (and successful) chip niche.

Once a company has decided the general area on which to focus, it can break that area down into subgroups that require different grades of product and service quality. This is what the Canadian Imperial Bank of Commerce did after it recognized the fact that it had a whole pool of high-income customers who could be served profitably if they were given kid-glove treatment. It was in the mid-1980s that CIBC realized it had ignored this select group by failing to deal with the market on a segmented basis. Although only about a quarter of the bank's customers could have been described as wealthy (with incomes over $150,000 and a net worth greater than $750,000), that segment was purchasing about 75 percent of its financial services from other financial institutions.

Since then, the bank has put in place a global private banking network covering 10 major Canadian cities and seven offshore financial centres, including London, Geneva, Singapore, and Hong Kong. Its investment will likely pay off, as it is predicted that the affluent segment will double during the next decade and the rich will likely become richer.

Subcategorization of the market segment has to be carried out with a certain amount of common sense. In the case of CIBC, it chose just one category—and a lucrative one at that. In the case of another company, which shall remain nameless, the market was divided into 10 subsegments; and, in an attempt to implement a democratic management model, each segment was given an equal amount of the company's resources to work with. After three years of this strategy, sales costs had crept up to 21 percent of revenues and the firm had to stop and take a look at its numbers. Apparently, the Pareto Principle had been in full force because some of the subsegments that brought in the worst returns were the most expensive to service. Although the firm felt it could not abandon any of its segments, it did a major shift in the allocation of personal and financial resources, investing more effort in the segments that had better profit potential.

It's important not only to define and target the right segments, but also to keep an eye on how they change. H.B. Fuller, the St. Paul adhesives company whose efforts to satisfy customers are legendary, met with its great success by locating sales offices, labs, and plants near customers so that it could deliver goods quickly even in the most difficult circumstances. This type of geographical subsegmentation worked perfectly when the company was small; but when the company grew, the very organization that allowed salespeople to give local, personalized service became the wedge that drove them away from their customers. "We were making 1,000 products for 100 different industries," said CEO Anthony L. Andersen, which meant that local salespeople could never hope to acquire detailed knowledge of any of their customers' needs. So Andersen divided the market into different subsegments, assigning 400 research, technical service, and sales people to separate industries so that they could develop expertise in specific product lines rather than particular geographical areas. "We had a rough period of a year or two when our customer service slipped because people didn't know their industry as well as their old geographical territory. But customers eventually started saying, 'You really know my needs.'" Since 1982, Fuller's revenues have doubled, and the company remains the world's largest publicly owned glue factory.

KNOW YOURSELF

Some enterprises get into trouble when they lose sight of what their image is in the eyes of their loyal customers. For example, two well-known companies spent a few years in the wilderness after forgetting who they were and where they should be going:

> Coca-Cola Co. is still clearing the debris from its decision to kill off its trademark brand and replace it with new Coke. The Atlanta-based giant failed to realize that Coke wasn't just a drink, but a part of North American life that should not be tampered with.
>
> That blunder taught Coca-Cola—and other watchful companies—that times have changed. Double-digit growth is a thing of the past, and

brand loyalty is an important factor that can no longer be taken for granted.

[The Canadian subsidiary of] Campbell Soup Co. Ltd. didn't make that mistake, but it did forget how powerful brand loyalty can be. It attributed sluggish soup sales to the dated image of its well known red and white label brand, and tried to give the product a new life as health food.

An ad campaign directed at healthy, active lifestyles was a flop, so Toronto-based Campbell went back to the drawing board. After more than 200 interviews with Canadian consumers, it discovered the product's strongest asset was the very feature the company had considered a drawback: its heritage.

"We realized we had walked away from our greatest equity," [said] John Cassady, Campbell's senior vice-president of marketing and sales [at the time]. "The most important thing was the warm feeling people had toward Campbell's."

Identity crises can also arise when companies overindulge in diversification or vertical integration. As one commentator has said, excessive vertical integration may be one cause of the troubles the American automobile industry has experienced in the past two decades. General Motors, for one, claimed at one point that its high degree of vertical integration allowed it to "[save] the supplier's profit by making its own components." By December 1986, however, GM had closed a component plant, reasoning that the plant would achieve lower costs if it operated as an independent supplier.

Even the venerable Hudson's Bay Company (The Bay), one of Canada's oldest businesses, was plunged into an identity crisis beginning in 1978 when it tried a new market focus by cutting back on low-margin hard goods such as appliances and concentrating on higher-margin items such as clothing and cosmetics. As the Bay renovated its stores to accommodate the changes, shoppers had trouble finding departments, and the changes in merchandise meant that some standard items were not available at all. Shortly after the Bay switched to soft goods, baby boomers started setting up house in earnest, and hard goods were in high demand. So, along with its identity as a hard-goods retailer, The Bay lost customers. (The firm still believes that its concentration on soft goods will pay off in the long run, however.)

Zellers, a deep-discount subsidiary of the Hudson's Bay Company, went through its own short image mix-up but soon found itself again and is now growing more than twice as fast as the department store industry as a whole. In an effort to evade the competition of new off-price operations such as Bi-Way and Bargain Harold's, Zellers tried to fancy up its image in the mid-1980s. By 1987, the store was floundering, and new management came in to bring the operation back to its senses. It adopted an aggressive pricing stance—"The Lowest Price Is the Law"—and it has returned to its position as a top-flight cut-rate merchandiser. "Our obsession is to be the absolute lowest-cost retailer," company president Hani Zayani has said. "We try to think of ourselves as good retail people—not flashy or fancy." Getting back to its roots has obviously paid dividends for Zellers—in customer satisfaction and profits.

THE DISTRIBUTOR AS CUSTOMER

A survey of large American manufacturers carried out in the mid-1980s revealed that nearly half the firms said that they reached the majority of their customers through distributors and middlemen rather than through their own sales staff. Agents, distributors, and retailers are taking on the role of customers more and more as they become the company's key contacts with the outside world. As New York-based management consultant Peter D. Moore has said:

> If your customers are beginning to look more like your distributors, . . . welcome to the new industrial revolution. Successful companies . . . recognize that controlling the output of goods is no longer enough to assure their access to profitable markets. Reaching the ultimate customer increasingly requires controlling the distribution system—and locking out the competition.

Moore goes on to point out how Citicorp, the financial services giant, has improved its position in the home mortgage lending business by targeting the real estate agent, rather than the home buyer, as its real customer. And the eight airlines that control more than 90 percent of all travel in the United States have taken the same tack—identifying travel agents, rather than passengers, as their key customers. With the convenience of the agents in mind (as well as their own interests), these airlines have set up computerized reservation systems that make life difficult for their smaller competitors, whose flights are less prominently displayed.

Treating middlemen as customers doesn't always mean sending them boxes of chocolates, as Robert Sinclair, president of Saab-Scania of America, discovered. When he came to Saab in 1979, he was shocked by the company's relationship with its dealers, whom he calls "my primary customers." Because dealers were not giving cars the proper amount of checking before letting them off the lot, owners were complaining about bad service. Sinclair realized that he had to fix the company's relationship with its dealers if the dealers were going to improve. He decided to use the old carrot-and-stick approach. Working with the dealers, he set up a process whereby mechanics were required to check every last item on the vehicle before it got into the customer's hands, and sales people were to spend at least one hour showing customers how to operate their new acquisition. Unless dealers agree to this procedure, Sinclair won't pay Saab's traditional delivery fee. The steel hand in the kid glove approach has worked. According to surveys by the research firm J.D. Power, Saab's relationship with dealers is now one of the best in the industry.

Professionals in the field of quality improvement use flow-charting methods to help identify all those who must be satisfied in delivering a product or service. By following the product from its creation through to its delivery, planners can identify all the customers who are affected along the way. This means, of course, that *employees working inside the firm* are as much customers as distributors and agents are. For the purposes of this kind of analysis, the term *product* is also given a broad definition— to include not only goods and services but also the processes by which they are produced.

Looking first at the external environment, the following customers would appear on the flowchart for an automobile assembler such as General Motors:

- Component suppliers, who require clear specifications and precise quantity forecasts in order to meet the assembler's need for timely delivery.

- Dealers, who receive finished automobiles from the assembler and are invoiced for the goods. They need advertising support and service training from the assembler.

- Drivers, who buy from the dealers and who have, of course, the full slate of customer requirements—including performance, features, image, and servicing.

- Shareholders, who have a vital interest in the success of the entire process and are concerned with the stability of earnings and the return on investment.

A supplier-to-customer chain for a footwear manufacturer such as Reebok would include these customers:

- The supplier(s) of raw materials needed for the shoe
- The designer and/or tester of footwear design
- The factory personnel who build the shoe
- The distributor in the distribution center(s)
- The retailer who sells the shoe
- The customer, the ultimate user

THE EMPLOYEE AS CUSTOMER

Looking inside the business, each department receives input from the others and produces output to be used elsewhere in the company. In other words, every employee has at least one other employee as his or her customer. To improve internal customer relations, managers need to keep in mind an "internal service vision," whereby external customer service strategy is turned inward and key groups of employees are targeted. This kind of internal marketing campaign should stimulate employees' awareness of the need for high quality and excellent service. It consists of four basic steps:

- Research: using employee surveys and interviews to uncover attitudes, concerns, and suggestions for improving product quality and service
- Segmentation: categorizing employees, for example, by number of years with the company and type of customer contacts, when considering training or retraining programs
- Media: using key employees as role models and publicizing their achievements through internal company publications
- Public relations: recognizing special individuals or groups with lunches, flowers, or other forms of special acknowledgment

Air Canada uses such methods as part of its "Customer Care" program. A key part of the airline's recent effort to improve quality of service has been to work to better understand and communicate with employees. The company believes rewarding and recognizing employees will keep morale at high levels. Exceptional employees are now individually honored at customer care conferences, by the president at an annual gala, and in Air Canada's triweekly newspaper, *Horizons.*

OWNERS AND SHAREHOLDERS AS CUSTOMERS

Owners, shareholders, and other sources of financial support for your company can also be usefully viewed as customers. In the past, corporate managers worked on the assumption that what was good for the business was good for shareholders, but times have changed. The flood of mergers, acquisitions, and takeovers in the 1980s demonstrated that disgruntled shareholders can lead to demands for new management. While executives must still manage the business enterprise for profitability and growth, they also need to satisfy investors' short-term goals and achieve fair value in the stock market.

There is a growing emphasis on stock price and a new militancy as shareholders insist that their interests as owners of the corporation be given top priority. In 1989, for example, when Honeywell Corporation proposed in a proxy statement the adoption of several antitakeover charter amendments, a group of private, institutional, and pension fund stockholders banded together to fight the changes. This was the first time public pension funds and private investors agreed to form a group for the purpose of soliciting proxies. And it was the first time such a group hired a proxy solicitor to work on its behalf against management. Within five business days, the group succeeded in blocking the shareholders' vote that management had sought.

A POSSIBLE PITFALL

Although it is essential to pay attention to the internal customer, the danger in focusing too intently on employees and their needs is that the *real* (external) customers might get left out in the cold. John Guaspari illustrates the problem this way in *The Customer Connection*:

> Below you are two separate groups of firefighters, each one holding a net for you to jump into. The net on the left was made by a company that faithfully used the internal customer model, with every department taking great pains to deliver that which was considered to be of value by the next department in the process. The net on the right was made

by a company that took great pains to make sure that everyone understood one basic fact: "We're here to build nets that will catch people jumping from the fifteenth floor of burning buildings."

Which net would you jump into?

Perhaps the most important difference between an external customer and an internal customer is priority. A company's success is determined by whether its products or services are better than competitors' and whether they satisfy customers. Internal customers are a vital part of the process, but they are still just a means to this end, and their needs must necessarily be subordinate. Recent advertisements used by Xerox sum up the right relationship between employees and customers. They say, "We answer to you."

In the changing business environment of the 1990s, the companies that make the grade will have to work as unified entities, in which each component of the operation has the same clear vision of who the customers are and the same dedication to giving them 100 percent satisfaction—if not more. This kind of devotion does not spring up overnight. It has to be cultivated and nurtured until everyone in the enterprise—from president to mail clerk—invests the same pride in creating value for their customers. In the next chapter, we will look at how the customer-value culture can be created.

3

Upside Down and Inside Out: Creating the Customer-Value–Driven Culture

Total Quality is everything, it's everybody. It's a matter of survival. And it is almost like a religion. To have total quality you're going to have to change your culture. You can't change your culture without an emotional experience.

> John C. Marous, chairman, Westinghouse Electric Corp.

To satisfy the customer, it means that everybody in the company has to understand that the total existence of a company depends upon the customer, so if the customer is not satisfied, he is not going to be a customer tomorrow, and if he is not a customer tomorrow, we don't have a business tomorrow.

> Harvey Lamm, president of Subaru of America

When John C. Marous first uncorked a bottle of champagne in the middle of a breakfast meeting, the 14 Westinghouse executives who were sitting at the table didn't know what he was up to. But people at the multibillion-dollar conglomerate are starting to get accustomed to the tradition now. It is all part of a new vision that is transforming the company's way of doing business. Old hierarchical structures have been supplemented by task forces, headed by top executives, which "have the job of cutting across the lines of command to ensure that a 'Eureka!' uttered anywhere in the company will be heard wherever it can be put to use." And every Monday morning, there is a breakfast meeting at which the firm's key executives meet to discuss whatever is on their minds. As for the bottles of champagne—one is opened whenever the company has made a major breakthrough or conquest.

All that would add up to only so much puffery if the results weren't beginning to show. From 1984 to 1989, the company's earnings per share increased 123 percent and its dividend nearly doubled. In a barely profitable position in 1975 (a 2.8 percent return on sales), Westinghouse received an estimated 10 percent return on sales in 1989. The key to the company's improvement has been a strategic-planning process called "VABASTRAM" (VAlue BAsed STRAtegic Management), which, in the words of Burton Staniar, chairman of Westinghouse Broadcasting, "forces internal units to make decisions that will increase shareholder value." This comprehensive approach, along with a Quality and Productivity Center that has inspired and implemented self-improvement projects throughout the corporation, is a model of what can happen when top management establishes a standard of quality and makes sure that vision is implemented all the way down to the grass roots.

STATE YOUR VISION

Singleness of purpose is part of the winning formula, which is why the first step in creating a customer-value-driven culture is to develop a clear mission statement. Since management by objectives came into style, managers and executives across North America have been writing mission statements and setting objectives, so this "company-wide vision" idea might sound old hat. You might say, for instance, that traditional mission statements and this new kind (some call them *vision statements*) are both intended to determine the firm's strategic and day-to-day operating decisions. So what's the difference? The vision statement is based on a whole different set of principles. Here are some of the more important ones:

1. Customer satisfaction is the main driving force behind the company's operations. Without customers, the company will not survive. This

philosophy has several implications: Employees in the company are obsessive about knowing, even better than the customers themselves, what the customers want; the company creates and manages customers' expectations; it designs its products and services to maximize customer satisfaction; and it "puts its money where its mouth is" by making a full financial commitment to customer satisfaction.

2. The company sets for itself "impossibly high" standards of product and service quality. Quality focuses on the presence of value rather than the absence of defects, and it is viewed as a starting point only. The aim is not to meet customers' expectations, but to exceed them.

3. Traditional bottom-line thinking is no longer the highest priority. As the Japanese quality authority Kaoru Ishikawa has said, "If a company follows the principle of 'quality first,' its profits will increase in the long-run. If a company pursues the goal of attaining a short-term profit, it will lose competitiveness in the international market, and will lose profit in the long-run." He goes on to point out some of the obstacles to this approach:

> In practice, many companies are still operating on the basis of profit first. They may proclaim "quality first," but at the shop they are only interested in cutting cost. . . . In many areas, America is still governed by an old-fashioned capitalism. The owner, the chairman, or the directors are the ones who scout and hire a new president. The president thus chosen must show a quick profit or else may be fired. He has no time to think about long-term profit. He is forced to choose a short-term profit, and in so doing loses his match with the Japanese.

Of course, Ishikawa is not saying the bottom line should be ignored. He is simply preaching freedom from the tyranny of the quarterly statement—which makes sense. After all, what is the point of having a neat-looking profit till the end of March if it means the company has failed to invest in the technology that will ensure its survival for the next five years? In other words, the company that is really interested in delivering value for customers will be more willing to make long-term investments, the impact of which can be felt only after several years; and it will accept lower profit levels on a particular product rather than eliminate features that are important to its customers.

4. Cross-functional management is recognized as a critical ingredient for success. The company is structured so that top management takes into full account the expertise of middle- and lower-level managers—

and cross-functional teams are set up so that people from different functional areas automatically have input into major decisions.

Proctor & Redfern Ltd., a Toronto-based engineering and architectural consulting firm, has used this approach to good advantage. (Its revenue grew from $18 million in 1985 to $41 million in 1988.) The company's CEO, Stuart Angus, says that senior executives "don't sit around like gurus and develop a strategy, then try to flog it to the troops. [They] get people involved in projects."

Fergus Groundwater, president of Advanced Dynamics Corp. Ltd., a custom designer and builder of industrial equipment based in Montreal, also endorses this approach:

> [In the past] I controlled everything—ideas had to be mine or pass through me. Eventually things got clogged at the top. [Now,]when a customer has a problem, an ADC project leader gathers people from all departments of the company and divides responsibility for solving it into smaller parts. . . . Often I burst into these brainstorming sessions with a total solution of my own and emerge with only 20% intact.

The participatory approach has been successful for ADC as well: Its sales went from $5.8 million in 1987 to $10.4 million in 1988.

5. All employees, including top executives, are required to stay close to the customer. At the Four Seasons Hotels, for instance, the Toronto-based chain that consistently has the highest occupancy rates and the most repeat business in the industry, executives' jobs are structured so that they *have* to stay in touch with customers' needs. The seven regional vice-presidents, who oversee three hotels each, must also serve as general manager for one of the three.

Keep It Simple

If a vision statement is really going to revolutionize a company's operations for the better, all the ingredients in the foregoing list have to be included. And the statement also has to be simple but challenging. Reuben Mark, Colgate's chief executive officer, has said that, even in a multinational operation, it is essential to establish a single global vision, rather than adapt that vision to different cultures. "You're never going to get anyone to charge the machine guns only for financial objectives," Mark says. "It's got to be something that makes them feel better, feel part of something." Colgate's own credo is short, sweet, and demanding: "We can be the best."

Mack Truck's stated vision, "We service our customers around the world through the innovative design, engineering, manufacturing and servicing of trucks and vehicles that meet their needs at low life-cycle cost," can be unpacked into specific corporate strategies that reflect many of the values listed above:

- Provide a strong and competitive field organization
- Maintain an effective global support system of parts and service availability for Mack products
- Maintain and strengthen product differentiation and quality
- Build on reputation for distinctive, durable products
- Compete on value; deliver products with the lowest life-cycle costs for customers

The vision statement published by the advertising agency Lintas is similarly emphatic about creating value:

- Valued for a total commitment to our Clients' winning
- Valued for having a true business partnership with our Clients, leading to mutual growth
- Valued and respected for the flair, integrity, and professionalism shown by every member of our team
- Valued for producing creatively stretching recommendations
- Valued for making our Clients' contact with the Agency the most stimulating part of their week

That sounds great on paper, you may be saying, but so do a lot of things. Is a vision statement really going to make things better at my company? In fact, a vision statement can easily turn into a lot of hot air if it isn't implemented, and it will never be implemented successfully without the total commitment of upper management. That means numerous visits to the trenches and leadership by example. J.M. Juran, one of the American deans of quality management (who told the Japanese how to do it before the Japanese told us), has warned that many attempts at quality transformation have failed because top executives have learned the lessons of delegation too well:

> Many upper managers have already tried to delegate to subordinates the job of meeting the quality crisis. The delegation process has generally consisted of a drive to exhort subordinates to develop "awareness." Such drives were conducted with the best intentions and with competent promotion: statements of support by top executives, meetings and displays to arouse interest, colorful posters, cleverly worded slogans. The assumption and hope were that such increase in awareness would somehow change behavior and improve results. With some exceptions, nothing of the sort took place.

> These drives were doomed to failure because they did not address the fundamentals. . . . The department managers continued to be judged based on meeting departmental goals, and those goals (with exceptions) continued to perpetuate the deficiencies of the past. No provision was made to determine "what should we do differently from what we have been doing." The fact that the upper managers' personal involvement (usually) ended with their speeches (made at the launching of the drive) tended to deny the assertions that the upper managers regarded quality as having top priority.

As if that weren't convincing enough, Ishikawa takes up the same theme:

> If only one or two company directors are dedicated to total quality control, that is quite insufficient. Unless the person in charge, the one who has the full power, that is, the president or the chairman, takes the initiative and assumes leadership in implementing quality control, the program cannot succeed. . . . Within a company, it is easy to become satisfied with the status quo. . . . But ours is the age of rapid technological innovation and worldwide competition. If the top management cannot assume leadership in breaking through the existing barriers, their company is going to be left behind. Japanese people used to think of caution as a virtue and said, "A cautious man taps a stone bridge before crossing." The question for our age is how fast one can cross the bridge after tapping. The age of excessive caution is over.

Caution may not be the problem in North America so much as too many department managers charging across their own bridges (meeting their own divisional goals) without getting together and deciding which bridge they should all be crossing *together*. Without a unifying vision and hands-on help from top-level executives, the corporation will never be transformed into a unified whole, and they'll never find the bridge that will lead them to excellence.

Connect It to Company Culture

The vision statement will also fade into thin air if the values on which it is based are not in harmony with the company's informal cultural values—the beliefs and company folklore that determine the attitudes and daily behavior patterns of management and, most particularly, those of front-line employees. Although company culture has only recently been recognized as an identifiable, and manageable, part of business strategy, it is becoming more and more obvious what a profound effect it has on business performance.

At the U.S. manufacturing operations of Honda Motor Car Ltd. in Marysville, Ohio, high-level executives have made concrete moves to make sure the company's informal cultural values are in line with the company's slogans: "associate involvement," "continual renewal," and "everything must improve." All Honda workers, from president Hiroyuki Yoshino to the assembly line workers, wear identical white shirts and pants. There is no corporate dining room, just cafeterias for all employees. There are no reserved parking spaces for top managers and all workers are referred to as "associates." Employees are constantly asked for suggestions on improving the operation, and courses on everything from leadership skills to Japanese and English are offered at the plant. "Honda hires the whole human being," says Jack McDonald of Stanford University's Business School. "They really want him or her to think."

Although most companies pay lip service to the importance of employees, Honda practices what it preaches to an unusually high degree. And this story has a neat twist: The effort to create a "Honda culture" has probably taken root more securely in this U.S. agricultural town than back in Japan. "It's a little bit like the analogy of people who come to the church by choice," says McDonald. The U.S. workers are "more pure and devoted" to the idea "than the people born into it" in Japan.

The results? For one, Honda is hoping to edge out Chrysler as the number three car company in the United States. For another, it rejects only one-half of 1 percent of all the goods destined for its cars. But "that's not good enough," says corporate spokesman Roger Lambert. "We didn't get to that level by being satisfied when [acceptances] were at 99 percent."

CROSS-FUNCTIONAL MANAGEMENT

Honda's "teamwork" approach might not appeal to the palates of many North American managers, for cross-functional management, as Ishikawa has said, is an "acquired taste." But without teamwork, the most high-minded pledges of allegiance to value creation will end up gathering dust in the company vaults.

It's no wonder that cross-functional management goes against the North American grain. For years *quality management* was considered to be the domain of experts such as Armand V. Feigenbaum, who managed manufacturing and quality control at General Electric staff headquarters in New York City in the 1950s and originated the concept of total quality control. He helped propagate the idea of quality control as a separate function by suggesting that total quality control be conducted mostly by quality control (QC) specialists.

On the other hand, the Japanese approach, as articulated by Ishikawa, has insisted (since 1949!) "on having all divisions and all employees become involved in studying and promoting QC." It is not that the Japanese have totally abolished hierarchical structures. Indeed, the "vertical line of authority" in Japanese companies was (and still is) so strong that QC specialists wouldn't have had the clout to be heard in individual divisions, let alone throughout the company, if a cross-functional approach had *not* been taken. To counter this problem, the Japanese have taken the tack of "[educating] everyone in every division and [letting] each person implement and promote QC."

The idea is not to destroy divisional distinctions, but to supplement and support them. Ishikawa's textile analogy best describes the intent:

> Industry has a strong top-to-bottom vertical bond while sectionalism hinders development of horizontal relations. For example, no matter how hard the division of quality assurance attempts to perform the function assigned to it, it cannot do so adequately within the existing organizational structure.
>
> Cross-function[al] management which has cross-function[al] committees for support can provide the woof to help the company run crosswise, making possible the responsible development of quality assurance.
>
> In textiles, the warp by itself remains a thread. Only when the woof is added, and when warp and woof are intertwined, will there be cloth. In a company, the analogy holds true. A vertical society resembling the warp is not an organization. It becomes a strong organization only

when various functions such as quality assurance are intertwined with the warp.... Organizational management is possible only through the intertwining of the warp, which engages in management by divisions, and the woof, which engages in control by cross-function[al] management.

In another way, cross-functional management is perhaps not so foreign to our way of thinking. Back to Dr. Juran: Company-wide quality management (another variation of the cross-functional theme), "is quite similar to the method long used to set and meet financial goals.... When properly done, the budgets ... are arrived at through extensive participation at all levels. The final result is financial goals at all levels: ..."

Just as it would be foolhardy for the company president to concoct a budget without the detailed input of marketing, operations, and all the other functional areas, planning for quality and customer satisfaction improvement initiatives can go badly astray when all input from all the relevant divisions is blocked. Juran cites some scenarios where divisions met their own goals but in so doing have subverted the greater good of the company:

- New products were developed to meet the needs of external customers but not the needs of internal customers. ...

- Multidepartmental planning projects such as new product launchings suffered perpetual delays because the various phases were carried out consecutively, with inadequate early warning of the damage done to later phases.

- A high cost of poor quality was perpetuated by being built into the cost standards.

Such problems being inherently multidepartmental in nature, [they] could be solved only by extensive multidepartmental means: joint planning, project teams, early warning systems, participation.

Why, then, doesn't everyone switch to cross-functional management approaches right away, if it makes so much sense? Largely because cross-function looks more like cross-purposes to managers used to thriving in the vertical system. Juran has noted that multidepartmental systems ("joint planning, project teams, early warning systems, participation") tend to "interfere with meeting *departmental* goals." [Emphasis added.] He cites an example:

A planning department is given a schedule to complete a specific planning project in twelve months. If the department were to bring its internal customers into extensive participation, it might benefit the company greatly. However, the department would then miss its schedule by two months.

Another purpose that gets thwarted when cross-functional management is introduced is that of getting a departmental monopoly over specific functions. The department manager who has added status and power because she has a high degree of control over her own area is not going to look kindly on anything that represents an invasion of her turf.

Conversely, cross-functional management might force another manager to act on one of the "grey-area" activities that keep cropping up between departments when he would rather not be bothered. This scenario, described in the journal *Quality Progress*, is typical:

> Consider the case of manager A saying to manager B: "I have a problem that is consuming company resources but the solution must come from your area." Manager B's response is, "Sorry about that, but it's not in my objectives, resources, or priorities."

Finally, let's be frank: Cross-functional management adds to the workload of already busy upper managers. Cross-functional teams, which are described in the next section, have to be headed up by a top-level manager if the company's vision is going to permeate all divisions. Furthermore, as Dr. Juran has remarked, it takes time to undergo the training necessary for quality planning, to create the company's vision and the policies, goals, controls, and incentives that will make it work as a whole, and to review performance against goals. Companies contemplating the implementation of cross-functional management will have to be realistic about these drawbacks; but if they hesitate too long at Ishikawa's "bridge," there might not be a bridge left for them to cross once they decide to go ahead.

Cross-Functional Teams

Once the company has accepted the notion of cross-functional management, a company-wide "customer value team" or "customer value council" should be set up. The chairman of such a team or council is usually the company president or executive vice-president, and its members are corporate officers. The functions of this team will vary, depending on the nature of the business and the customer value problems it has to address, but the following basics should be carried out:

- Coordinate establishment of quality goals
- Coordinate preparation of plans to carry out the goals
- Review progress against goals
- Coordinate the administration of the reward system

In cases where a vision statement has not yet been created, the team will have to develop one before it does anything else, and it will have to set up the systems by which customer value will be delivered. In order to build these systems, it will be useful to create a backdrop in the form of a *value proposition*, which is similar to the vision statement, but more focused on the company's core proposition, or promise, to the market. The value proposition clearly defines the company's target customers, the benefits and price levels to be offered compared with those offered by competitors, and the cost structure necessary to deliver value to customers at a sufficiently attractive profit margin.

At different points in a company's life, it may be important to set up other cross-functional teams, to address specific issues that may be hampering the delivery of value to customers. Divisional cross-functional teams (as opposed to company-wide ones) should be chaired by the general manager, and team members should be chosen from his or her staff.

Possible Pitfalls: Forewarned Is Forearmed

It will take a while for the cross-functional teams to produce results. As with any new system, the bugs will have to be worked out before the committees are really effective. Some of the problems are predictable, however. A list of possible pitfalls (and ways to avoid them) follows—in Ishikawa's no uncertain terms:

1. Some companies convene a meeting only when there are problems. They consider cross-function[al] teams to be project teams and ad hoc in nature. That approach must be avoided.

2. Some people erroneously assume that once cross-function[al] management is established, the company can dispense with control by division. Both are necessary.

3. Some people feel that all specialists and all affected divisions must be included in the committee. No, the cross-function[al] committee is of a higher order than that.

4. Do not regard cross-function[al] committees as your project teams. Let us assume that you have a cross-function[al] committee for profit control and your profits have not reached an established goal. Does your committee establish quotas for the line divisions to reach certain profit goals? No, these are to be determined by the line divisions themselves (through management by objectives).

5. Initially, company directors who are named committee members tend to represent only their sectional interests in their capacities as heads of the design division, accounting division, etc. This must not be allowed to happen. What they must strive for is to build a company-wide perspective from the outset.

6. Some people may genuinely believe in their devotion to the functions to which they are assigned, but continue to interpret everything that comes before the committee in terms of their own divisions. For example, a cross-function[al] committee on quantity control must be concerned with the overall product amount for the entire company. However, a committee member from the production control division may not pay any attention to events in other divisions. Similarly, an accountant on a cross-function[al] committee may forget the overall picture and only discuss accounting procedures.

7. The work of cross-function[al] committees cannot go smoothly unless information is gathered routinely through all channels within the company.

8. Do not increase the number of cross-function[al] committees excessively. When there are too many committees, they may engage in inter-committee disputes and create a situation very similar to inter-divisional rivalries.

A PORTRAIT OF THE BUSINESS AS A VALUE CREATION PROCESS

Although each cross-functional committee will of course have a unique set of problems to tackle, one of the most useful tools for pinpointing problems is to view the company as a *business system* made up of many processes, which must be orchestrated toward the goal of delivering superior value to customers. Apart from the top-level customer value team, most cross-functional teams should be looking at one process within the system and deciding how it could be improved. A process can be as simple as the process for following up on unpaid invoices, or it can consist of all the factors affecting the operations of, say, the accounting department. The different factors affecting manufacturing, operations, design, purchasing, sales, data processing, human resources, and administration can also be considered processes. Any process consists of a collection of *cause factors*, which can be defined and therefore controlled to obtain better effects. By understanding all elements of a business process, each element can be managed to create a more consistent, high-quality performance.

The following process model is an adaptation of models used by Kaoru Ishikawa and Philip Crosby (of *Quality Is Free* fame). The cause factors in this model are as follows:

1. Outputs
2. Activities
3. Inputs (including equipment and facilities, and training and knowledge)
4. Performance standards

It is important to remember that the whole purpose of the exercise is to find ways of ensuring that customers feel they are getting value for their dollar—not to get caught up in analyzing the process. That said, however, it is essential to do a comprehensive analysis of the business process at hand in order to root out cause factors that are hampering productivity and the delivery of value.

Outputs

The first job of the team is to define the desired output. If it is assessing shipping as a process, for instance, the output might be on-time delivery of goods 98 percent of the time, with zero breakage. A committee assessing the marketing division would define the desired output more broadly—perhaps as satisfied buyers who become loyal, repeat customers.

Activities

This category is a "process within the process" and includes all the tasks—or work steps—and operations required to produce the desired output. Flow charting, which we discussed in the last chapter to identify all the *customers* that a company comes in contact with, can also be used to identify all the steps that make up the activities in a process.

When it comes to getting things down on paper, the conventional flow-chart symbols can be used to define each of the activities. (An oval represents the first activity, a box denotes each process step, a triangle indicates a decision to be made, and another oval stands for the last activity. All the symbols together will add up to a sequence of activities [do this first, do that second] and conditional branches [if this condition, then do that].) Once the entire sequence is represented visually, it is easier to pinpoint inefficiencies and blockages.

When this flow-charting method is applied to the diagnosis of processes as deliverers of value for customers, it is often called *blueprinting*. Jane Kingman-Brundage, a specialist in the technique, calls a detailed blueprint an "expert system." Such a system can be the first step in developing an automated expert system. American Express uses one such system. Kingman-Brundage writes that

> [d]rawing on the technology of artificial intelligence, the expert system of American Express assists their customer representatives [in making] . . . credit decisions. Through careful blueprinting of the various service steps and decision conditions typical of a service representative's interaction with a customer, American Express has thought through, in advance, the best responses. This ensures customer satisfaction, while at the same time protecting the company's interests.

Inputs

Inputs are all the means employed in the process to produce the output. They include *information or materials* (the raw inputs to be transformed), *methods* (the specific *ways* in which activities are performed), *equipment* (the machinery or other productive "hardware" used in the process), and *people* (the individuals who operate within the process, their training and skill levels as matched to the tasks to be performed). No matter how well a process has been designed, it will not produce the desired output if the inputs are not aligned with it. For this reason, many companies are seeking ways to more actively manage their relationships with the suppliers of raw materials and components.

Evaluating inputs is also a useful way of thinking about the relationships between internal company departments. One department's output is usually the input needed for the process of another. Through discussions and clarification of the needs of both parties, the hand-off step between them can be improved and the overall process upgraded. Often, non-value-adding steps are eliminated as unnecessary departmental boundaries are taken down, resulting in a seamless flow of value-adding activities.

Performance Standards

This category is essentially self-explanatory. Standards must be defined in precise, observable terms—such as those used by some pizza operations. Domino's Pizza, for instance, doesn't just promise "fast delivery." It promises delivery within "30 minutes or the pizza is free." Because the standard of performance is clearly articulated, the business process can be more easily aligned to meet the standard.

As the employee team assesses the process, it should establish both the actual performance level of the process and its performance capability (potential performance level). Juran puts it this way:

> [A]ll processes have an inherent capability for performance. That capability can be evaluated through data collection and analysis. By changing the process procedures and definition, you also change the capability to produce the results you want. Process capability may be likened to the "capacity" of the system to produce. Process performance is what a process actually does. Process capability is what a process could do if you removed the significant causes of poor performance.

If the team is not satisfied with the output of the business process, the input, activities, and performance standard variables should all be reassessed. It is tempting for managers to assume that it is the employees who are always to blame for poor outputs (which, of course, they *sometimes* are), but if the process is poorly designed or inputs are incorrectly managed, no amount of shouting, whining, or cajoling will improve the output one bit. In fact, most performance problems can be traced to faulty management and administrative processes that were designed on the basis of outdated assumptions, inaccurate perceptions, and poor process principles. Most experts in the field of quality management believe that poor design of business processes is responsible for 80 percent or more of output problems. Through the use of simple business process models, however, managers and cross-functional teams can expose the integrated and interdependent nature of the "cause factors" within a process and of the processes within the whole business system and discover ways of improving the effectiveness and efficiency of the process. This is the first, essential step in improving the value of the product or service that is ultimately delivered.

You might be thinking this sounds all very well in theory, but who has the time and resources to carry out this kind of painstaking analysis in practice? An assessment such as this *does* take time and money; but if an enterprise is looking for ways to deliver value to its customers, it can't afford *not* to look at its business processes. If the company's executives don't take the time to go through this exercise, they will never know where the rough spots are and what can be improved; and in the end they'll have to work twice as hard to get the same result as a company that overhauled its processes. There is a lot of validity in the expression, "If it ain't broke, don't fix it," but first you have to spend some time finding out whether "it" really is working as well as it appears to be.

Case in Point #1. This case study amply demonstrates the insidious nature of process defects and the kind of analysis that it took to uncover the problems. The company in question sold a custom-made product, and the process being examined started with the salesperson entering a customer order. It ended with the shipment of the product to the customer. The process was a cross-functional one, with activities carried out by order entry, production control, purchasing, manufacturing, and distribution. The problem with the output was this: Although the product was of excellent quality, deliveries were much later than the promised 60 days, and customer satisfaction was eroding. At the same time, customers were asking for even faster turnaround on orders.

A quick examination of the process showed that the order entry system had a lot of aborted runs because orders either lacked necessary information or had conflicting information from the salesperson. Special expediting had to be undertaken frequently, since 85 percent of all orders were entered into the production control system late. A lot of time was spent in reworking orders that had changed or in giving status reports on the phone. The special expediting and order changes were causing continual starts and stops, which translated into manufacturing inefficiencies.

A cross-functional team of middle managers was set up to analyze the process and they came to the following conclusions:

- There was no adequate way to measure the process (a "performance standards" problem).
- Sales people were not penalized for sending incomplete or inaccurate information to order entry (an "input" problem and a "performance standard" problem).
- Of the 85 percent of orders that were entered into the production control system late, 62 percent did not have all the information needed to correctly process the order (another "input" problem).
- Upper management was unaware of the key problem: inaccurate information from sales representatives.

A traditional approach to this problem might have been to give the sales people a pep talk about accuracy. But the problem would have continued, because they would have been given no support to change their ways.

The cross-functional team concluded instead that the problem was with the process, and the following actions resulted:

- Sales people were told about order-entry requirements and the consequences of their errors. They were also trained in a new order-entry procedure, including a system prompt that made errors and omissions less likely.
- An "exception procedure" was established to be used when delivery got behind schedule. Reports on these cases were given to marketing management.
- The 60-day lead time was reduced to 15 days for the most common custom orders. This simplified the order entry process, and the shorter lead time encouraged customers to order one of the standard configurations.

In spite of the detailed work that was required and the headaches that generated, the whole analysis procedure paid off. The average shipping time for 60-day orders was reduced to 50.8 days, and the people associated with the process were reduced from 35 to 19 (because there was less need to expedite orders and there were fewer phone calls about the status of orders).

Case in Point #2. The cross-functional team just described took a re-active approach to process analysis and improvement, addressing a major problem and solving it. Other teams are set up to take proactive measures as well as to fight fires. Because the 130 staff members of the Productivity and Quality Center at Westinghouse are dedicated only to quality management and are not pulled from separate functional areas, they can't properly be called a cross-functional team. It is cross-functional in its approach, however, and it performs many of the activities of a cross-functional team—but on a grander scale. It has its own sense of mission: "When you accept the challenge of doing the same work in half the time, you *must* improve quality," says Carl Arendt, the Center's marketing manager. "By definition, bad quality is a waste of time." President Paul E. Lego describes the Center's angle: "When most people think of quality they think of the product; we try to think of the process."

Any business unit at Westinghouse can ask for a "Total Quality Fitness Review" for its operation or some part thereof whenever it feels it is necessary. A team from the Quality Center then comes in and conducts interviews and analyses at all levels of the organization—examining all the processes, great and small, that make up the unit's business system. After the team has identified weak links in the chain of training, processes, and products, the results are recorded on a Total Quality scorecard and presented to the manager. Then the Quality Center helps the manager set up teams to look for and implement improvements. "The approach is unique," says Tom Davenport, a senior research associate at the Harvard Business School. "It has a heavy emphasis on process redesign and more of an information technology component than others."

PULLING IT ALL TOGETHER

These sweeping applications demonstrate the flexibility of business process analysis. But none of this analysis will be of much use if it is not done in an environment that encourages the entire business system to operate as an integrated, *customer-value-driven process*. Which brings us right back to the principles of cross-functional management. The business system must be structured in such a way that the combined skills of marketing, operations, and human resources, all drawing on infor-mation technology, are directed towards giving the customer value for money. More important, each functional area must *see* itself as part of the integrated whole.

In the past, department managers were encouraged to work away in their own little silos, meeting and surpassing (and occasionally missing) divisional objectives but not having any incentive—or time—to work for the common good except in the most abstract sense. When the rubber hit the road and the pressure was on, the department manager would always opt to make his part of the picture look good, even if it was at the expense of another department—and thus possibly at the expense of the company as a whole. ("If it's a choice between me and him—I opt for me.") Part of the problem was, of course, the selfishness of human nature—and that's not bound to go away even in the most smooth-running cross-functional environment. But the other part of the problem was systemic. The corporate hierarchical structure was not (and, in many companies, still *is* not) set up to reward managers who invest their time and resources in supporting the efforts of other departmental areas—even though the combined efforts of these managers could often introduce significant efficiencies and save the company from expensive gaffs.

But things don't have to stay that way.

Benson P. Shapiro, writing in *Harvard Business Review,* has identified several characteristics of market-driven, or customer-oriented, companies. They all depend on cross-functional structures and behavior:

- Information on all important buying influences permeates every corporate function. A company can be market-oriented only if it completely understands its markets and the people who decide whether to buy its products or services. . . . To be of greatest use, customer information must move beyond the market research, sales, and marketing functions and "permeate every corporate function"— the R&D scientists and engineers, the manufacturing people, and the field-service specialists. When the technologists, for example, get unvarnished feedback on the way customers use the product, they can better develop improvements on the product and the production processes. . . .

- Collaboration among the various functions is important when pinpointing the key target accounts and market segments. . . .

- Strategic and tactical decisions are made interfunctionally and interdivisionally. Functions and divisions will inevitably have conflicting objectives that mirror distinctions in cultures and in modes of operation. . . .

- The customer-oriented company possesses mechanisms to get these differences out on the table for candid discussion and to make trade-offs that reconcile the various points of view. The marketing department may ask the R&D department to develop a product with a certain specification by a certain date. If R&D thinks the request is unreasonable but doesn't say so, it may develop a phony plan that the company will never achieve. If, on the other hand, the two functions get together, they are in a position to make intelligent technological and marketing trade-offs. They can change a specification or extend a delivery date with the benefit of both points of view.

• Divisions and functions make well-coordinated decisions and execute them with a sense of commitment. If the R&D vice president thought like the financial vice president, she wouldn't be effective in her job. On the other hand, if each function is marching to its own drum, implementation will be weak regardless of the competence and devotion of each function. Joint opportunity analysis, in which functional and divisional people share ideas and discuss alternative solutions and approaches, leverages the different strengths of each party.

The kind of company-wide cooperation that Shapiro has described took place at Esso Chemical Canada when executives there realized they had to do something about the late orders, invoice errors, and customer complaints that were occurring because the different distribution elements of the company were poorly coordinated. Now, one centralized marketing services organization—including the old marketing, customer service, and physical distribution departments—handles everything from the receipt of the order to post-invoicing functions. Under this whole-job concept, each customer service representative takes ownership of a complete transaction, including its physical distribution aspects (dispatching, making routing decisions, and managing off-site inventory). A core group of distribution operations personnel establishes guidelines for all these activities. The customer service rep is also responsible for contacting the client when a delivery cannot be made in time.

In other cases, organizations encourage greater cooperation between different functional areas in the face of drastic internal and external changes. When the AT&T Network was broken up in 1983, for instance, it caused disorientation and turmoil among the people within the old Bell system, and among customers and shareholders. Suddenly the old rules and norms that had governed the relationship between these parties was torn apart.

The one Bell company that seems to have pulled itself back together the fastest, at least from the customer's point of view, is BellSouth. According to studies conducted by third-party research companies who track the telecommunications industry, BellSouth's customers give the company high ratings for responsiveness, installation, repair service, and clear communications (including billings!).

These high levels of customer service have been achieved through specific programs that promote employee cooperation between departments and divisions. BellSouth defines service to include not only external customers, but also the things employees do to help each other perform their jobs more effectively.

One program, called "Count on Me," aims to identify, recognize, and publicize front-line employees who go to interesting and sometimes even amazing lengths to satisfy external customers or help other employees in serving customers. Through this program, BellSouth encourages all employees to see every action as having an effect on the customer and to see that all employees depend on each other in servicing customers properly. Thus, the company has gone to extraordinary lengths to integrate its internal functions and employee activities in order to, as the company states in its vision statement, "deliver service in a manner that causes our customers to perceive value added." The program has worked because it is based on a clear company vision statement, which focuses on creating value for customers, and because it is backed up by efforts to bring the company's informal values into harmony with the main goal.

As in the case of BellSouth, cross-functional management thinking proved effective at Motorola Inc. when that company found itself face-to-face with a badly shrinking market. In the early 1980s, Motorola was losing cellular telephone customers to Japanese firms. By 1988, the firm had become the first recipient of the prestigious Malcolm Baldrige National Quality Award, which recognizes companies that have adopted effective quality and customer satisfaction processes. *USA Today* stated that, by winning the Baldrige Award, Motorola was "the highest quality company in the U.S.A."

The company started its turnaround after a particularly electrifying meeting held in 1981. Chairman Robert W. Galvin had called his top officers together to review business results. Although the financial results looked good, the future looked uncertain. Several officers reported that the quality of the company's cellular phones did not stack up to the Japanese competition: Many of the phones produced by Motorola had simply died in customers' cars.

Galvin appointed Jack Germaine as quality director with the mandate to examine the entire organization and get quality back where it should be. Germaine looked across all functions and discovered that every part of the company had a role to play in fixing the problem.

He turned first to the manufacturing area. More than 75 plants were examined. The number of defects was tracked and analyzed. Managers were given a goal: a ten-fold reduction in defects by the end of a five-year period through implementation of improved manufacturing practices.

Germaine then sent teams to other companies' electronics plants to see how defects could be further reduced. The results of this research suggested that more effort should be concentrated on altering product designs so that they could be manufactured more easily. When this was done, the number of parts in each phone plummeted from 1,378 to 523.

Motorola then reexamined its training and human resources practices to ensure that they encouraged the achievement of quality improvement. The company boosted its spending on employee training to $100 million a year. About 40 percent of this sum is devoted to the procedures and skills that workers need in order to build perfect products or provide error-free service. Workers who learn extra skills and improve quality can earn hefty rewards: Bonuses of up to 30 percent of salaries are given.

The payoff has been substantial. Motorola has not only overcome problems in its cellular phone business, but it has also boosted performance for other product lines. Dataquest Inc., which has recently done a survey of 168 electronics companies, says that Motorola makes the highest-quality semiconductors in the industry. The company has also grabbed the number-one spot in the brutally competitive Japanese pager market. And the company reports that it has reduced annual production costs by $250 million mostly by eliminating rework and repair. That money flows directly to the bottom line, says Richard Bueton, a Motorola vice-president.

This kind of revolution would not have happened without input from all the company's functional areas—or management's renewed devotion to delivering the best-value product to its customers. As Jack Germaine discovered, every department had something essential to offer in solving the problem.

Cross-functional management is obviously not a frill but a necessity for the company that aims to deliver value to its customers. Within each functional area, however, there are strategic tools that can be used to enhance and support the value-delivery process. As we mentioned in Chapter 1, the separate parts of most organizations have always focused on some kind of quality control or customer satisfaction effort. In the marketing area, customer satisfaction has traditionally consisted of using the tools of market analysis and research, competitor benchmarking, and customer satisfaction measurement. In human resources, the focus has been on customer service, organizational

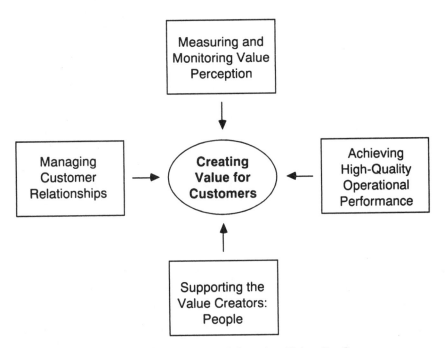

Figure 3–1. The Important Elements of Creating Value for Customers

processes, staff development, rewards and incentives, and the means of changing a culture within a company. Finally, operations brings the burgeoning methodologies of product quality and service quality improvement.

As these approaches merge to form the all-embracing concept of creating value for customers (see Figure 3–1), it is perhaps especially useful to take a close look at what each functional area has to offer. Then, with a deeper knowledge of the techniques and methods specific to each area, managers will be able to choose the most useful tools for their own purposes—and understand the value creation techniques their colleagues in marketing, operation, and human resources are already using.

4

Measuring Customer Satisfaction and Value Perception

Many companies think *they know what quality means in their industry; few have taken the time to back their hunches with careful research ... it is not those who offer the product, but those whom it serves who have the final word on how well a product fulfills needs and expectations.*

David Garvin, Managing Quality

Companies with reputations for satisfying their customers have a common denominator: They set high standards for the dimensions of their business that create value in the minds of their customers. And they have methods for measuring how well they are meeting customer expectations. Successful improvements in value creation are built on good customer research.

This is where the marketing department comes in. Sometimes referred to as the "voice of the customer," it is the part of the business that usually has the most contact with customers and their requirements. Executives who do not have a marketing background need to become familiar with some of the basic tools and techniques of marketing research that can be used to assess customer satisfaction.

Historically, marketing research has had a relatively narrow focus.

In the words of one marketing executive, it has been used to evaluate "a product, a concept, an advertising theme." Customer satisfaction research—that is, the broader application of marketing research techniques to the value creation process—"calls for a different philosophy than traditional marketing research." Now, "customer satisfaction and service quality measurement programs are often spearheaded by top-level management outside the marketing department—managers who are coming to view customer satisfaction data as part of the overall 'management information system' that guides their decision-making." Hence, the scope of the marketing research function is being expanded to include, among other things:

- An emphasis on understanding the buyer-seller relationship over time
- A focus on assessing customer satisfaction compared to competitive offerings
- An increased emphasis on determining how employees affect customer satisfaction

In other words, customer satisfaction research looks at all aspects of the company's interaction with prospective and already established customers. It seeks to define the long-term links between producer (or service provider) and buyer and the degree to which these contact points increase or decrease customer contentment.

In spite of the strategic value of customer-satisfaction measurement, many managers still do not feel comfortable with the idea. Since it is a perception held by buyers, it seems too fragile and subjective a notion to be measured—especially for businesspeople who are used to dealing with "hard facts" such as financial data. "How are we supposed to manage the feelings of our customers?" they ask. That is why the "soft data" of customer feedback needs to be translated into quantitative terms.

The ubiquitous management expert Tom Peters has some useful advice to offer on how this can be done. First of all, feelings are often based on observations of measurable deficiencies or points of excellence. Secondly, a single customer complaint often points to a large, system-wide problem. In *Thriving on Chaos*, Peters points out a number of the objections most commonly raised by managers who are not convinced that customer satisfaction can be quantified—and suggests some ways to make customers' responses at least more concrete, if not strictly numeric:

Seemingly innocuous terms can lead us way off course with the measurement of customer satisfaction. Here are five loaded phrases:

1. "Not symptomatic": A bank executive was discussing customer satisfaction measurement. He said that when a problem only showed up once—a particular error on a statement, for instance—then there was little or no follow-up beyond a cursory apology, because it was "not symptomatic of a larger problem." . . . *Every* customer complaint *is* symptomatic of a shortcoming—moreover, it usually represents a lurking improvement opportunity. Treat every snafu (a) as symptomatic of impending doom and (b) as a budding opportunity for market creation and product redefinition—and act accordingly.

2. "Objective" versus "subjective": One manager insists: "Cleanliness is subjective. By definition, it can't be measured." First, cleanliness can be measured. Just add a question to your next survey: "How clean was the store, on a scale of one to ten, where ten is 'like an operating room'?" Or: "Relative to fast-food places where you've eaten recently, how clean was our operation?" Choices might include "awful," "below average," "average," etc.

So anything can be measured and made 'objective.' But measurement per se does not ensure objectivity.

3. "Ninety-seven percent satisfied": An IBM executive says, "We make 300,000 components. Don't say to me, '97 percent are okay'." Say instead, '9,000 were defective.' Sounds a little bit different, doesn't it?" He adds: "You don't really want 9,000 angry customers, do you?"

4. "On average": The use of averages is downright dangerous. For instance, "On average, we ship parts within 37 hours of order entry," or "The average customer requires 0.84 service visits per year." But more study reveals that the 37-hour "average" also means 89 hours for the "worst-off 10 percent"; and the 0.84 service visit translates into two or more visits for 26 percent of your customers. *Gear your measures to focus attention on the worst-off 1, 5, 10, or 25 percent of customers.*

5. "Unsystematic": I'm all for systematic surveys of 700 randomly selected customers or non-customers. But I also applaud very unsystematic rituals, despite the disdain they draw from MBA analysts. Once a month, George Gendron, editor-in-chief of *Inc.* magazine, calls a half-dozen people who have not renewed their subscriptions. When I saw him last, he was flying off from the East Coast to Denver just to talk to one of those unhappy subscribers. "Her notion of what was wrong and what could be improved was positively brilliant," he said. The MBA's conception of "systematic" didn't apply in this case, but the business was well served.

Once the credibility of customer satisfaction measurement has been established and an effective measurement program has been put in place, chances are that the results will speak for themselves. In *The Service Edge*, management consultant Ron Zemke discovered that many of the 101 companies he earmarked as top-level service providers paid scrupulous attention to customer satisfaction measurement. They measured formally and frequently, and used the results to assess and modify the way they did business. And they supplemented the formal measurement systems with informal ones. Hotelier Marriott, for instance, conducts both

> [S]cientific, third-party sampling [and] a less formal, more open, Guest Satisfaction Index (GSI) compiled from the in-room survey forms people voluntarily fill out and turn in. John Dixon, general manager of the Marriott in Washington, D.C., calls the GSI at his hotel "a reality check." It answers the question, "Are we as good as we think we are?"

Zemke even found that research and development projects—so often viewed as unknown quantities—could be assessed for customer satisfaction. The Battelle Memorial Institute, which was instrumental in the development of xerography, and works on projects worth more than $600 million at any one time, assesses its customers' satisfaction through a detailed "service-and-satisfaction questionnaire," which it sends out at the end of every project. Says Zemke,

> Even though the unpredictable nature of R&D makes it hard to assess satisfaction, Battelle asks anyway—but it does so in the context of process and expectations, not outcomes. In other words, the research itself may not prove out. But the client should feel that some advantage has come from the knowledge gained, and that its needs were fully and conscientiously attended to. More than 70 percent of Battelle's industrial clients respond. Well over 90 percent consistently say the lab has met or exceeded their expectations.

Although the evidence is stacked in favor of carrying out frequent, comprehensive, and actionable customer satisfaction research, few companies have good indicators to record customer satisfaction performance or measures for managing the processes by which value is created and customer satisfaction is achieved. For example, in a 1989 survey of the Canadian manufacturing, retail, hospitality, business services, and franchising sectors, it was discovered that fewer than 50 percent of respondents undertook frequent assessments of their customer service, relative to the competition.

INGREDIENTS FOR SUCCESS

If a customer satisfaction research program is to succeed, it must, first of all, fit in with the company's overall objectives; and it must have the full support of upper management. A good example of top management involvement in customer satisfaction research is the previously mentioned Total Quality Fitness Review (TQFR) used by Westinghouse Electric Corp. The TQFR method uses an in-depth internal employee interviewing process that measures the performance of a division against the total quality performance of the company. To underline management's commitment to the project, the task force that administers the review is composed of members of senior management.

Management commitment has to be more than visual and personal, however. It also has to be financial. In *Creating the Service Culture,* consultants Brown and Martenfeld report that Apple Canada Inc. spends close to half a million dollars a year on research, "just to get . . . measurements on an ongoing basis." Those measurements include an annual 250-question research study that assesses Apple's performance in relation to the competition.

As for the research tool itself (and there are many, several of which will be described later in this chapter), it has to be designed according to certain basic principles.

1. It should focus on customer expectations (the quality and type of service or product customers expect to receive) and on customer perceptions (what customers believe they are receiving), not on what the company thinks it is delivering.

2. It should focus on the quality of the product or service, not on laying blame on an individual or group. American Express Canada president Morris Perlis has stressed the importance of avoiding anything that looks like "witch-hunting." In 1988, American Express sent out 12,000 questionnaires "[n]ot to demonstrate that Mary Jane made a mistake, but 'here's what we did well, and here's how customers give feedback to each department.'"

3. Employees must be involved in developing the customer satisfaction measures, so that the measures will be more relevant to their day-to-day jobs. One major Canadian insurance company held a series of employee workshops to debate proposed service measures and standards. This resulted in improvements to the measurement approach as well as employee acceptance of the metrics that were ultimately introduced.

Also, staff-developed standards are usually more demanding than the ones management would recommend.

Ron Zemke discovered the importance of making measures relevant to the everyday experiences of employees when he acted as a consultant to a theme park in the upper Midwestern states. He and his colleagues hit on four measurement criteria—friendliness, cleanliness, service, and show—and asked guests who were leaving the park how they rated the place in those four categories. When the results were presented to the front-line workers, they were met with a cool reaction. In Zemke's words, the workers said,

> "What you have is nice for management, but it doesn't help us. When you ask about cleanliness, it would help to know exactly when and where they saw us doing good or bad." [So Zemke] put back the detailed items on clean restrooms, clean sidewalks, clean parking lots, and so forth. . . . The refined measurement and feedback system may not have enhanced our statistical model, but because it did increase the coverage of customer encounters, an interesting thing happened. Employees and supervisors suddenly weren't satisfied knowing they had achieved a 4.8 on bathroom cleanliness. They insisted on knowing how things were perceived by shift, by type of restroom, and by time of day. They simply couldn't get enough feedback.

4. Both qualitative and quantitative data should be gathered. As Marriott's John Dixon notes, "The specific comments explain the numbers."

5. Questions in the survey or interview should be specific; and, if the research is to be carried out along with other work activities, it must be easy to collect and record.

6. The research instrument should be designed so that management and/or employees can take action or implement change, based on its results. As one consultant has put it:

> A major problem with much of today's customer satisfaction research is that product management [this applies to any kind of management] is given six answers [as] to why customer satisfaction is low—without being given priorities. Some things impact customer satisfaction more than others—without priorities, there is no basis for determining what to fix first. Moreover, in much of today's research, the reasons for market damage are not specified in terms which allow action to be taken. To simply say that service is a major cause of market damage, for

example, is useless. Conversely, to say that service technicians can't fix a problem the first time is an actionable statement.

Equally problematical is information that is provided too late for employees to act on or that is directed to employees who have no control over changing the situation.

In an interview with consultants Brown and Martenfeld, Jim Black, senior manager of Service Development and Customer Relations at Nissan Automobile in Canada, said that his company's customer research can be taken so seriously that it alone once formed the basis of a new policy. After preparing a detailed criticism of their own operations in 1985 and asking their dealers and their customers "what they were doing wrong," the research was compiled and used to form new policy and procedures, to revamp the warranty on new vehicles, and to change the way dealers had ordered their parts or vehicles, among other things.

7. Finally, rewards for bringing about positive changes based on the results of a survey should be visible and valuable.

EVERYTHING—INCLUDING THE KITCHEN SINK?

Measurement for the sake of measurement is a useless exercise, of course, but since most companies err on the side of not subjecting enough things to scrutiny, it is safe to say that managers should consider measuring every aspect of their operation that affects customers' perceptions of value. By doing some preliminary exploration (more on that later), researchers can identify all the product and service attributes that determine customer satisfaction and value perception. These attributes will then form the basis of the research instrument.

The appropriate attributes to measure will be different for every company, but the following list shows some of the most important ones:

- Product quality, including

  Performance—the functional product
  Features—options and line extensions
  Reliability—failure rates
  Serviceability—ease and cost of repair
  Aesthetics—design and packaging

- After-sales support and, in particular, delivery and product or service support, including

Speed of delivery—length of time from order
Consistency—ability to meet promised performance schedules
Order fill rate—completeness of shipped orders
Information—status of orders
Emergency response—ability to handle nonstandard requests
Returns policy—procedures to handle damaged goods

- The interaction between employees and customers, including

Timeliness—speed of response to customer inquiries
Employee appearance—cleanliness and appropriateness of attire
Courtesy and response to complaints—helpfulness in resolving
   problems

In addition to these basic attributes, individual businesses should evaluate the key elements of their operation that affect customer satisfaction, as did the customer service division of TRW Inc. The division provides maintenance, repair, and support services for computers and other information handling systems for customers around the world. It had been using traditional measures of quality—response time and repair time—but then added the following criteria to its list: system availability, protocols for calling for service, emergency repairs, preventive maintenance activities, and problem-escalation procedures. All these new indicators provided more detailed measures on how well the company was serving its customers.

UNDERSTANDING THE COMPONENTS OF CUSTOMER SATISFACTION

In order to design appropriate questions about key service and product attributes, the researcher needs to know some basic principles of customer satisfaction. One simple definition says that customer satisfaction is "the state in which customer needs, wants and expectations, through the transaction cycle, are met or exceeded, resulting in repurchase and continuing loyalty." In other words, if customer satisfaction could be expressed as a ratio, it would look like this:

$$\text{Customer satisfaction} = \frac{\text{Perceived quality}}{\text{Needs, wants, and expectations}}$$

If customers perceive that the quality of the product or service *exceeds* their needs, wants, and expectations, customer satisfaction will be high—or at least greater than "1." If, on the other hand, customers perceive that the quality of the product or service *less than* meets their needs, wants, and expectations, the customer satisfaction ratio will be low—a fraction of 1.

Since customer satisfaction depends so much on the customer's own perceptions and expectations, researchers need to know some of the factors that influence those perceptions and expectations. The following are some of them:

1. "Needs and wants": These are related to a perceived *problem* that the customer is trying to *solve* by entering into a transaction with a company. If the customer's needs or concerns are great, expectations of performance will be high, of course. Conversely, low-risk concerns create lower expectation levels.

2. Previous experience with the company's products and services and with those of competitors.

3. The experience of the customer's peers. Word-of-mouth communication can have a powerful influence on customers' perceptions, particularly where they perceive high risk in the potential purchase and where the information source is considered credible.

4. Advertising and marketing communications also contribute to customer expectations—a good reason for making sure that sales personnel and advertising campaigns do not raise customers' expectations beyond levels that can actually be met by the product or service being sold.

Ironically, by exceeding a customer's expectations today, a business may actually be making it more difficult to meet future expectations. The innovation that gives a company the "value edge" soon becomes the industry standard, leaving all competitors scrambling to find a way to meet or exceed the customer's new expectations. In his book *Why People Buy*, J. O'Shaughnessy has said, "A firm should not just assume the consumer's want is fixed and given . . . current consumer satisfaction is always conditional on rival offerings being less attractive." Today's acceptable customer satisfaction ratio may be tomorrow's rotten report card. That is why customer satisfaction measurement has to be done frequently and in a timely way.

Customer satisfaction can be expressed in both specific and general terms, and the researcher should design questions that allow for both aspects to be surveyed. J.W. Marr, of Walker Research, has developed a "satisfaction pyramid" (see Figure 4–1), which shows the different levels of a company's operation at which customer satisfaction can be affected, including macro and micro components. Customer satisfaction research should therefore include both

- A *general* evaluation of product or service quality
- An evaluation of *specific* product or service attributes

The customer satisfaction survey questionnaire shown in Figure 4–2 shows a mix of both "general evaluation" and "specific attribute" questions.

Marr's pyramid also points to the fact that customer satisfaction does not hinge only on external factors, such as the customer's perception of quality. Specific activities internal to the organization are obviously linked to, and affect, the external attributes judged by customers. For

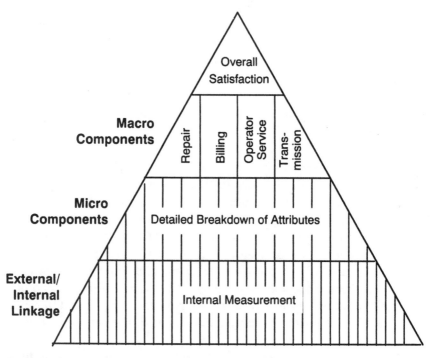

Figure 4–1. The Satisfaction Pyramid.
Reprinted by permission of Marr, Walker: CSM

Measuring Customer Satisfaction and Value Perception

Introduction/Screening

(To switchboard/person answering)

A. Good (morning/afternoon). May I please speak to (name on sample card)?

If yes	*	Continue
If RNA	*	Arrange callback
If no such person/wrong number	*	Discontinue
If refuse/reject	*	Discontinue

(Clarify that we have correct respondent.)

B. I'm _____ from Marketing Research. I understand (you use/your company uses) cellular mobile communications. We are conducting a short survey about cellular mobile phone service, and would like to include your opinions.

C. Are you currently using cellular telephone service?

Yes	—	1
No	—	2* Discontinue
DK	—	X* Discontinue

Satisfaction

1. Overall, how satisfied are you with your cellular telephone service? Are you (READ LIST) . . .

Very satisfied	—	4
Somewhat satisfied	—	3
Somewhat dissatisfied	—	2
Very dissatisfied	—	1
(DO NOT READ) DK/REF	—	X

2. For the following, please rate your satisfaction with each service offering, using a scale from 1 to 4, where "4" means "very satisfied," "3" means "somewhat satisfied," "2" means "somewhat dissatisfied," and "1" means "very dissatisfied." How satisfied are you with (READ FIRST EXAMPLE/NEXT OFFERING). (IF NECESSARY, REPEAT SCALE.)

(continued)

Figure 4–2. Cellular Telephone Customer Satisfaction Study

Source: The Burke Institute, "Customer Satisfaction Research," seminar given in Cincinnati, Ohio, March 6–7, 1989. © 1989 The Burke Institute, 800 Broadway, Cincinnati, Ohio 45202.

Rotate		VD	SD	SS	VS	DK
_____	Billing	1	2	3	4	X
_____	Customer service	1	2	3	4	X
_____	Quality of transmission	1	2	3	4	X
_____	Ability to complete calls on the first attempt	1	2	3	4	X
_____	Geographic size of service area	1	2	3	4	X

Problems/Contacts

3A. During the past 30 days, have you experienced transmission problems such as fading, static, background noise, or voices that have required you to hang up and reestablish the call?

Yes	—	1
No	—	2
DK	—	3

(Ask Q.3B and Q.3C if "Yes" to Q.3A; otherwise skip to Q.4.)

3B. Did you contact (name of company) to resolve the problem?

Yes	—	1
No	—	2
DK	—	X

3C. Was the problem resolved to your satisfaction?

Yes	—	1
No	—	2
Not yet resolved	—	3
DK	—	X

Usage

4. Thinking about your cellular telephone usage, how many calls would you say you make, on average, in one month?

(Record number)   # _____
                    DK-XXX

Figure 4–2. *(continued)*

5. What is your average monthly bill, excluding any rental, lease or access charge?

   (Record dollar amount) $ _____
                                          DK-XXX

Demographics

6. What is your age?   (Record exact) _____

7. Which one category best describes your business or industry of employment? (DO NOT READ LIST.)

Ad agency/consulting	—	1
Accounting/banking/finance	—	2
Communications	—	3
Computer (hardware/software)	—	4
Construction	—	5
Chemicals/petroleum	—	6
Engineering/R&D	—	7
Health/medical	—	8
Insurance	—	9
Real Estate	—	0
Legal	—	X
Manufacturing	—	Y
Trade (retail/wholesale)	—	1
Transportation	—	2
Other	—	3
DK	—	X

   Thank respondent.

(Record sex)	Male	—	1
	Female	—	2

Figure 4–2. (*continued*)

example, perceived operator service could be affected by how quickly inquiries are answered. Internal response times can be measured to obtain a clearer idea of operator service.

Improved internal response times have been the object of a value creation program launched by *USA Today*. Under the program, the following standards for handling telephone customer inquiries were set (the company receives about 2,500 per day!): Handle each customer

1. Which of the following reasons *best describe why you closed your checking account* at Valley National Bank (VNB). (Check all that apply.)

1 [ ] Moved (outside of Arizona) * PLEASE SKIP TO QUESTION 12 AND CONTINUE

2 [ ] Interest rates (on deposit accounts) not competitive

3 [ ] Could not get errors corrected

4 [ ] Needed money to buy something

5 [ ] To consolidate one or more accounts

6 [ ] This VNB Branch no longer convenient

7 [ ] Don't have free checking

8 [ ] Fees/service charges too high

9 [ ] Discourteous/unfriendly personnel

A [ ] Slow service/long lines

B [ ] Unable to get loan

C [ ] Unable to get Visa/Mastercard

D [ ] Made too many errors

E [ ] Due to a change in marital status

F [ ] Lost or stolen purse/wallet/checkbook

G [ ] Inconvenient banking hours

2. Which of these would you say was the *main* reason for closing your account? (Check only *one*).

1 [ ] Interest rates (on deposit accounts) not competitive

2 [ ] Could not get errors corrected

3 [ ] Needed money to buy something

4 [ ] To consolidate one or more accounts

5 [ ] This VNB Branch no longer convenient

6 [ ] Don't have free checking

7 [ ] Fees/service charges too high

8 [ ] Discourteous/unfriendly personnel

9 [ ] Slow service/long lines

A [ ] Unable to get loan

B [ ] Unable to get Visa/Mastercard

Figure 4–3. Valley National Bank Closed Account Questionnaire

C [ ] Made too many errors
D [ ] Due to a change in marital status
E [ ] Lost or stolen purse/wallet/checkbook
F [ ] Inconvenient banking hours
Other (specify)

_____

_____

3. How did Valley National personnel respond to your request to close your account? (Check only one)

1 [ ] He/she asked why I was closing my account, but did nothing to retain my business.

2 [ ] He/she asked why I was closing my account, then offered to attempt to resolve my problem and/or concern.

3 [ ] He/she did not ask why I was closing my account.

4 [ ] Other _____
        (please specify)

4. After you closed your checking account at VNB, did you open a new checking account at . . .

1 [ ] Another financial institution * CONTINUE TO QUESTION 5

2 [ ] The same VNB branch

3 [ ] Another VNB branch

4 [ ] Didn't open a new checking account

Please skip to Question 7 and continue

5. Where did you open your new checking account?

1 [ ] Arizona Bank
2 [ ] Chase/Continental Bank
3 [ ] Citibank/Great Western Bank
4 [ ] First Interstate Bank
5 [ ] Great American/Home Federal Savings
6 [ ] MeraBank
7 [ ] Pima Savings
8 [ ] United Bank
9 [ ] Western Savings

(continued)

Figure 4–3. (*continued*)

A [ ] Valley National Bank
B [ ] A Credit Union
Other (specify)

_____

6. Why did you choose that financial institution?

1 [ ] Convenient hours
2 [ ] Convenient location
3 [ ] Recommended by a friend/family member or business associate
4 [ ] Already had other accounts there
5 [ ] Attracted by the advertising
6 [ ] Free checking
7 [ ] Overall reputation of the institution
8 [ ] Directly solicited by one of its employees
9 [ ] Attracted by a special premium offer
A [ ] Lower fees/service charges
B [ ] Interstate network
Other (specify)

_____
_____

7. In the past 12 months, have you moved within Arizona; that is, have you changed residences, but remained in the state?

[ ] Yes [ ] No * (SKIP TO QUESTION 12)

8. Did you close your account at Valley Bank at the time of your move?

[ ] Yes [ ] No

9. Did you open a new account after the move?

[ ] Yes [ ] No * (SKIP TO QUESTION 12)

10. Where did you open your new account?

1 [ ] Arizona Bank
2 [ ] Chase/Continental Bank

Figure 4–3. (*continued*)

3 [ ] Citibank/Great Western Bank
4 [ ] First Interstate Bank
5 [ ] Great American/Home Federal Savings
6 [ ] MeraBank
7 [ ] Pima Savings
8 [ ] United Bank
9 [ ] Western Savings
A [ ] Valley National Bank
B [ ] A Credit Union
Other (specify)

_____

11. If you moved to an area where there was a Valley National Bank branch conveniently located, but did not open an account there, why not?

_____

_____

12. Compared to other financial institutions (banks, savings and loans, credit unions, brokerage firms, etc.) you may have used or know about, how would you rate VNB on: ("X" THE APPROPRIATE BOX FOR EACH ITEM).

	5 The Best	4 Better Than Most	3 The Same	2 Not Quite as Good	1 The Worst
a. Providing quality service in the branch	[ ]	[ ]	[ ]	[ ]	[ ]
b. Innovative products and services to meet customers' needs	[ ]	[ ]	[ ]	[ ]	[ ]
c. Convenience of locations	[ ]	[ ]	[ ]	[ ]	[ ]
d. Advertising message that applies to your needs	[ ]	[ ]	[ ]	[ ]	[ ]
e. Safe, strong, secure	[ ]	[ ]	[ ]	[ ]	[ ]
f. Arizona/community minded	[ ]	[ ]	[ ]	[ ]	[ ]
g. Delivering value to its customers	[ ]	[ ]	[ ]	[ ]	[ ]

(*continued*)

Figure 4–3. (*continued*)

13. Regarding other personal accounts you may also have had or have at Valley National Bank, please mark an "X" in the appropriate box.

		1 Closed When Checking Closed	2 Continue to Have at VNB	3 Never Had at VNB
a.	Regular Savings	[ ]	[ ]	[ ]
b.	Certificate of Deposit	[ ]	[ ]	[ ]
c.	Money Market Savings	[ ]	[ ]	[ ]
d.	Credit Card	[ ]	[ ]	[ ]
e.	Loan	[ ]	[ ]	[ ]

Other (specify) _____

14. How long did you have your checking account at Valley National Bank?

1 [ ] Less than 1 year   4 [ ] 6 to 10 years
2 [ ] 1 to 2 years   5 [ ] Over 10 years
3 [ ] 3 to 5 years

The following information will be used to accurately group your answers for analysis purposes. PLEASE "X" THE APPROPRIATE BOXES.

15. SEX

[ ]   Male
[ ]   Female

16. AGE

[ ]   Under 25
[ ]   25 to 34
[ ]   35 to 44
[ ]   45 to 54
[ ]   55 to 64
[ ]   65 or older

Figure 4–3. (*continued*)

request with one phone call, answer each incoming call within 20 seconds or four rings, start up all subscriptions within four days, respond to incoming letters within 48 hours, resolve all complaints within five days, and spend no more than two minutes per customer call. By carefully managing each of these components, *USA Today* hopes to improve customer perceptions of its service levels.

Although one of the purposes of carrying out a customer satisfaction study is to discover what makes customers *dissatisfied*, these points of friction will not always be mentioned as a matter of course. Specific questions have to be designed to unearth difficulties that customers might not otherwise articulate. The customer dissatisfaction part of the research should focus on

> [T]ypes and frequency of customer problems, to determine their impact on customer satisfaction and dissatisfaction, and to use this information to establish priorities for corrective action. . . . The problems that occur most frequently and . . . have the greatest negative impact on customer opinions are [then] targeted for management action.

Some research instruments focus only on the negative reactions of customers—as in the case of the document shown in Figure 4–3. Even in general surveys, however, it is important to leave room for negative comments from customers. In some cases, customers being surveyed will come up with a specific complaint that they either did not bring up before or did not resolve with the company. A follow-up procedure should be built into the survey so that the complaint can be channeled to the right person and dealt with.

CHOOSE YOUR WEAPON

The tools of customer satisfaction research range from simple customer comment cards to in-depth surveys carried out in person, by mail, or by telephone. The choice of research approach will depend on variables such as the following:

- The need to reach diverse segments of the population
- Geographic coverage
- The need to know the identity of respondents for future reference
- The complexity of information required

- The amount of assistance the interviewer needs to give
- The quantity of information required
- The speed with which data has to be collected
- The funds available for collecting data

The personal preference of the interviewer or researcher will also have an effect on which instrument is chosen. J.W. Marr, who developed the satisfaction pyramid mentioned earlier, swears by *telephone surveys* as the "best all-around method of collecting data from customers." He says,

> Telephone contact produces a more random data set than does a mail-out, self-administered questionnaire, at least relative to customer satisfaction issues. This is largely because those who take the time to respond to a mail survey often feel strongly about the issue at hand, so that you get very polarized responses. Those who are more neutral on the subject may not fill out a questionnaire, but will often participate in a brief telephone survey. Personal interviews provide another option, but they have their own logistics—and cost—problems.

Telephone surveys also have the following advantages: It is easy to gain access to telephone lists, interviewers can help respondents with prompts and guidance, and information can be presented quickly. However, telephone surveys do not allow visual information to be obtained, and interviews can usually not last longer than 15 minutes because of respondent fatigue.

Mail surveys have a relatively low cost per respondent and they are quite adequate when the information required is simple and straightforward. However, it is difficult to obtain proper mailing lists, response rates are low, and response times are lengthy. Furthermore, information can be incomplete if respondents fail to fill out parts of the questionnaire.

In-person, face-to-face interviews are particularly useful when the issues to be researched are complex or sensitive, or when the interviewer may need to explain and probe. Among the disadvantages of in-person interviewing are the length of time needed to complete the interview process and the relatively high cost of sending interviewers to meet with respondents in their homes or places of business.

Most large enterprises use a variety of customer satisfaction research tools—from 800 numbers to mystery shoppers, from formal surveys to informal chats with clients.

When Armstrong introduced its no-wax line of floor coverings, it began to receive calls from customers who thought that "no-wax" meant "no-care." Detailed maintenance instructions had been packed in with the products, but most of Armstrong's customers were not bothering to read them. Finally someone happened on the idea of providing an *800 number* for customers to call as soon as they receive their shipment. Because the number is printed in removable ink right on the flooring, customers have to phone to find out how to take the number off.

Now Armstrong's 800 number is used for more than giving cleaning instructions. The consumer affairs representatives on the phone lines also give product information, dealer locations, installation instructions, and even decorating ideas. The service has become a research tool as well. The phone representatives track their callers, "analyze them, cross-reference them, and communicate their inclinations and interests to product planners and field sales people."

Although *customer comment cards* are a difficult form of customer satisfaction research to administer, since clients do not always have the time or motivation to fill them out, they remain an excellent source of information. Ron Zemke describes how some Marriott hotels have solved the motivation problem:

> Some managers . . . make a contest of it—they will buy something like a two-hundred-dollar briefcase and park it on the registration counter: You fill out your rating card and toss it in the briefcase along with your business card, and every week or month or whatever they'll pull out a business card (the ratings will long since have been read and acted upon) and award the briefcase to that guest. . . . Each property has a quota of forms to pass out in order to maintain a high response rate, because the higher the response rate, the more complete and accurate the GSI [Guest Service Index] reading, and the better Marriott can respond to what's happening to guests in the hotel.

How seriously does the Marriott chain take the results of these informal surveys? For one thing, the data is circulated to every department for employees to see where improvements can be made. For another, Bill Marriott, the company chairman, himself reads hundreds of comment cards every month.

Another operation that takes its suggestion box seriously is Stew Leonard's Dairy, a single store in Norwalk, Connecticut, that has become legendary for its good service. Every morning the suggestion box beside the front door is emptied, and by 10 A.M. the suggestions have been transferred to comment sheets and circulated to all department managers, tacked up on the wall in employee break areas, and left on the tables in the lunch room. Within 24 hours, one of the store's managers—often Leonard himself—has followed up with a phone call to the customer who gave the suggestion. Unscientific, perhaps. Effective, absolutely.

Mystery shopping, or secret shopping, is a relatively recent technique whereby trained researchers posing as customers visit company outlets and later prepare reports on their observations and experiences. It is becoming a more and more popular way of gauging customer satisfaction. Carol Cherry, president of Shop 'N Chek Inc., one of the earliest mystery shopping services, reported in 1989 that firms like hers are attracting more business all the time—and from a wider range of enterprises. Although her initial client base came from the retail sector, she is now getting requests from manufacturers as well. Automakers, for instance, "have determined that service departments of dealers determine the sale of cars" and so have hired mystery car shoppers to do research for them.

Domino's Pizza, which seems to make an appearance in every other article or book on excellence in customer satisfaction, has characteristically honed mystery shopping to a fine art. It employs 8,000 inspectors (two per store per month) to check up on 22 different aspects of each outlet's operations. Their reports become the basis for both product- and service-quality control, and they are entered into a database that gives headquarters and regional managers access to performance levels across the United States.

Among the more recent innovations in research tools are videotaping and *visual imagery profiling* (VIP). With video cameras, researchers record responses from customers right at the point of purchase—after they've walked out of the appliance store with their new microwave oven or while they're waiting in line for a movie. Eleanor Holtzman, a founder of the New York research agency Consumer Verite, has pointed out that "video frees researchers from the confines of the focus group room and the limits of the pad and pencil." The video tends to capture more honest, spontaneous responses, and it also records that all-important truth communicator, body language.

Visual imagery profiling is a McLuhanesque research method that uses "groups of photographs to help consumers express their attitudes in nonverbal ways." Perfect for the TV generation, which sometimes has trouble saying what it means in writing, this tool presents interviewees with several series of photos, from which they are asked to choose those that either (a) "best represent the typical buyer of a particular brand of product" or (b) represent what a company or brand name means to them. One hotel company asked its interviewees to identify the types of people (as represented in photographs) who would stay at its hotels and the types who would stay at competing hotels. This way, the company learned how customers perceived its "personality," and whether its advertisements effectively communicated that personality.

Most enterprises that are devoted to satisfying their customers use many research techniques at once. As Ron Zemke puts it,

> Among the Service 101 [the top service companies, which were profiled in his book *The Service Edge*], we found that the measurement of service performance is a systematic effort that depends on no single measure to tell all. These organizations seem to wear both belts and suspenders, just in case. Technically speaking, they value "nonrepetitive, redundant" measures of their frontline performance, customer satisfaction, and service quality—they measure the same thing in a lot of different ways. The more information, the better, they maintain.

The First Pennsylvania Bank, for instance, uses a mystery shopper program, an advertising tracking study, a benchmark study, a banking services study, and customer comment cards. The Eastman Kodak Company uses customer survey cards; customer "field trips" in which employees visit customers to learn about their needs; and customer "help desks"—central comment and complaint desks that customers can visit in person or can reach through a telephone hotline. Apple Canada Inc. uses two kinds of surveys: a customer satisfaction survey designed to elicit responses about service and support and a broad market survey, which addresses "many other issues, ranging from how people are using personal computer systems, how many applications they are using, what are some of the issues they are facing, . . . would they rather deal with the manufacturer or the distributor, etc." Burger King uses three measures of customer satisfaction: a restaurant progress report based on in-depth studies by franchise and company district managers, an operations audit performed by an outside research team that measures restaurant services from the customer's point of view, and an annual restaurant operations review of product safety and preparation, service, and cleanliness.

Although formal surveys must be used to bring in the hard data, the value of informal techniques should not be underestimated. John Cleghorn, president and COO of the Royal Bank of Canada, spends a lot of time traveling around the country interviewing his managers and tellers. And when a manager from a competing bank joins the Royal, he asks what

> [M]ajor differences she perceives between the two banks. "I wouldn't know if we had problems with our mortgage system, for example, unless I was out there, hearing from our people," [he says]. He sets himself a target to visit a hundred branches, as well as over a hundred clients, every year. "And I don't just sit there and buy them lunch! At the end I say, 'I hope you've had a nice lunch. Now, could you give us some suggestions on where you think we should improve. Give us some kudos, too, if we deserve them but where do you think . . .'".

The Body Shop, the British-based cosmetics and perfume chain, also has a predilection for informal methods of research. Margot Franssen, president of Canadian operations, says the company has created "customer focus groups," made up of "good customers" that each store has picked out. (To be considered a good customer, a person doesn't have to spend a lot of money, they just have to visit the store frequently.) "We bring them in, offer them a coffee or danish, or maybe drinks and hors d'oeuvres at night, and let them have a blast at us." They use customer suggestion cards, too, which are sent into the head office every month, after a written reply has been sent to the customer by store staff.

Although different companies use different combinations of research methods, some techniques are more popular than others. In an American Management Association (AMA) consumer affairs report published in 1987, companies were asked to rate the effectiveness of the following techniques:

- 800 telephone numbers for comments, questions or complaints
- Comment cards enclosed with merchandise
- Mail/phone questionnaires
- Focus groups on existing product lines
- Consumer education materials
- Employee training in consumer relations
- Regular company-wide programs on customer relations
- Assigning non-sales personnel to point-of-purchase stations

The most favorably rated techniques were open-ended, high-touch approaches. Of these, 800 phone numbers were rated the most effective method by 36 percent of the sample. Fifty-three percent of the companies surveyed were using 800 numbers at the time.

Customer focus groups were rated as the second most effective customer listening tool; 55 percent of all respondents were using focus groups. This method was reported to be especially useful in making customer needs more concrete to company personnel, particularly management decision makers who have little day-to-day customer contact. They were also reported to be an effective tool for providing insight into new trends.

Focus groups and 800 numbers were seen to be effective because they are relatively unstructured approaches that allow customers to express their concerns in their own terms. Also, the two-way communication process for these activities was rated highly, since it put a "human face" on the customer feedback process.

BENCHMARKING

No customer satisfaction research program can be considered complete if it focuses only on the company's own product and service quality. It has to include a probing survey of what the best of the competition is doing. This concept may not sound new, but in its current incarnation—*benchmarking*—it is more comprehensive and systematic than old-style competitor research. Kaiser Associates, Inc., a consulting firm that specializes in this type of work, has identified the following steps in the benchmarking process:

- Determining which functional areas within your operation will benefit most from benchmarking;
- Identifying the key factors and variables with which to measure competitive cost and quality for those functions;
- Selecting the best-in-class companies for each item to be benchmarked . . . Best-in-class companies can be your direct competitors (domestic or foreign) or even companies from a different industry. . . .
- Measuring your own performance for each benchmark item;
- Measuring the performance of the best-in-class companies for each item, and determining the *gap* between you and the best-in-class;
- Specifying programs and actions to close the gap;
- Implementing these programs successfully by setting specific

improvement targets and deadlines, and by developing a monitoring process to review and update targets over time.

In the benchmarking process, it is important to look not only at competitors in one's own industry but also at enterprises outside the industry. Air Canada, for one, uses this kind of extra-industry benchmarking. According to Leo Desrochers, Air Canada executive vice-president of Marketing, Sales, and Service, the airline has looked not only at competitors in its own field, but also at

> [R]etail companies, the service industry, the non-airline service industry. It comes through reading and getting feedback, trying our own product, trying their product, seeing what happens in a customer/ employee interface. And we used some of that to develop our own thinking.

In another case, a large multidivisional chemical firm with operations throughout the United States and Canada did benchmarking research that showed it was highest rated on all customer satisfaction attributes. However, customers found all suppliers to be poor in answering their questions, resolving their complaints, and providing order status information. A new opportunity to increase customer satisfaction was thus identified. The company subsequently held marketing strategy planning sessions to design and implement programs that would open up better communication channels with its customers.

THE BASIC STEPS IN CUSTOMER SATISFACTION RESEARCH

Regardless of the purpose or kind of research being undertaken, a common framework can be applied to most customer satisfaction research processes. The basic steps are as follows:

- *Define the management problem.* The first step is to determine what customer satisfaction issues need to be resolved; this may include developing preliminary solutions, which can then be tested through the research.

- *Set research objectives.* These objectives must specify how the data collected will contribute to resolving the management problem defined earlier.

• *Search for secondary data.* Before beginning any *primary*, or original, research, a search for data already available should be undertaken; the results of the secondary data search may lead to a redefinition of the original research objectives.

• *Carry out exploratory research.* Preliminary qualitative research, such as focus groups or a limited number of personal interviews, should be conducted to further clarify the issues to be addressed.

• *Plan the primary data collection strategy.* Four decisions need to be made at this stage: first, *how* the information should be collected (the kind of research or survey); second, from *whom* (what customer groups) it should be collected; third, the *size* of the survey; and fourth, *how frequently* the data should be collected.

• *Design the customer satisfaction research instrument.* Produce the questionnaire or interview guide.

• *Collect data.* After the questionnaire has been designed, the predetermined number of customers should be contacted and asked to respond.

• *Process and analyze data.* The questionnaire must be collected from customers and individual answers tabulated and analyzed.

• *Interpret and apply results.* Draw conclusions and make recommendations after evaluating the data in light of the management issues set out at the beginning of the process.

Setting Objectives

Once the management problem has been defined, clear research objectives must be set. The following questions can be used to clarify objectives:

• How satisfied, overall, are your customers with your products or service?

• What are the specific needs and expectations of your customers? How important is each expectation as a determinant of satisfaction? Do expectations differ depending on the market segment to which the customer belongs?

• How well does your company meet customer expectations? How do you compare to competitors, as perceived by customers?

• What are the biggest complaints or problems that customers have with your company? Which complaints are made most frequently?

• Which complaints have the greatest potential effect on customer happiness?

• How is your company, and its offerings, perceived and evaluated by key customer sub-groups within the overall market?

• What are your company's key strengths in satisfying customers? What are your key weaknesses in and greatest opportunities for improving quality and satisfaction?

Search for Secondary Data

The first place to look for secondary data is in *internal company records*. Previous research data should be reviewed to determine whether information pertinent to the research objectives has already been collected. Some companies find complaint files a valuable source of secondary data. One such company is Winnebago Industries, which manufactures recreational vehicles. It has set up an Owner Relations Department to manage buyers' information requests and complaints. When a complaint is received, it is first coded by product, service, or part; relevant information about the problem is noted, then the complaint is added to the computer bank. Information may be retrieved electronically in a variety of combinations, such as service complaints according to service district and percentage of total retail sales complaints generated by each dealer.

External sources of information can also shed light on customer satisfaction research issues. Many federal, state, provincial, and local governments publish industry information and studies that may include an analysis of customer needs and requirements. Other sources of information include colleges, universities, and other nonprofit organizations; professional and trade associations; and industry newsletters and trade publications.

On-line information searches have improved dramatically in recent years and are also becoming an important means of gathering data. Nearly every directory, manual, handbook, newsletter, newspaper, journal, thesis, and textbook of significance is available through electronic information retrieval. This creates an instant library for researchers, regardless of their geographic location.

On-line information is available in the following formats:

• *Bibliographic.* Any combination of bibliographic information is available, from author, title, and publisher listings to more detailed bibliographies, which could include abstracts.

- *Full-text or abstract.* Most on-line services allow customers to choose between receiving a complete chapter, article, paper, etc., or simply receiving highlights.

Exploratory Research

After secondary sources have been combed for background, the information they have yielded can be used to revise and refine the study objectives. Then, other types of exploratory research can begin.

Interviews with the company's top management will help clarify their perspectives on the firm, its industry, and its customers. The most senior managers of the company usually have the best overview of the company and its position in the market and can therefore give the researcher a good start on the research process. These interviews will also unearth information about existing value creation and customer satisfaction policies.

Here are some questions that could be asked:

- What has been the evolution of the industry in which we compete?
- How is the customers' environment changing?
- . What are the strategies and activities of our competitors?
- How are new technologies, government regulations, and social trends affecting our business?
- What are the specific corporate philosophies and objectives that relate to value creation, including customer satisfaction and quality standards and specification?

Exploratory interviews with employees are also fruitful in the early stages of a research program. Front-line employees often have an even better appreciation of customer problems and requirements than does senior management. Since they are the critical interface between the company and its customers, front-line employees can provide a valuable perspective on the effect of company policies on customer happiness. The following are questions that might be used in an exploratory interview with such employees:

- What are current levels of satisfaction among your customers?

- What are the key sources of customer problems and what can be done to solve them?
- What are the causes of substandard product and service quality?
- How do employees perceive management's commitment to value creation—including quality improvement and customer satisfaction?

Employee input can carry a lot of weight in the final design of the research instrument. This happened when Pacific Gas & Electric Company organized employee discussion groups in local field offices to determine which factors should be measured to establish benchmarks of service quality. The factors identified by employees were incorporated into the company's "Quality of Service Evaluation Questionnaire," with few changes.

Customer interviews should also be carried out in the preliminary stages of the program, for two reasons. First, the interviews will help the researcher develop a broad overview of customer needs and expectations, sources of satisfaction or problems, and how competitors are perceived. Second, the researcher will be able to ensure that the survey instruments employed in the latter phases of the project feature vocabulary that is understandable and relevant to customers. The following types of questions should be asked at exploratory interviews with customers:

- What needs and expectations do you have with regard to the company and its products and services?
- What are your biggest problems and complaints?
- What criteria do you use to judge product and service quality?
- How do you see the company and its competitors?

Among the most effective and popular exploratory research techniques are in-depth interviews, focus groups, and critical incident analysis. These qualitative research techniques are used to probe for underlying problems and sources of satisfaction and dissatisfaction. After this kind of research has been done, quantitative techniques can be used to validate or elaborate on the preliminary findings.

In-depth interviews. These are personal interviews conducted at length with individuals who have been selected from the respondent group. Although the interviewer usually has an interview guide that sets a framework for discussion, the session should be freewheeling enough to allow new and important ideas to surface.

This technique is most useful when the customer satisfaction issues to be researched are not yet clear. It is also helpful in situations in which respondents would feel uncomfortable responding to questions in a group setting, or where the subject matter is complex and the participants are knowledgeable.

The focus group. This consists of about eight to 10 participants who meet under the guidance of a trained moderator to discuss and explore particular issues. As in the case of in-depth interviews, an interview guide must be prepared to help the moderator direct the flow of discussion.

The unique value of focus groups is that the interaction between participants will often spark new insights. Focus groups work best when the subject matter is not too complex and when participants feel comfortable discussing the subject in a group setting. This technique also helps the researcher get a better grasp of customer attitudes through the tone of voice and body language of participants as they interact with each other.

In the mid-1980s, focus groups helped Ford Motor Company stay in touch with its customers as it recommitted itself to customer satisfaction. Through the groups, Ford discovered four major problem areas in automotive service quality: courtesy of service technicians, price, convenience, and technical competence. Many of the customers in these focus groups were videotaped so that a permanent record was created. This record helped Ford develop a new statement of its "mission, values and guiding principles" for improving customer satisfaction.

Other manufacturers are also beginning to recognize the value of the focus group technique. In 1981, Caterpillar Inc. started using customer focus groups in which buyers were asked open-ended questions about the criteria they used to judge Caterpillar's service quality. A mail survey was developed from the responses, which is now sent to customers to measure dealers' service performance.

Critical incident analysis. With this method, the researcher asks customers to describe their interactions with the company and to identify the *critical incidents* that have influenced their opinion of its products and services. For the purposes of this kind of questioning, a critical incident is defined as behavior that is either "outstandingly effective or ineffective with respect to attaining the general aims of the activity." In other words, customers are asked to identify specific behavioral traits that they associate with satisfaction or dissatisfaction.

This approach is useful in identifying satisfaction and dissatisfaction issues that arise from specific contacts customers have with the company. For example, a customer might be interviewed to determine the effect of a retail clothing store's merchandise returns policy on customer satisfaction. The following story is typical of those that evolve from such discussions:

> I discovered a few flaws in the fabric and returned it to the store. I had to wait several minutes before a saleswoman was available and then asked for a replacement. The saleswoman said that a replacement was not available in the store. I asked if the saleswoman could phone another store under the same chain to see if they had one. She stated it was not company policy to telephone other stores, but that I could go there myself. Not pleased with this policy, I asked for my money back. The saleswoman politely stated that this too was not company policy, but that perhaps I would like to pick out something else in the store. I left the store with an item of clothing I was not pleased with, and would not have purchased in the first place.

This "critical incident" story not only makes it very clear that the store's merchandise returns policy leaves customers with a bad impression, but it also highlights the specific points of friction.

Once the preliminary research is complete, the researchers will have gained insights into the key factors that contribute to customer satisfaction in the industry. To confirm and validate these conclusions, more detailed primary research may have to be undertaken.

Planning the Primary Data Collection Strategy

Detailed primary data collection can occur in the context of in-person interviews or mail or telephone surveys. The chief benefit of this type of research is that it offers the opportunity to validate the preliminary findings. Although primary data collection is not always strictly quantitative, it should include questions that will solicit answers in hard numbers. Most often, detailed customer satisfaction research is done in the form of a survey or questionnaire.

Before these can be designed, however, the researcher has to determine (a) *from whom* to collect data, (b) the *size* of the survey, and (c) the *timing and frequency* of the data collection.

Whom to survey. In *Thriving on Chaos*, Tom Peters suggests that measurement of customer satisfaction should include "over time, all functions, all levels from line workers to top management. Suppliers, wholesalers, and other members of the distribution channel should also take part, formally and informally." Furthermore, he says, the satisfaction of all direct and indirect customers should be measured: "the ultimate user and every member of the distribution channel—dealer, retailer, wholesaler, franchisee, rep, etc." Within these target groups, a variety of people might also be surveyed. A food service company, for instance, might conduct annual in-person interviews with food service managers in three different kinds of customer organization: hospitals, educational institutions, and airlines. A manufacturer of office equipment might conduct monthly mail surveys of 10 percent of its customers, divided according to product type: photocopiers, word processors and printers, and information storage and retrieval systems.

The most obvious target for a customer satisfaction survey is, of course, the *end user* of the product or service. This target group can be subdivided into current customers (both long-term and new), prospective customers, former customers, and the customers of competitors. The Burke Institute of Cincinnati, a well known marketing research company, has identified the kinds of information that can be obtained from each of these groups. Current customers are the principal population of interest and the final judge of quality; former customers are sources of information on dissatisfaction and of competitive intelligence; prospective customers can define image-driven expectations (for example, the expectations generated by advertising); and customers of competitors can provide multiple brand or vendor usage patterns and benchmarking information.

Within the current customer category, it is important to survey both long-term and new customers, since long-term customers will have a broader overview of the kind of quality and service the company provides, while new customers will focus on the "front-line" activities: selling, installation, and set-up, in the case of a product.

Cantel, the Canadian manufacturer of cellular phones, has made this distinction by conducting a comprehensive telephone survey to learn how clients feel "just one month after starting the service, how the dealers and agents have been treating him/her, etc." The answers to the questions are fed back to dealers. "That's their report card, and they have to improve things before the next issue of those reports come in," says Maureen Ladly, assistant vice-president, Customer Service.

Intermediaries in the distribution channel should also be surveyed.

General Motors, for instance, sends satisfaction surveys to owners, sales managers, and service managers in all dealerships. Each manager is questioned on his or her respective area of responsibility and overall opinion of General Motors. Typical questions focus on sales, service, and product information, training programs, the effectiveness of General Motors' district managers, and merchandising programs.

Internal customers, including managers and employees, should also be assessed. The *survey of managers* measures the degree to which management and supervisors are aware of, and responsive to, customers' needs. It also touches on how satisfied are senior executives with the way they themselves are managed. Such questioning might lead to the removal of internal problems that hinder management's ability to focus on customer priorities.

The *employee opinion survey* tells supervisors and managers what employees think and how they feel about their bosses, pay, benefits, working conditions, security, and so forth. It is difficult to motivate employees to focus on customers' needs if they do not feel well treated themselves.

A specialized type of employee survey, the *internal client survey*, is useful in diagnosing how well the internal business departments meet each other's needs in operating the company. This type of survey uncovers interdepartmental conflicts that may distract employees from focusing on customer requirements.

Other employee surveys, which are premised on the assumption that employees have an important, indeed critical, role to play in creating happy customers, determine the factors that employees feel are major contributors to customer satisfaction and perceptions of value. These employee surveys are often compared with customer satisfaction surveys, with sometimes interesting results.

In one case, the customers of a large urban transit company were surveyed to establish how they expected to be treated by bus drivers, and the bus drivers were asked what they thought passengers expected from them. The passengers said they expected good drivers to help passengers who needed assistance, provide information on routes, manage crowds of passengers effectively, and be neat and well groomed. The drivers thought that passengers expected route and fare information but, surprisingly, did not view passenger assistance and crowd control as important concerns. This difference obviously had great potential for eroding customer satisfaction. The study results prompted a rebalancing of the company's marketing resources. In addition to continuing to direct their marketing efforts to passengers, the company implemented an extensive employee-training and incentive program to motivate employees to display customer-satisfying behavior—in line with the customers' actual expectations.

Determining the size of the survey. After researchers have determined which groups to survey, they must establish a sampling strategy. That is, they must decide how many customers should be contacted in order to draw valid conclusions about the population they represent. Among the possible sampling strategies are the census, random samples, stratified samples, and judgment samples.

In a *census*, researchers contact *everyone* in a particular population. This method is useful where the customer population is small and each individual opinion is important. For example, management consulting firms often have the senior partners contact each client after a project is finished to see if the client is satisfied. These inquiries are, in turn, summarized to provide an overall view of client satisfaction and opportunities for improvement.

A *random sample* consists of a small number of respondents—selected at random, of course—from the population that is the subject of the study. If the sampling is done properly, this group will accurately represent the wider group. Depending on the needs and size of the survey, the random sample may consist of anywhere from 100 to 1,000 respondents or more. A database of 100 respondents is usually an absolute minimum unless the total available population is much smaller. Household goods manufacturers often randomly select small groups of consumers to answer their questionnaires. This is done by contacting shoppers at random in shopping malls, by telephone, or by mail.

The *stratified sample* sets predetermined targets for the number of contacts to be made within specific subsegments of the customer population, which ensures that the researcher will obtain the views of a true cross-section of buyer types. Wang Laboratories Inc. has used stratified samples for its surveys, first analyzing company records for patterns and categories, then telephoning at random until they find the right number of respondents for each segment. In this way, they can be assured that the most appropriate people within each subsegment are interviewed.

In a *judgment sample*, the number and variety of contacts is based on the researcher's knowledge of the structure of the industry and market. In an industry where the customer group is divided into a few large buyers and many small ones, for instance, the sample might consist of all the large buyers and none of the small ones, since the small buyers would not have a great influence on business.

Timing and frequency of surveys and questionnaires. The timing and frequency of data collection will depend to a great extent on the characteristics of the industry or company and the purpose of the survey. Tom Peters offers advice in this regard. "Formal surveys every 60 to 90 days are a must," he says, "and these should be supplemented by informal monthly surveys and an annual image survey done by a third party." While the formal surveys will give a comprehensive view of customer satisfaction issues, monthly, quarterly, and semiannual surveys help a company keep its finger on the "pulse of performance." It also "measures any seasonal changes, and can provide an early warning system of quality changes."

The Burke Institute suggests that researchers ask themselves two critical questions in determining the timing and frequency of surveys: (1) "How quickly can my organization assimilate and respond to the results of a customer satisfaction survey?" and (2) "How long will/should it take for managerial actions to produce an impact on the customer satisfaction measures?" Xerox Canada, for instance, generally processes and responds to its surveys within two months.

Charles Bultmann, assistant vice-president of Operations Support and Quality Assessment at the GTE Service Corporation, a leader in the telecommunications industry, has put it this way: "Satisfaction measurement can't be treated as a one-time event... [because] ... regardless of what industry you are in, customer expectations and perceptions ... change over time." A number of other companies also subscribe to this philosophy. The Ford Motor Company sends questionnaires to buyers 30 days following the purchase of a new car or truck, to evaluate not just the product, but the selling process as well. A second survey sent out nine months after the sale covers any maintenance or warranty work the customer may have had occasion to use. Amdahl Canada Limited asks for

> [A] relative assessment on how [they] are doing against . . . [quality, timeliness, and professionalism, how well the firm appears to under-stand his or her needs] this time 'round, compared with the last time we conducted the survey... [because] a customer may be satisfied, but somewhat less so than at some previous point, and we need to measure that difference and deal with it.

Developing Questionnaires and Interview Guides

Regardless of the type of customer satisfaction survey being used, researchers have to prepare some form of questionnaire as the means of gathering information from respondents. And to design an effective questionnaire, they must first determine their information needs and the types of questions to be asked. Typically, a questionnaire will ask buyers to provide:

- An overall evaluation of their satisfaction level
- An indication of their needs and expectations with respect to the category of products or services that the company provides
- An evaluation of the company's performance against these expectations
- An indication of any specific problems or complaints they might have
- Customer classification information, which will allow the researchers to analyze customer responses by subgroups after all the data have been collected

Although a number of types of questions appear in customer satisfaction research, open-ended questions and closed-ended questions are the two most commonly used.

Open-ended questions give respondents a high degree of freedom in the way they answer. This type of question often appears on the questionnaires distributed at the end of conferences and seminars. The following are some examples of this type:

- Why did you decide on this seminar?
- What did you hope to learn from it?
- What did you think of the speaker?
- Did the speaker cover the subject adequately?
- Were you disappointed in the presentation?
- Did you learn anything new?

Closed-ended questions let respondents choose between preselected options and usually appear in the form of ranking and rating scales, multiple choice questions, or checklists. The Sheraton Hotel chain uses closed-ended questions in its patron survey, which is designed to determine whether staff are friendly, courteous, efficient, enthusiastic, and helpful in resolving problems. Customers rate each of these items by checking off categories labeled "below," "met," "exceeded," or "does not apply." Closed-ended questions also appear on surveys conducted by the Pacific Gas & Electric Co. They ask whether the user owns or rents the residence billed, what type of residence he or she lives in (single home, mobile home, house trailer, apartment, or condominium), the total cost of household utilities during a year, and the age group and total annual household income of the user.

Process and Analyze Data

To develop precise measures of customer satisfaction, some knowledge of statistical theory is needed. Although the development of such customer satisfaction metrics is best left to a marketing research professional, managers should become familiar with some of the basic concepts so that they can direct the professional's efforts most effectively. At least two questions should be asked: "What level of measurement is needed to provide the greatest insight into customer satisfaction perceptions?" and, "What are the key variables that will determine those perceptions?"

For example, the company conducting the survey may want an overall measure of customer satisfaction or it may want ratings on specific attributes that contribute to customers' overall perception. Most research practitioners recommend that businesses develop, at minimum, a measurement scale that addresses customers' overall perception of the company's performance. Since customer satisfaction consists of many interlinked influences, it is important to design a measure that allows customers to consider all these influences together as they rate their satisfaction and the value of the company's products and services.

Attribute ratings, on the other hand, give customers the opportunity to express their opinion on more detailed characteristics. For example, customers might be asked to evaluate the in-flight service of an airline by commenting on specific attributes such as the quality of food and beverages, the attitude of flight attendants, and the selection of current magazines. One major hotel's comment card asks patrons to give separate ratings of the front desk, reception, the hotel room, and the restaurant and lounges. Within the hotel room segment of the questionnaire, customers are queried further on linens and towels, TV and radio, lighting, air conditioning/heating, plumbing, mattress and pillows, telephone service, and carpeting!

In addition to asking both general and specific questions, you must distinguish those product or service components that address the *minimal* requirements of performance from those that are perceived as *adding value* to the customer experience.

There are many methods for establishing the relative importance of different customer satisfaction criteria. Most research practitioners prefer to let customers reveal their preferences through some form of direct questioning, such as the *paired comparison* technique. For example, a question might read as follows: "Which of these two factors is more important to selecting your computer hardware vendor: high-speed technology or quick-response service capability?" A list of such trade-off questions will establish the relative importance of each criterion.

Key variables affecting customer satisfaction can also be determined by presenting respondents with *problem experiences.* These measures indicate the frequency with which customers experience specific problems, whether they contacted the company to have the problem resolved, and whether the problem was handled in a satisfactory way.

After the key attributes have been identified, rating scales are constructed. There are basically three to choose from: "quality" ratings, "satisfaction" ratings, and "value" ratings.

A *quality rating* typically allows the customer to assign a rating through answering questions such as: "How would you rate the quality of the meal served at this restaurant, using a scale from 1 through 10, where '1' represents 'poor' and '10' represents 'excellent'?" In its quality audit survey, for instance, Herman Miller, the furniture maker, asks its clients, "Overall, how do you rate our . . . product and service quality, . . . the Herman Miller sales representative and the dealer?" The rating options range from "excellent," "good," and "average" to "poor" and "unacceptable."

A *satisfaction rating* question uses slightly different wording, such as, "How satisfied were you with the meal served at this restaurant?" Speedy Muffler King uses a rating scale that allows a customer to evaluate overall service as "exceptional," "meets expectations," or "below expectations."

A *value rating* question explicitly takes into account the price paid by customers in relation to the benefits they feel they received from the purchase. A question like this might read, "Do you feel you received a good meal for the price you paid?"

In addition to designing questions like these, the researcher should do statistical analyses that evaluate "the relative importance of attributes as well as [the company's] performance in these areas." As marketing research consultant J.W. Marr has pointed out, "[m]easuring the importance that customers place on different attributes can help managers make important resource-planning decisions." The grid shown in Figure 4–4 shows how relative importance ratings can be used in resource planning.

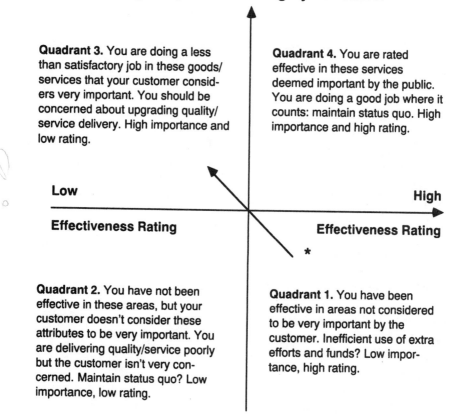

High importance rating by consumer

Quadrant 3. You are doing a less than satisfactory job in these goods/ services that your customer considers very important. You should be concerned about upgrading quality/ service delivery. High importance and low rating.

Quadrant 4. You are rated effective in these services deemed important by the public. You are doing a good job where it counts: maintain status quo. High importance and high rating.

Low

Effectiveness Rating

High

Effectiveness Rating

Quadrant 2. You have not been effective in these areas, but your customer doesn't consider these attributes to be very important. You are delivering quality/service poorly but the customer isn't very concerned. Maintain status quo? Low importance, low rating.

Quadrant 1. You have been effective in areas not considered to be very important by the customer. Inefficient use of extra efforts and funds? Low importance, high rating.

Low importance rating by consumer

*The arrow shows the direction in which to shift resources.

Figure 4–4. Attribute Rating Map. Importance—Effectiveness
Reprinted by permission of Marr, Walker: CSM

Interpreting and Applying the Results of the Survey

As important as the measurement phase is, all the data gathered and compiled will be of no relevance if they do not help management make better strategic decisions or develop constructive action plans. For this to happen, survey results must be analyzed and appropriately applied.

A survey by consultants Brown and Martenfed found that the Four Seasons Hotels, for example, have a rigorous data collection and analysis system, whereby both a guest survey and an employee survey are conducted in every hotel in the chain. The guests' remarks are compiled by category and performance in each hotel and compared with that hotel's performance the previous year. The employee surveys are analyzed and discussed by a committee of line employees, who meet once a month with the general managers to go through all the employees' comments. Executive vice-president John Sharpe underlines the importance of not only collecting data, but also using it intelligently: "The first thing you have to do is ask the right questions. Then, once you have the answers, what do you do about it? Do you stick it in a drawer?" Obviously, they do not.

The ways of following up on survey data range from the extremely informal to the highly structured. When customers call the 800 number printed on many of Procter & Gamble's products, the calls are recorded so that the data can be communicated to the appropriate departments and individuals. Barbara Fraser, the general manager of P&G's Disposable Products Division in Toronto even listens to tapes of the calls in her car. "As the G.M. of disposable products, I now know when someone is calling from New Brunswick or Montreal to complain about Luv Diapers, and why they're concerned."

Jeffrey Marr suggests that quality review sessions or teams should be set up before data collection even begins so that they can review the research as soon as results are available. In other cases, a formal consumer affairs department may be set up so that customer feedback is incorporated into the strategic decision-making process. In the 1987 AMA report on consumer affairs mentioned earlier, it was found that about half of the respondents had set up consumer affairs departments. However, only 64 percent of the companies surveyed said that the department was headed by someone from middle management. And only 21 percent of the companies had a consumer affairs department headed up by a senior manager. This deficiency meant that vital customer feedback was not reaching the top level of many companies. Since most consumer affairs departments have not yet achieved sufficient status to have direct reporting relationships to most senior executives, it is not surprising that customers often complain about the poor responsiveness of large businesses while, at the same time, top executives are bewildered by their inability to grasp customer needs.

Whatever the context—customer value committee or consumer affairs department—the analysis of customer satisfaction information can be done in two ways: (1) to describe the behavior and attitudes of customers and (2) to diagnose the underlying causes of customer behavior. It is also important to prioritize the results—to decide which ones really need to be acted on immediately and to determine the level of resources that should be applied to changing undesirable situations.

The Burke Institute has identified a few simple guidelines for results analysis:

- Be problem-oriented, not technique-oriented [that is, don't fall in love with the surveying techniques; remember that the goal is to improve value for customers],
- Use results as input, not [as a] substitute, for managerial decisions,
- Exploit the complementarity of various techniques [that is, look at qualitative and quantitative, formal and informal research results as parts of a whole, not as separate entities in themselves],
- Focus on the meaning, not the mechanics, of analysis.

Ron Zemke points out that it is important not to turn customer satisfaction research results into "generic measures": Marketing research firms, he says, which

[M]ay have done some nice research are extrapolating from that data the five or six "most important" factors of customer satisfaction and are then selling them as systems that promise, "If you measure these X number of things, customer satisfaction nirvana will be yours." The problem with that is twofold. First, one size does not fit all whether it be pantyhose or instruments. If the information is not something very specific that people all the way to the front line of the organization can look at and say, "Oh, now I know what I need to change," then it's not actionable. Second, if you and everyone else are using those factors, you're not looking for ways to distinguish yourself in the marketplace. You're just trying to not be worse than anyone else. The point of customer satisfaction data is not to level the playing field, it's to unlevel it.

How, then, should customer satisfaction research be applied? It should be related to specific areas of the company's operations and integrated into strategic planning.

Strategic planning. Although benchmarking research, which can give insights into competitive advantage, is an obvious strategic tool, other forms of customer satisfaction data can be used to develop a company's strategy as well.

When the Royal Bank learned from its research "that the greatest satisfier out there [was] to stop the number of errors [they made], as well as [their] reluctance to put them right," management formulated a new service guarantee: "Error-free service or your money refunded."

For IBM Canada, research data resulted in a reorganization. Although the company thought that their billings were a problem, customers did not think they were an important issue; but they did point out that the company's "responsiveness and reliability" were key factors in determining customer satisfaction. With this knowledge (and after some internal validation), IBM Canada reorganized itself into business centers with telephone access.

Analyses of customer research data can also be applied to the distribution, operations, marketing/advertising, and human resources areas of a company; and it can be used to improve complaint handling and customer relations management.

Operations. By tracking the relationship between different levels of operational performance and customer satisfaction ratings, internal standards can be aligned to enhance customer satisfaction. Through this process, companies are learning how the operational variables that they control internally can affect the external perceptions held by buyers. Hewlett-Packard, for instance, collects performance measurements from internal events and process tasks and compares these to data on customer perceptions of service quality levels. The company is seeking to clarify the linkage between the day-to-day operating variables and customer satisfaction. The goal is, ultimately, to develop a management system that focuses on the tasks considered most important by its clients.

Marketing/advertising. If customer satisfaction research is designed to give a company a clearer portrait of the individuals who make up its market, it can help the company launch more effective marketing programs and advertising campaigns. In some cases it may be useful for a company to determine whether its key customers are "high-sensation seekers" or "low-sensation seekers." High-sensation seekers tend to be responsive to information transmitted through mass media and special interest media, and they are more likely to be attracted by promotional appeals stressing risk and novelty. They also are more likely to react well to informative advertising, and they tend to evaluate a product or service based on their own experiences. Low-sensation seekers, on the other hand, tend to evaluate the merits of products and services based on the advice of a trusted celebrity or expert as reference points. If customer satisfaction research is analyzed in terms of high- and low-sensation seekers, the company can determine whether it will target one group or the other—or both—with a two-pronged promotional campaign.

Customer satisfaction research can also be used to help a company understand how its buyers view its strengths and weaknesses compared to those of its competitors. And, using information gathered about customers' expectations, the company can actively influence those expectations by carefully aligning advertising with the company's actual ability to perform. In this way, gaps between customers' expectations and their actual experiences with the business can be avoided.

A few years ago, Vicks developed a liquid cold remedy that promised quick but prolonged relief. The product was successful except for one drawback: It caused extreme drowsiness. When the company got feedback about this, it remedied the problem and lured customers back to the product by renaming it Nyquil and promoting it as a night-time remedy. The product remained the same, but the gap between expectation and actual experience was closed. Sales rebounded and Nyquil became a market leader.

Human resources. Over the years it has become more and more obvious that traditional compensation systems often do not motivate employees to improve their service to customers. This is where customer satisfaction research can be used as a motivator. One marketing research expert suggests that the salaries and bonuses of all employees should be linked with the results of a consistently administered customer satisfaction research program, and that the link between executives' salaries and bonuses and customer satisfaction ratings should be closer than the same link for line employees. This is because executives have greater responsibility for allocating resources.

Tom Peters suggests that customer satisfaction be made a "prime motivator" in sales incentives (instead of volume of sales) or that it be used "at least . . . as a 'go-no go' switch (e.g., if a person is not in the top half on the continued customer satisfaction measure, he or she is not eligible for any awards based on the volume of sales)."

Northern Telecom has adjusted its compensation program to encourage employee behavior that supports the company's goal of improved response time to customers. Using a "pay-for-skill" program, employees receive pay increases for each new skill they learn. This allows employees to be used in more than one job task and has helped Northern Telecom eliminate some job categories. Responsiveness to customers is also increased because employees can be moved more easily to fill in where they are needed during peak demand times.

Customer satisfaction feedback can also be used to form the basis of employee training programs. Through customer research, one major airline identified a list of dos and don'ts for employees dealing with customers and used the list as a basis for training. Among the dos relating to "employee response to customer needs and requests" were the following:

- DO recognize seriousness of need
- DO acknowledge
- DO anticipate
- DO attempt to accommodate

Among the don'ts were the following:

- DON'T ignore
- DON'T promise but fail to follow through
- DON'T embarrass the customer
- DON'T laugh at the customer

These guidelines were based on actual situations in which travelers were either very pleased or very displeased with service quality. The fact that the results were tabulated in the form of "DO" and "DON'T" lists enabled their use in training sessions using case studies, role playing, and employee round table discussions.

If customer satisfaction research instruments are designed to produce specific, actionable information, they can be applied to all areas of a company's operations. By investing time and resources in effective research, executives are sending a message to both their customers and their employees: They care enough to find out *exactly* what customers want. This kind of care and attention to detail goes a long way in establishing a company's reputation for value creation, and it is one step in the process of managing relationships with customers.

Although relationships with customers have always been a crucial part of any business, only enterprises that are focused on creating value for customers emphasize the *management* of those relationships. While in the past, customer relationships have been the specialty of the sales/marketing and customer service areas alone, they are now a basic part of the value creation effort of every area of the company. In the next chapter, we will look at how the management of customer relationships adds to the value-building process.

5

Managing Customer Relationships

*Your next sale, next product, next idea, next success depend a lot on
your external relationships. A good relationship is an asset. We can
invest in relationships and we can borrow from them. We all do it,
but we seldom account for and almost never manage it. Yet, a
company's most precious asset is its relationship with its customers. It
is not who you know, but how you are known to them.*

Theodore Levitt, The Marketing Imagination

Building relationships with your customers is akin to opening an
emotional bank account. The more positive or helpful the relationship,
the greater the deposits. Withdrawals, on the other hand, occur when
the focus of the business effort reverts away from the customers and their
needs and to the product. Augmenting this type of bank account is the
equivalent of sustaining repeat business. This can be accomplished by
treating the sales process as "relationship marketing," instead of
"transaction marketing." This means providing the consumer with a
helping experience at all points of contact with your organization:
before the sale, during the sale, and after the sale. As a result, the
customer learns to trust, and eventually feel that he or she is receiving
full value from the company's service and products.

Harvard Business School professor Theodore Levitt suggests that relationship marketing can be distinguished from transaction marketing as follows:

Transaction Marketing	*Relationship Marketing*
Single sale focus	Continuous sale focus
Product is feature-oriented	Product is system-oriented
Modest service component	High service component
Limited commitment to buyer	High commitment to buyers

When you continually meet or exceed customer expectations, you create satisfied customers who provide repeat business. Sometimes, customers sense a gap between their expectations and your actual performance, however, and then they become unhappy. Customer expectations, then, need to be managed. There's a certain irony in this, however, as Karl Hellman, of the Atlanta-based consulting firm Hellman & Lock observes: "Most customers often do not know what to realistically expect from a service or product until after they have received it."

A company can manage customer relationships effectively by:

• Telling the customer what to expect; otherwise he or she may not think your quality is high. Hellman tells of an experienced repairman who found a unique way to meet or exceed customer expectations. The repairman simply added one hour in estimating his normal repair time. That way, when things went as planned, customers were pleasantly surprised. When the repairs took longer, he had a time buffer to solve the problem and meet the expectations he set.

• Explaining to the customer the internal company processes that are responsible for service or product quality. Then your customers can appreciate more fully what you are doing for them.

• Learning to know the customer's needs better than the customer does and communicating to the customer you have what is desired.

In order for relationship marketing to succeed, you must have enough information about your customer to make recommendations that fit his needs and really solve his problems. It is a process that must be handled carefully and subtly. "Stand in the shoes of your customers. Try to understand what it is that will make them so pleased with your company's service that your competitor's discount won't interest them."

One company that has turned knowing a customer's need into the "foundations of their business," is Minneapolis-based Mackay Envelope Corporation. As mentioned in Chapter 2, CEO and chairman of the board Harvey B. Mackay advises keeping a "trivia file" on each and every customer. This sort of information can be gleaned during friendly lunches or through formal research.

Things to look for? Everything from a golf handicap to views on the federal deficit, from the size of a home to a favorite vacation spot. In a word, anything that can help *personalize* the relationship. This, notes Mackay, "Establishes you as an effective listener. Effective listeners remember order dates and quality specifications. They are easier to talk with when there's a problem with a shipment. Effective listeners sell more to customers and keep them longer."

Mackay's other secret weapon for customer satisfaction is the "Mackay 66," a questionnaire designed to elicit such information as the contact's educational background, career history, family, special interests, and lifestyle. "It's continually updated and it's studied to death in our company. Our overriding goal is to know more about the customers than they know about themselves." Armed with this information, the Mackay salesman has the tools to be more perceptive and empathetic to customers' needs, which conveys to them the sincere message, *"I care."*

METHODS FOR MANAGING CUSTOMER RELATIONSHIPS

All parts of your company have the potential to influence customers' perceptions. Senior executives, however, need methods of analysis to manage all elements of the customer satisfaction process. Here, the concept of *blueprinting* is useful. Blueprinting means looking at the basic systems and structures of your organization to better understand the business as a *process* that creates satisfied customers.

First, identify all points of contact that a customer has with your organization. From here, you can map your underlying business processes to identify blockages to customer satisfaction. Then, use the information you glean for implementing improvements. There are several frameworks that are useful in carrying out a blueprinting exercise, as follows:

- Cycle-of-service analysis
- Value-chain analysis
- Story-boarding

Cycle-of-Service Analysis

The cycle-of-service analysis will show you how the customer experiences each contact with your organization. Each point of contact with your firm is a "moment of truth" for the customers and for their perceptions of value delivered by your business. Every contact point has the potential to increase or decrease customer satisfaction levels. And each contact point forms a continuous chain of events for the buyers, even though the customer may deal with many departments within the organization.

Yet, service providers and manufacturers often fail to think of the process as a single flow of connected experiences. Instead, they think of it in terms of their own individual tasks and activities. Each department sees only one part of the picture. No one sees the whole process from the customer's point of view. Who has not had the frustrating telephone experience of being passed from one department to the next hearing the refrain "It's not the responsibility of my department." With this kind of treatment, the customer might wonder if your employees are working together under the same roof and for the same company.

Value-Chain Analysis

Value-chain analysis, previously discussed in Chapter 2, is a method of analyzing a business to understand its sources of competitive advantage. The value chain strips down a firm into its component activities so that you can understand how it provides value for its customers. Value is created from the discrete activities a firm performs in designing, producing, marketing, delivering, and supporting its products. An example of how value-chain analysis could be applied to the production of newspapers might be as follows:

- Inbound logistics—delivery, handling, and storage of ink and newsprint
- Operations

    The editorial board oversees the general design and direction of the daily newspaper
    The managing editor confers with department and city editors and decides which stories to pursue
    Stories are assigned to reporters who then submit copy to copy editors
    Copy editors proof the stories, check facts, and write headlines

- Production—the composing room produces each page
- Photo engraving—plates are cut after produced pages are photo-graphed and developed into large negatives
- Printing (usually on site or at a plant)—the paper rolls off the presses
- Outbound logistics—bundling, sorting, and distributing papers to independent operators who supply vendors
- Marketing and sales—selling advertising space, soliciting new sub-scriptions, and buying time on radio and television and space in other print media
- Service maintenance—conducting market research on content and updating and upgrading the content of the newspaper

Each of these activities adds value to the final product—the news-papers delivered to customers each morning. Through examining each step in the value-adding process, blocks and opportunities to build customer satisfaction can be identified.

Story-Boarding

This approach combines elements of the two previous concepts to provide insights into how your company interacts with its customers. As a customer-analysis technique, story-boarding was developed by the Walt Disney organization in designing its theme park. Disney executives wanted to choreograph every aspect of their patrons' experiences with the park's attractions to ensure the highest possible degree of "customer happiness." Appropriately enough, for a company that earned its reputation producing cartoons, they borrowed from movie-making a technique known as story-boarding.

In making a movie, each scene is carefully planned in advance of actual filming. This is done through a series of cartoon-like sketches, called story-boards, which are arranged in sequence. Using this frame-work, you can portray exactly how a customer comes into contact with your organization and rearrange the "scenes" to improve your customer satisfaction levels, then build the business processes necessary to make the scenes come alive.

All of the above approaches are tools that will help you see your business as a process that works toward a goal of creating satisfied customers and identifying ways to improve procedures for maximum customer value. This, in turn, will help you become a long-term partner with your customers.

HOW TO TURN THE COURTSHIP INTO MARRIAGE

Long-established customers are the most profitable because they buy more, refer new business, and usually are willing to pay higher prices. Levitt likens the evolution of such relationships to courtship and marriage:

> The relationship between a seller and a buyer seldom ends when a sale is made. Increasingly, the relationship intensifies after the sale and helps determine the buyer's choice the next time around. The sale then merely consummates the courtship at which point the marriage begins.

What, then, can a company do to make the marriage last?

Frequent Patron Programs

These started in the early 1980s and are now practiced by many companies in the service industry as a way to recognize the importance of building lasting relationships with repeat purchasers. For example, the Marriott Hotel chain instituted a program that offered travel perks to long-time frequent customers. The program allowed customers to earn points toward discounts on room rates after so many stays. As for its success in retaining customers, the frequent patron program was more effective and cheaper than advertising, Marriott discovered. It was better to build upon an existing patron base than to continually chase new business. Frequent patron programs are now standard throughout the hospitality industry and have altered the competitive balance by changing the way customers perceive their choices. Many customers now use the availability of such benefits as a criterion in assessing where to stay or on which airlines to fly.

The Personal Touch

For some companies, getting to know a customer is not just a matter of studying written data on a page. Rather, a little more intimacy is sought. Wink Vogel knows the value of such personal contact. Each year, the president of Cloverdale Paint Inc. in Surrey, British Columbia, treats his top industrial clients to a fishing excursion. In the spirit of the outing they all stay up and talk into the wee hours of the morning. By that time, the president has forged or renewed some personal acquaintances, which, of course, helps business. Vogel also applies the same personal attention when addressing customers' problems.

His approach has paid off. The company has more than 10 percent of the British Columbia and Alberta markets and has become a major supplier of paint and other coating to homeowners and contractors, and the leading supplier to industrial users. Sales have risen an average of 15 percent per year in recent years, reaching $30 million in 1988.

Making It Easy to Do Business

In your quest for long-term customers, you must make it easy to do business with your company. One factor in retaining patrons is the attitude of your sales representatives, their promises of performance, and their commitment to work closely with customers to meet their needs.

Sometimes it starts with basic appearance and courtesy. In one American supermarket chain, Super Valu Stores' Club Food Market, managers teach workers how to smile and walk erectly; and, in some instances, they must even specify that workers come to work with their shoes tied and shirts ironed.

Faced with the double challenge of a labor shortage in the service sector and the demand for quality service from customers, many U.S. companies are revising their strategies to attract—and keep—higher-quality service personnel. As consultant Frederick Reichheld of Boston-based Bain & Co. puts it, "Customer retention and employee retention feed one another."

In its quest to provide better customer service, American Express Travel Services Group, for example, began to solicit employment applications from more educated workers, enticing qualified personnel, such as busy mothers who are college graduates, with flexible hours and richer job content. Other companies, such as Super Valu, are offering similar flexibility to college students who can, if necessary, work a partial shift, write a Chemistry exam, and then return to work the same day.

Other factors that contribute to a customer perception that it is easy to do business with your company include the ease of getting information about your offerings and the smoothness of the transaction. Some companies have achieved great success by making service convenience a priority.

Parisian is a well known chain of 17 stores operating in four southern states. The company pays its sales personnel higher-than-average wages and staffs its floors at a higher level than most retail chains do in order to give customers greater personal attention. Employee training alone takes 45 hours; then there are refresher courses to ensure that customers are served by knowledgeable staff. In addition, the stores provide a shuttle service to carry customers to their parked cars, and they offer such welcome perks as free giftwrapping service and no interest charges for six months on items charged to the store's credit card. As a result, Parisian has seen healthy profits; and it maintains a strong competitive position in its trading region.

Like any long-term relationship that's worth having, you must keep working at your relationship with your established customers. Sometimes, just adding some extra perks here and there can remind your regular customers that you value their business and will encourage them to keep coming back. For example:

- *Reward customers.* Nothing elaborate; it's the thought that counts. For example, Cy Mann Tailors in Toronto gives away a free tie with each custom-made suit it sells. The cost of one tie is insignificant compared to the cost of the suit, but the customer walks away feeling that he has been given something extra.

- *Offer them more of what they buy or something compatible.* This is a way to be sensitive to their needs. If, for example, you are aware they purchase a lot of pencils, ask them if perhaps they need any paper.

- *Reward them for telling a friend about your company.* This promotes one of the most effective means of advertising—*word of mouth.*

Customer Support after the Sale

As mentioned, a good company/customer relationship is only consummated after the sale. Then it's up to the company to nurture the marriage. One way companies do this is by providing value-added service. This is especially vital for those that manufacture big-ticket machinery. Glegg Water Conditioning Inc. of Guelph, Ontario, knows this. The company has eight service engineers ready to jet anywhere in North America within 24 hours, 365 days a year, to service the demineralizers it sells to paper mills, power plants, semiconductor-makers, and other manufacturers that require pure water. To GWC president Robert Glegg, customer service is essential enough that he would rather "have more engineers than necessary."

A well developed customer retention strategy is not only useful for those who are end-users of your product but also for others in the relationship equation who can also be considered as customers: distributors, dealers, shareholders, the financial community, and even employees.

For example, Gillette's vice-president of Business Relations is responsible for cultivating relationships with major retailers and distributors through entertainment at conventions and the organization of special events for major accounts. Through these efforts, Gillette builds strong customer relationships with its major accounts.

Business relationships can atrophy, however, with lapses in sensitivity and attentiveness. A healthy business relationship requires constant maintenance effort.

It becomes important for you, the seller, to regularly and seriously ask yourself some very common-sense questions. Levitt suggests these:

- How are we doing?
- Is the relationship improving or deteriorating?
- Are our promises completely fulfilled?
- Are we neglecting anything?
- How do we stand in the relationship compared to our competitors?
- What concrete actions can I take to keep key account relationships from deteriorating?

The pharmaceutical products industry keeps these questions in mind. Sales representatives regularly check back with physicians to whom they have sold items, to find out how the products have been received and whether the products will be purchased by the physician in the future. Medical sales people regularly conduct physician surveys and constantly monitor their relationships with physicians. They also attempt to woo medical students and doctors alike with dinners, gifts, and information on the newest technical developments in the field.

The key is to take the initiative by showing concern for buyers and their problems. The seller should nurture mutual interest with the buyers. Here are some dos and don'ts for sellers to enhance the positive relationships between them and their important customers and create helping partnerships:

- Initiate positive phone calls, instead of only returning calls.
- Make recommendations, instead of justifications.
- Be candid instead of accommodating.
- Don't write when you can use the phone.
- Show appreciation when you can. Don't wait for misunderstandings.
- Make service suggestions instead of waiting for service requests.
- Use "we" problem-solving language instead of the "you-us" legal language that creates barriers.
- Tackle potential problems head-on instead of responding to them after they arise.
- Communicate clearly and succinctly instead of in long-winded communiques.
- Be open about personality problems. Air them out and resolve differences instead of keeping them smoldering.
- Plan for "our future together" instead of talking about correcting past mistakes.
- Make prompt response the routine. Don't use fire drill/emergency responses.
- Accept responsibility instead of shifting the blame.

Keeping Industrial Customers

If your business serves primarily industrial or commercial customers, it makes sense to pay special attention to your "key accounts," those relatively few buyers that typically account for the majority of business.

Levitt suggests three steps to improve your key account relationships:

- *Awareness.* Show that relationship management is a problem, and that the problem has costs. Show that it is an opportunity, and that the opportunity has benefits.

- *Assessment.* Establish regular reporting on individual relationships and then on group relationships so that these can be weighed against other measures of performance.

- *Actions.* Make decisions and allocations, and establish routines and communication, on the basis of their impact on the targeted relationships. Constantly reinforce awareness and actions.

AUGMENTING THE VALUE OF PRODUCTS AND SERVICES BY USING RELATIONSHIP STRATEGIES

There are at least three dimensions to product augmentation and gaining market leverage through stronger customer relationships. Each of the following, or their combination, should be considered:

- Improved physical distribution
- Better product support
- Stronger service orientation

Improved Distribution

When considering manufactured goods, product availability is both a key to customer satisfaction and a highly valued benefit. Thus, the physical distribution system between buyer and seller must be assessed for opportunities to enhance the total benefit package to be offered. Such is the case with The Brick Warehouse, a Canadian-based furniture store chain. It has set speedy delivery as one of its major customer-value-enhancing goals. Its fleet of 125 vehicles ensures that customers can enjoy their purchases almost immediately after making their selection. In fact, the company makes a guarantee to customers that furniture and appliances will be delivered within 24 hours.

The following components of physical distribution contribute to strengthened customer loyalty:

- Accurate billing procedures
- Fair returns policies
- Accurate order-filling processes
- Minimum delivery lead times
- Easy handling of claims
- Availability of accurate order status information
- Speed in answering emergency orders

Renowned catalog retailer L.L. Bean developed a loyal clientele using such elements. For example, the company is extremely flexible with customers who want to return products they are unhappy with. In addition, phone staff have been trained extensively to provide accurate order-filling services. The company also has invested heavily in computer technology that allows for a quick check of inventory and order status, and it gives customers different delivery options depending on whether they are in a hurry.

Better Product Support

These are the services and features that enhance the usefulness of your product after purchase. For example, electronics and communication company ITT Canada offers comprehensive customer training programs so that clients' employees can install, calibrate, and maintain the precision process-control and measurement instruments sold by the company. This keeps the systems running smoothly and builds customers satisfaction.

Following are some elements to consider when forming your post-purchase strategy:

- Locate service facilities near markets
- Provide service telephone "hot lines"
- Offer longer warranty periods and wider coverage
- Provide product loans and "stand-bys" to minimize down time
- Use modular product designs to facilitate quick component exchange

General Electric, for example, offers the longest warranties in the industry for its telephones, TV's, and electric skillets. G.E. also has an exclusive "quick-fix system" for do-it-yourselfers that includes readable instruction manuals with simple step-by-step procedures. Thus, if anything goes wrong with a G.E. appliance, the customer can choose whether to incur the expense or inconvenience of a service call.

Stronger Service Orientation

Just as important as the quality of the tangible product you sell to the customer is the quality of care or concern shown by your employees to customers. The Four Seasons hotel chain, for example, has profited on the care and attention it provides its guests, many of whom are travel-weary, but well heeled, executives. They can expect such frills as 24-hour room service, plush bathrobes, hair dryers, and extensive fitness facilities. But, more importantly, personalized needs are quickly attended to as a result of a higher-than-average staff-to-guest-ratio. The hotel's computer files on regular guests keep track of needs such as whether they are smoking or non-smoking, whether they require a king or queen size bed, which credit card they pay with, and so on.

Factors that help to enhance perceived service quality include:

- Responsiveness to customer inquiries
- Easy buyer access to required information
- Courtesy in buyer interactions
- Competence of service personnel
- Clarity of communications with buyers

Software manufacturer Microsoft Corporation implemented some of these when their switchboards overloaded with calls several years ago after introducing 17 new and revamped products. The company swiftly added 80 employees and many extra phone lines to provide more accessible support. In addition, this team operates in an open rather than closed office environment so that customer support information is easily shared. To Microsoft, service support is just as important as technical sophistication.

Identifying Customer-Support Needs

It is necessary to segment markets carefully to develop the best approach to customer support needs. Management consultant Barbara Bund Jackson suggests that markets can be divided along two dimensions: *switching costs* and *buyer risk exposure.*

Switching costs are the degrees of difficulty or disruption that a customer will experience in changing suppliers after the initial purchase has been made. *Risk exposure* is the perceived negative consequences to the buyer if his or her purchase decision proves wrong. From a customer-support perspective, products that have low switching costs and low perceived risk require less after-sales support. This product category includes such mass-market items as food and toiletries where buyers are most interested in price and performance.

By contrast, products with high switching costs and high perceived buyer risk—personal computers, for example—require more highly developed product-support strategies. Not only are consumers of these items concerned with price and product performance, but they also require the assurance of ongoing vendor support.

Different types of products require different types of after-sales support. In his book *The Customer Is Key* Milind Lele, a professor at the University of Chicago's Graduate School of Business, defines four generic product types that have their own unique after-sales support requirements:

• *Disposables.* Risk costs are low here, so the best strategy is to encourage disposability through simple product design and low price. Successful examples of this type of product are disposable lighters and razors.

• *Repairables.* These items have a high replacement cost. Customers are receptive to them when they are designed for high reliability and easy repair. Successful examples of companies with this type of product include appliance manufacturer Maytag and some Japanese automobile companies.

• *Rapid response.* The user of this type of product can little afford down time. That's why the support strategy here includes use of rapid-response repair teams that can be quickly dispatched to resolve problems. Computer systems are one example of this type of product. Power supplied to industrial users by electrical utilities is another.

• *Never fails.* When customers cannot tolerate product failure due to the high cost and risk to their own business, vendors must move towards "redundancy" support programs. Suppliers then should provide back-up capability in the event of product service or failure. Tandem Computers for example, are designed with parallel processing systems so that the alternate processing unit can take over if there are system problems.

Customer-Support Strategies

As seen previously, customer relationship strategies need to be tailored to the specific market segment or type of customer you are servicing. Three additional variables need to be considered in the formulation of your relationship strategy:

• Product and service design
• Systems support
• Buyer risk reduction

Product and service design. This focuses on the opportunities to improve the product's reliability, repairability, or ability to function even if some parts of the system fail. Long-lasting performance should be built-in through better design. For example, leading children's toy manufacturer Fisher-Price strives to provide consumers with the safest and most durable toys possible. It is part of the company culture. Quality is every employee's responsibility, from the product's conception to its delivery to a customer. At every stage of production, the firm's Quality Control Division runs quality checks to ensure the product is safe, durable, and reliable. New product qualification requires a series of tests to certify compliance with Fisher-Price specifications, foreign and domestic government regulations, and fitness-for-use requirements. Each part purchased from other vendors must also be rigorously tested before it becomes part of a Fisher-Price toy.

Systems support. This is the means by which a buyer is assured of continued product performance. The key elements to consider are response time (how long it takes to respond to a customer problem) and repair time (how long it takes to get the customer back in operation or to have the full use of your products or services).

Consider AT&T. In a telecommunications market where competition has heated up as a result of deregulation, AT&T has remained a strong leader. The company's Post-Warranty Maintenance Program offers customers continued maintenance after their warranty has expired. For a fixed price, AT&T will repair its customers' equipment for a post-warranty period of from one to four years. Its Service Plus program can be added to any product under warranty, lease, or maintenance contract. Response time is prompt. A single call to AT&T with this service takes care of any equipment or signal problems. For most "system-down" problems, AT&T is at the site within a couple of hours and can repair or replace the equipment on the spot.

Buyer risk reduction. This refers to the activities your company can undertake to reduce exposing customers to significant financial loss due to product or service malfunction. This reduction in perceived risk can be achieved, for example, through warranties and service contracts such as those discussed earlier. An illustration of this is found in how Audi of America uses its comprehensive warranty program to reassure potential buyers. The company's warranty pays for all maintenance and repairs for three years or 50,000 miles. The unlimited mileage corrosion protection warranty is good for 10 full years. Essentially, Audi buyers pay for nothing more than gas, tires, and insurance during the warranty period. The warranty is one of the most comprehensive car coverage programs in the country and helps to increase consumer confidence in the company's products.

The most important principle in implementing a customer relationship-building program is to follow an integrated approach. Customer relationships must be viewed within the context of your company's overall value-building strategy. Customer support alone will not offset poor products, weak marketing communications, or rude and inconsiderate employees. But with these other elements in place, adding a strong customer support effort will create an unbeatable combination.

6

Delivering on Your Promise: Achieving High-Quality Operational Performance

---

The bitterness of poor quality and service remains long after the sweetness of low price is forgotten.

John Ruskin

By definition bad quality is a waste of time.

Carl Arendt, Westinghouse Quality Center

It is called the Quality and Productivity Center. Installed in a former Chrysler warehouse outside of Pittsburgh, it is Westinghouse's quality think-tank, a place where 130 computer gurus, consultants, and engineers work, meticulously helping business units "do the right things right the first time." Company president (now chairman) Paul Lego describes the center's mandate: "When most people think of quality they think of the product; we try to think of the process." The center's job is to improve everything that goes into the product process "from engineering to plant maintenance to billing. The goal is customer satisfaction—the result of emphasizing quality rather than productivity."

More than 100 times a year, teams from the Quality Center are deployed to perform Total Quality Fitness Reviews that any business unit can request for all or any part of its operation. Even the chairman's office is subject to a regular fitness review. After rigorous analysis, including interviews and customer surveys, the team identifies weaknesses in the process. The results are recorded on a Total Quality scorecard and presented to the manager. Then, the Quality Center helps the manager implement improvements.

This is but one example of how Westinghouse is approaching a standard of excellence known as corporate-wide quality control (CWQC).

In his book *What is Total Quality Control?* Japanese quality guru Kaoru Ishikawa says "company-quality control" is a way of operating where everyone in every division in the company must study, practice, and participate in quality management. The business journal *Quality Progress* reports that CWQC is "a system or means to economically produce goods or services which satisfy customers' requirements...." The journal notes that "implementing (CWQC) effectively necessitates the cooperation of all people in the company, involving top management, managers, supervisors, and workers in all areas of corporate activities...."

CREATING YOUR CWQC PROGRAM

The previous chapters have introduced to you the techniques for better understanding customer requirements and their perceptions of value. However, knowing what customers want is hardly sufficient for actively satisfying them. Instead, you must manage the operations of your business to meet customer requirements. You need to understand how your systems, procedures, and production processes contribute value toward meeting customer needs. The term "operations" is defined, for the purposes of this chapter, to be the manufacturing activities, or the "plant," in goods-producing industries, or the "back office" for service organizations. It is the physical setting that enables the service to be rendered. If you do not have an operations background, you may be bewildered by the emerging techniques of quality management. Perhaps you may think that quality management is the responsibility of the "plant people," and not something you need to be concerned with. However, some of the most powerful ideas for making your company more customer-responsive can be found among the new concepts of quality management. You should, therefore, become more familiar with the key quality management ideas that can be applied to your customer-value-creation efforts.

Among them is corporate-wide, or company-wide, quality control. It consists of five principles:

- Attention to quality in management
- Involvement of all functions
- Involvement of all employees
- A belief in continuous improvement
- A strong focus on the customer

Attention to Quality in Management

Managing quality is not a narrowly focused process based just on improving a product's technical attributes. Top executives must practice innovative, conscientious management practices as well, auditing the system rather than the product, emphasizing change for quality improvement. Such was the case three years ago at Union Pacific Railroad. Chief executive officer Mike Walsh found that 18 percent of the bills it sent out contained errors. Walsh appointed a special team to look at the problem. Using statistical analysis, the team concluded that the billing errors stemmed from 20 different causes spread across every department, from finance to shipping. Twenty different teams were set up to handle each problem.

Involvement of All Functions

Quality management permeates all company activities and extends beyond the domain of manufacturing and operations. Customer satisfaction and value creation, the key objectives, are most effectively achieved in a situation where the company's cross-functional linkages work smoothly so that the "voice of the customer" is heard throughout the company as it plans customer satisfaction programs.

Fuji-Xerox kept this in mind during the late 1970s when it geared up to penetrate the small copier market with the 3500 copier. Intertwined with this effort was a rethinking of the company's culture that eventually would revamp the way business was conducted throughout the organization. Prior to this, Fuji-Xerox had been a company plagued by fragmented and inconsistent leadership and complacent and arrogant managers who had lost their sense of urgency. There was little or no focus on customers, and product development was undisciplined and sloppy. Worst of all, there was little cross-functional cooperation.

"It was very important for us to improve cross-functional co-operation as we were already a big bureaucratic company full of sectionalism. The buzzword for all of us was to 'break the wall,'" recalls Hidy Kaihatsu, the company's director of International Relations. With this in mind, Fuji-Xerox reorganized; and top management teams attended product review meetings at the factory each month to work out the trial-and-error details. Development and support of the new product was the obsession of every staff member, with personnel, accounting, and marketing researchers all participating.

What resulted was a "super-product" that was delivered in half the normal product development time and was accepted and favored unanimously by customers. The 3500 copier won the prestigious Deming Award for quality in 1980.

Involvement of All Employees

Corporate-wide quality control means the involvement of all employees—at all levels—in solving quality problems and improving the quality management process. Employees closest to the problem areas should participate in the development of solutions. To accomplish this goal, the Japanese use "quality circles," which consist of teams of employees who meet regularly to discuss quality problems, devise methods for improving quality, and participate in extensive training in problem-solving techniques.

Quality circles have been adopted in some North American companies. At General Motors, for example, "Workers who were once expected to shut up and follow orders are now encouraged to use their brains." To this end, a team of hourly and salaried employees came up with a way to reduce the number of parts in the rear floor of Cadillacs and big Oldsmobiles from 52 to 30. What resulted was a reduction in the number of stamping dies from 93 to 38, and in the number of presses used from 93 to 10. General Motors realized a savings of $52 million as a result of this effort.

Massachusetts-based Paul Revere Insurance Companies also derived enormous benefits from its "Quality Has Value" program. Introduced in 1984, the program made use of participative management, quality teams, and value analysis. The company gained 4,110 new quality ideas from its more than 1,200 employees. These, in turn, led to significant quality improvements that reduced costs by $8.5 million in the program's first year.

A Belief in Continuous Improvement

Inherent in CWQC is the conscious effort to set improvement goals, take action, measure results, and then learn from them. It emphasizes that progress is best accomplished through making many small improvements daily, rather than expecting dramatic results from breakthrough projects.

At the BASF Corporation, a multinational chemicals producer, the company's quality improvement program is managed daily by quality improvement teams (QIT) made up of managers representing each plant or business group. With a maximum of 10 managers per team, each group acts as liaison between the work force and upper management. Each QIT also has the authority to create a subcommittee responsible for solving recurring errors.

Certainly, this is the case at the Westinghouse Productivity and Quality Center mentioned earlier. If, during one of the more than 100 fitness reviews conducted each year, weaknesses are found in the quality process, the quality center then helps the department manager set up teams to look for and implement improvements.

A Strong Focus on the Customer

CWQC emphasizes the need for the voice of the customer to be heard throughout the company and to be the primary guide in corporate decision making. Careful market research is a must. Quality standards should be formulated through listening to customer feedback, not by adopting internal operation standards developed for the convenience of the producing company. The result of the quality management process should be products and services that meet customer needs and expectations better than your competition's products and services do.

This type of thinking was used by Techsonic, a Eufaula, Alabama-based manufacturer of Hummingbird depthfinders. Here, "the customer literally developed" a successful product. Depthfinders are used by fishermen to measure the water beneath the boat. Techsonic, however, had met with several product failures. To rectify the situation, chairman James Balkcom decided to interview 25 groups of sportsmen across the United States. Using their input, Techsonic developed a successful product that grossed $80 million in sales in 1988 and captured 40 percent of the U.S. market share despite fierce Japanese competition.

CWQC incorporates customer feedback into the very earliest phase of the product and process design. The approach of deploying customer needs and requirements directly into product development is known as "quality function deployment" (QFD) and will be described later in the chapter.

MOVING FROM QUALITY "INNOCENCE" TO QUALITY "EXCELLENCE"

Corporate-wide Quality Control, also known as Total Quality Management (TQM), is one of the more recent phases in the quality revolution that roared into full throttle in Japan after World War II. The Japanese had considerable incentive to embrace quality management thinking, for it was a time when goods "made in Japan" were considered inferior by the rest of the world. With the desire for a lasting strategic advantage, the Japanese popularized the concept of *statistical quality control*, which had been put forward before the war by such American quality management pioneers as W. A. Shewart. Best known for his ground-breaking book *Economic Control of Quality of Manufactured Product* Shewart introduced the use of probability and statistics to measure the inherent variability of products compared to the standards set. Quality management activities at this stage, however, were considered to be the domain of manufacturing or operations executives.

From statistical quality control evolved *quality assurance*, the uncovering and permanent eliminating of the "root cause" of quality failures. Quality problems had begun to be addressed not only by operations but by several functional departments as well, including product and process design and engineering. The challenge was now to build in quality from the beginning and to eliminate those poorly designed products that did not mesh well with operations processes.

Then came the concept of *total quality control* (TQC). Total quality control broadened the definition of quality management to include all functions within a company; and TQC programs encouraged the establishment of customer-oriented quality principles in marketing and engineering functions as well as in operations and production. This broadening of responsibility for quality evolved into total quality management (TQM), which covers the entire production cycle from conception to customer service and is facilitated by a company culture built around teamwork, communication, and an entrepreneurial spirit.

Recognition of the importance of the right company philosophy, quality awareness, and sufficient employee motivation for high-quality performance characterizes the *zero defects* quality movement that has become popular in North America. For senior management, this means the continuous need to have programs that promote a constant desire among employees to do any job "right the first time." It results in only one acceptable standard—defect-free.

As with corporate-wide quality control, the zero-defects philosophy emphasizes the importance of instilling the right attitudes in employees to motivate high-quality performance. Ways to accomplish this include training, special recognition events, posting of quality results, goal setting, and personal feedback. Continuous education of management and staff is also necessary.

One of the more recent phases in management theory about quality may be termed *strategic customer satisfaction*. Incorporating several of the quality principles mentioned previously, it has three components: First, customers' perceptions are the key standard by which to judge quality. Second, high-quality performance is an essential part of your business strategy, especially since it wins customers away from competitors. Third, because customer-satisfying quality is a strategic issue, it is primarily the responsibility of the senior management team.

Getting back to CWQC, for many companies this state of excellence is still a dream. Many have yet to begin the time-consuming process of change. Some experts recommend that senior executives be prepared to devote up to five years for managing their companies through the transition. Achieving quality excellence requires substantial modification in the work processes, culture, structure, operating style, and spirit of the organization. But it will be worth it. Once the changes have been implemented and are working smoothly, companies can look forward to "costs of poor quality" of less than 3 percent of sales revenue compared to 15 to 20 percent initially. The cost-of-quality concept is discussed later in this chapter.

Manufacturing consultant Douglas Cudlip of Coopers & Lybrand Consulting Group in Toronto likens a company's transformation to a state of quality excellence to a journey with the following five recognizable stages:

- Innocence
- Awareness
- Understanding
- Competence
- Excellence

Recognizing the evolutionary stages is not enough, however. Five management processes work in tandem with each stage. Assessing how each management process will operate in conjunction with the change process is necessary before setting the changes in motion. These five management processes embody a wide range of issues that make up the fabric and culture of the company. Briefly, these five management processes are:

• *Communication:* Informing customers about product quality in a timely and open manner.

• *Managing change:* Planning and anticipating new ways of doing things. This involves education and training of employees.

• *Total quality management:* The processes and technologies of managing for excellence in customer value creation. They are a subset of overlapping and interdependent management practices, policies, concepts, and technologies that can be found in an organization.

• *Human resource management:* Employee training often accompanies any organizational change that involves quality improvement. Inherent in this process is performance measurement, reward, and feedback to help people reach their personal best.

• *Leadership and commitment to improvement:* Management's demonstration of commitment to quality is essential. The appropriateness of this leadership needs to be assessed, for it is management's own "sweat equity" in fulfilling internal and external customer satisfaction.

These management processes in combination with the recognition and understanding of the stages of the journey to "quality excellence" can help you to anticipate the issues you will need to confront and to manage the process more effectively.

To help you understand the stages of this journey of change, the five stages are explained in more detail.

Quality Innocence

Few senior executive teams commit themselves to excellence in quality overnight. The decision usually develops over months or years as executive teams begin to recognize some of the ongoing problems that may be causing the company to lose business because it is not producing high-quality, customer-oriented products or services. Some signs to look out for: lower earnings; a declining market share; failure to compete successfully with those firms that have quality strategies in place; adversarial external relationships, i.e., with suppliers and customers; a large number of customer complaints.

The internal climate may also be a fragmented and negative one, characterized by poor communication, low morale, pessimism, and a lack of teamwork within and between departments. Management style is dictatorial and resistant to change. When it comes to problem solving, reactive or scattered responses amount to little more than crisis management or fire-fighting techniques. Many programs are being launched to solve problems without studying the situation for its root causes. Meanwhile, the cost of poor quality is still high because the causes of variation in performance have not been investigated. The result: quality improvement is erratic and short-lived.

Quality Awareness

At this point, senior management has acknowledged that quality improvement is crucial to competitive success. The message is also communicated to, and intellectualized by, employees. Still, there is a lack of readiness and of commitment to action. This also means that improvement efforts are not understood by enough people. But, quality performance analyses and data collection have begun. Quality problems are analyzed and prioritized. Some causes of performance variance are uncovered and corrected. Quality improvement efforts begin to be more proactive, and quality gains take better hold at this stage as underlying causes become better understood.

Quality Understanding

At this stage, your company is consistently involved in measuring and reporting its costs of poor quality and using this information to set priorities for its improvement activities. The causes of any variances from quality standards are being identified and corrected. Preventive thinking is beginning to permeate the company as is the philosophy of "doing the job right the first time."

Quality and value creation have been defined in customer terms, have become a predominant part of corporate strategy, and these are being communicated to all parts of the organization. Teamwork within and between departments has emerged as a predominant method for solving problems and addressing quality-improvement opportunities. The particularly encouraging characteristic of this stage is that quality improvement actions are emerging even without management direction. Quality improvement initiatives "take hold" and sustain long-term improvement.

Quality Competence

At this stage, external relationships are no longer adversarial. Suppliers and vendors are working more in partnership. This is a sign that you are on the way to success. Patricia Sellers, writing in *Fortune* magazine on how to hold on to loyal customers, points out:

> Successful companies listen to everyone in the distribution chain—dealers, distributors, retailers—as well as to the fellow who carries the package home. They eliminate the bureaucracy that often makes it difficult for customers to register complaints or render suggestions and they know the relationship doesn't end with the sale.

At this point of quality competence, a state of equilibrium exists for the customers as they perceive that the value of the product meets their needs. Should there be any variation in quality performance (which at this point should be minimal), thorough, accurate, and timely data collection will be used effectively to discover the causes. On the management level, quality improvement strategies become a unifying force between functional departments that are also enjoying good internal communications.

Quality Excellence

Companies that have achieved this final stage of the journey experience a significant competitive advantage. They have achieved a high level of performance and find they have made gains in reputation, market share, and profitability. At this level of development, strong partnerships now exist between both customers and suppliers, enabling the creation of real benefits throughout the value-added chain. Improvement activities are ongoing throughout the organization, occurring without direct management intervention. Most of all, the real competitive advantage is in the development of people who can anticipate and address changing factors of competition with confidence and mastery.

WHAT IS QUALITY, ANYWAY?

Quality "excellence" sounds like a wonderful place to be. However, it won't be too long into your journey before differences of opinion surface within your company as to what this elusive state called "quality" actually is.

In the minds of most executives, the words *quality* and *customer satisfaction* are intimately interwoven. North American business is moving toward the Japanese concept of quality and customer satisfaction, which embraces all the "hard" and "soft" attributes discussed previously. Customer value can be perceived as the outcome of your performance compared to expectations. But this begs the question "Whose expectations?"

Everyone claims to "know what customers want." They "know quality when they see it." The differing definitions within your organization about what quality and customer satisfaction really mean usually reflect the functional bias of the background of the executives involved. The differing views on quality can serve as the basis for developing consensus within your management group. The "right" answer may not be as important as having a definition that everyone understands and is committed to.

In his book *Managing Quality* David Garvin categorized varying definitions that provide insight into the concept of quality and, by inference, customer satisfaction and value.

Transcendent

If you believe in transcendent quality, you believe in an innate beauty and excellence as the means to customer satisfaction. Certain brand names have become famous for their perceived high standards. Names such as Dom Perignon, Cadillac, and Gucci are synonymous with fine quality. This cachet applies as well to services, such as American Express credit cards and travelers checks, and to retailers such as Saks Fifth Avenue and Bloomingdale's.

Definitions from the transcendent school have been articulated by some well known authors:

- "Quality is neither mind nor matter, but a third entity independent of the two . . . Even though Quality cannot be defined, you know what it is."
- "It is a condition of excellence implying fine quality as distinct from poor quality . . . Quality is achieving or reaching for the highest standard as against being satisfied with the sloppy or fraudulent."

Product-Based

Product-based definitions of quality and customer satisfaction are markedly different from transcendent concepts. A product-based view holds that quality is measurable and high quality, and, by extension customer satisfaction is achieved by having more of something—increased quantities of an element or attribute. Illustrative definitions of quality from a product-based viewpoint include:

- "Differences in quality amount to differences in the quantity of some desired ingredient or attribute."
- "Quality refers to the amounts of the unpriced attributes contained in each unit of the priced attribute."

An example of product-based quality is seen in the recent influx of premium beers, specialty teas and coffees, and extra-rich ice cream and chocolates. These products claim their high-quality status because they contain premium ingredients or higher levels of critical components such as butterfat.

User-Based

A *user-based* definition of quality and customer satisfaction is founded on the premise that only the customer can truly judge what quality is. Users' perceptions of how well your company satisfies their wants and needs are the benchmarks for evaluation success. Garvin cites the following user-based definitions of quality:

- "Quality consists of the capacity to satisfy wants . . ."
- "In the final analysis of the marketplace, the quality of a product depends on how well it fits patterns of consumer preferences."
- "Quality is fitness for use."

General Electric exemplifies user-based quality and customer satisfaction. The company designs and makes products that best meet the needs of "most customers," and sums up its mission as that of providing a level of ". . . overall performance and attitude that makes General Electric the natural choice of our customers." In making this declaration, General Electric is saying that customer preference is the best judge of quality.

Operations-Based

The *operations-based* view of quality and customer satisfaction often bring its supporters into conflict with those who prefer user-based definitions. Central to the operations-based definition of quality is the concept of *conformance to requirements*. Your operations executives may insist that quality be measurable, objective, and manageable. The appropriate measurement is how closely the product or service meets the "specifications" set for it.

Many North American manufacturers, in defending themselves from Asian and European competitors, are revamping their manufacturing processes and employing a quality standard known as "zero defects." Defects are defined as deviations from a predetermined quantified standard of performance.

Here are some examples of operations-based definitions of quality:

- "Quality [means] conformance to requirements."
- "Quality is the degree to which a specific product conforms to a design or specification."

Value-Based

The final definition of quality may be termed *value-based.* By this definition, quality is expressed in terms of conformance to requirements, including the price and cost of meeting them. Your product or service has more value and, therefore, more quality, when you meet customer needs at a price, or cost, that is lower than that of competing offerings. Value-based definitions of quality include:

- "... The degree of excellence at an acceptable price and the control of variability at an acceptable cost."
- "... [what is] best for certain customers' conditions. These conditions are (a) the actual use and (b) the selling price of the product."

Some observers believe that customers consciously or unconsciously decide upon a price range for a particular category of goods or services and look for quality within it. Quality is, therefore, measured in accordance with price, resulting in a judgment about "affordable excellence."

Although differing definitions of quality, value, and customer satisfaction can produce conflict within your executive team, multiple perspectives can be beneficial, as well. Debate will help them consider the full range of possibilities and challenge "sacred cows" when it comes to customer requirements.

SLASHING THE COSTS OF MISTAKES

At some point on the road to quality excellence, it will be necessary to start measuring and reporting costs of quality (COQ). These are the costs that a company incurs in its daily operations in order to meet the standards of quality it has set for itself. Quantifying all the variables of the process of product making and/or service delivery—and seeing the results in black and white—can help a company plan for future improvements and lower overall costs.

As mentioned before, many world-class quality performers report that their costs of quality are approximately 3 percent of sales revenue. Most companies, however, do not have specific mechanisms in place to reduce these costs. As a result, they may find their quality cost as high as 15 to 35 percent of their sales. To manage COQ more effectively, a company must understand that costs incurred by its operations are either *value-adding* or *non-value-adding*. By adopting COQ management approaches, your company can significantly reduce costs by eliminating non-value-adding activities, defined as those that are not contributing to customer satisfaction. That, in turn, enables a company to focus more on activities that add a perceived benefit, those that customers are willing to pay for. Examples of these can be manufacturing and packaging of a product and, perhaps, certain necessary support services.

However, many costs are perceived by the customer as non-value-adding. These include housekeeping, invoicing, inspecting, testing, and engineering. It is important to know the magnitude of such non-value-adding activity costs and to lower these costs as much as possible. This will improve your profits and free up resources to invest in enhancements that your customers will value.

When these costs are reduced through the use of proper management techniques, they have high profit-leverage effects. A moderate reduction of COQ—by 15 percent for example—could double or triple profits. Many companies have demonstrated that a 10 percent reduction in quality costs requires little more than simple awareness; a 20 percent reduction can be achieved with more work; and even 30 percent can be accomplished with an aggressive strategy.

Quality costs can also be divided into these four categories:

- Prevention
- Appraisal
- Internal failure
- External failure

Prevention

These costs involve non-value-adding support activities that prevent reccurrence of product or process failures such as defects, waste, and unscheduled down time. In a manufacturing environment, the prevention costs category includes:

- Quality-related training
- Quality system development and the upgrading of quality circles or employee-improvement teams
- Quality-improvement training and motivation materials
- Engineering efforts to improve products and processes, such as quality function deployment studies
- Improved testing and inspection methods and equipment
- Programs for establishing qualified suppliers
- Market research and customer surveys that gauge the effects of

product and service characteristics on customers' perceptions of product quality

- Quality-improvement planning and activities for all functional departments, including purchasing, sales, operations, warehousing, maintenance, material management, and personnel

In a service environment, additional activities can be included in the prevention category, such as:

- Customer relations training
- Improved service delivery systems and order entry systems

According to cost-of-quality studies by Coopers & Lybrand's manufacturing consulting practice, in most companies prevention costs account for only 0 to 10 percent of total quality costs. In high-performing companies, those with world-class levels of quality, prevention costs are relatively much higher. World-class performers understand that it is better to incur higher prevention costs in order to reduce appraisal and failure costs. In other words, they do it right the first time. It is essential, then, to increase investment in those prevention activities that in turn help lower overall COQ.

Appraisal

These are quality costs associated with evaluating, measuring, inspecting, and auditing products, processes, components, and materials to ensure that they conform to customer and internal requirements, expectations, and specifications. Typical appraisal cost categories include:

- Quality system and procedures audits
- Supplier reviews and ratings
- Testing, maintenance, and calibration of inspection equipment
- Incoming materials inspection
- Product quality audits
- Prototyping
- Process capability studies
- Testing of materials (incoming and in-process)
- First article inspection

- Obtaining endorsements from outside standards-setting bodies
- Carrying out quality of inventory audits
- Proficiency testing of operators and laboratory personnel

Costs associated with the appraising of and inspecting for quality typically account for 20 to 40 percent of total COQ. Appraisal is, therefore, a key opportunity area for COQ management and reduction, but only after prevention measures have proven effective!

Du Pont, for example, is one of many companies that has improved its manufacturing operations by employing a methodology called statistical process control (SPC), which measures and controls variances in operating processes, resulting in reduced appraisal costs. In one plant that produces electrical connectors, SPC helped the company to eliminate high costs caused by overplating the wire used in the connectors. In making the connectors to meet the customers' different sets of specifications, the plant failed to have precise control measurements that would meet the standard for each order, and therefore overplated the wire to exceed the minimum requirement for each order.

By designing a control system that eliminates overplating by more accurately measuring the process and adjusting it to meet each customer's specifications, Du Pont reduced the total costs of plating by 200 percent. The connectors are now being made right the first time, which greatly reduces appraisal costs because there is much less need to inspect products to ensure that they meet the buyer's requirements.

Internal Failure

This is typically one of the largest COQ categories and, once defined, should be a key priority in COQ improvement efforts. These costs are associated with evaluating, testing, analyzing, correcting, reworking, repairing, and scrapping defective products, materials, or components before the customer receives any product or service. Internal failure costs typically include:

- Design failures (design does not meet customer specifications)
- Rejected lots
- Scrap, waste, and damage
- Retesting and reinspecting
- Reworking, repairing, and touching-up

- Segregating inventory into "firsts" and "seconds" and lost revenue due to downgrading of product
- Overtime due to quality-related production losses
- Expediting and rescheduling
- Surplus inventory carrying costs

For example, before reducing its internal failure costs, Velcro USA threw away anywhere from 5 to 8 percent of finished product due to defects. The company produces a variety of fastener products, such as tape for binding car seat parts together and strips that bind fabric to the roof of the vehicle. They successfully implemented a new program that stressed improved manufacturing quality management at all steps of the production process. Its reduction of internal failure costs was impressive. During the program's first year, Velcro saw a 50 percent reduction in waste from the year before. In the second year, a further 45 percent reduction was achieved.

External Failure

These are costs associated with customer-detected deficiencies in products, materials, or services. They are particularly important for two reasons. First, they are non-value-adding costs, contributing nothing to perceived customer satisfaction, adding up to a very costly burden for your company. Second, external failure directly affects customers' perceptions of your company's products and services. Failures can ruin your reputation and lead to reduced repeat purchase.

Certainly the Korean car manufacturer Hyundai can attest to that. In 1986, Hyundai became an overnight success story when it invaded the automobile market. By 1988, however, it was widely known that many quality problems had surfaced in Hyundai cars. Canadian and U.S. sales plummeted by a third as buyers spread the word to their friends. Price-conscious car purchasers, the core group comprising Hyundai's target market, started to turn to used-car lots where they felt they could get better value for their dollar. Constantly replacing your customer base because you have driven your buyers away with shoddy goods or services means higher marketing expenditures are necessary to attract new business. Clearly, lowering external failure expenses is critical to cost-effectively managing your business and achieving customer satisfaction.

External failure costs include:

- Returned material and products
- Reworking
- Inventory segregation and carrying costs
- Replacement materials reshipped to customers
- Complaint investigation and response
- Warranty and recall costs
- Field service and retrofitting
- Product liabilities
- Customer order cancellations
- Field service, spare parts, and excess inventory

GETTING A HANDLE ON QUALITY COSTS

The first step to quantifying your COQ is to establish base-line measures and to set up a tracking mechanism for evaluating your COQ improvement efforts. Without a COQ measurement program, you will be unable to systematically gain control of the component variables.

First, establish the COQ categories that you will use. Since these categories are typically not part of your current cost-reporting procedures, they will have to be developed. You will need a company aggregate estimate and specific departmental estimates so that the locus of opportunity can be identified. Then, COQ data must be collected. This information may not be readily available, and estimates will have to be made. Typically, the following company materials can form the basis of estimated COQ information:

- Product cost breakdowns
- Inspection and test reports
- Vendor information
- Field repair reports
- Customer return reports
- Customer survey reports
- Process capability studies

- Engineering change order information
- Quality audit reports

Efforts to identify your COQ should be comprehensive and practical. It is better to reduce the 90 percent of COQ that is readily identifiable than to wait until you have verified the final 10 percent that requires more analysis.

After COQ data have been collected, establish a current baseline position. Usually, total COQ are compared against some productivity indicator in order to determine whether quality is indeed improving as changes in volume or service activities occur. Several bases (used as denominators) are commonly employed. For example, the dollar value of COQ can be expressed as follows:

- Per hour of direct production labor
- Per unit of production
- Per dollar of direct production labor
- Per dollar of standard manufacturing costs
- Per dollar of sales

Once COQ categories are defined and expressed in terms of an index of productivity, COQ analyses can be performed to find the major cost areas. Then, COQ savings can be projected through the carrying out of specific improvement projects.

Develop a reporting mechanism for senior management to track COQ efforts and results. The timely publication of the report is crucial if COQ are to be used as a management tool. At the very least, the report should be distributed on a quarterly basis. A monthly report is usually best for operations and management feedback. For example, 3M's transportation department and its affiliated carriers joined forces to establish the Partners in Quality (PIQ) program as a means to develop service strategies and to organize a manageable carrier base by reducing the number of carriers used. Part of this program is a quality improvement process that defines service performance targets and measures actual service performance. A quality improvement plan is developed annually, and specific items related to the PIQ program are identified in the document. The costs of quality associated with PIQ are monitored and reported on a quarterly basis. As a result, transportation efficiency has improved, and the timeliness of delivery is averaging 95 percent or higher.

USING COQ AS A MANAGEMENT TOOL

The COQ techniques are tools for quality management in a company's pursuit of quality and profit improvement. They give all company members the common goal of working on how the business can practically and cost-effectively create a competitive advantage through superior quality. Several implementation issues need to be addressed:

- Forming a COQ steering committee
- Developing system documentation
- Carrying out appropriate training

A COQ steering committee analyzes study results and establishes plans to commit resources for the indicated improvements. Priority areas for cost reduction must be identified, and project teams from different departments should be set up to resolve problems in these areas. The steering committee should coordinate COQ projects and monitor the overall results of the company's total COQ.

Documenting the procedures of the COQ system is also necessary. This includes recording the purpose of the system and the goal of COQ management, the elements, required steps, and cost sources; the responsibilities, report formats, and distribution.

To ensure that your COQ system functions properly, management and affected employees should be properly trained from the outset. Such training should explain the philosophy and concepts of COQ while emphasizing the use and benefits of COQ as a performance measurement tool. Ultimately, employees should be made aware that the real value of a quality program is determined by its ability to contribute to customer satisfaction and profits.

Immediate education needs of project teams include problem-solving process training, teamwork skills, and meeting management. For example, the COQ program in use at the Westinghouse Electric Corporation teaches employees to analyze each process, or activity, within the organization by evaluating what it refers to as the "cost-time profile." The profile shows the aggregation of costs over a time period. The goal of the program is to reduce overall costs and time by improving the process—or to "shrink" the profile while improving quality performance. The company also uses a similar technique called an organization profile to measure information flow and work patterns in its office operations.

By using COQ management techniques, a company can reduce costs while at the same time improving quality, which ultimately results in better meeting customer needs even as cost-competitiveness is increased.

MORE WEAPONS FOR FIGHTING IN THE QUALITY CRUSADE

A number of well known tools for quality improvement can be applied directly to your value-creation programs. One group of techniques is the "seven tools" of statistical quality control closely associated with Japanese quality control consultant Kaoru Ishikawa. These techniques help employees to identify the factors that are causing quality defects in products or services. By using the seven tools, workers can sort out complex industrial and service delivery processes.

The tools display data for analysis and organize the salient factors so that people can see patterns and relationships that lead to the root causes of problems. Teaching employees how to use the seven tools will help them become more analytical and effective in their value-creation problem-solving projects.

The tools are as follows:

- Check sheets
- Pareto diagrams
- Cause-and-effect diagrams
- Histograms
- Stratification charts
- Scatter diagrams
- Control charts

Check Sheets

In any process, some products are bound to be defective over a period of time. Merely observing the total number of defective items is not useful in itself in determining the source of trouble. Check sheets (detailed data observation charts), however, can be used to divide the faulty output by type of defect and identify the source of trouble more readily; for example, those with cracks, those that are the wrong size, those that are not hard enough, and so on.

A few years ago, the Florida Power & Light Company (FPL) became alarmed at the number of days its nuclear units were off line or unavailable for unexplained reasons. One nuclear unit, in particular, showed a trend toward increased down time over a four-year period. The utility decided to observe the problem unit more systematically to discover the root of the problem. Initial observation indicated that failures of a reactor coolant pump were the primary source of trouble. More detailed analyses, using check sheets, compared the causes of pump failures and found that two separate situations (or types of defects) were responsible for 92 percent of the failures. Using these comparisons, FPL discovered which problem or problems to eliminate to improve the coolant pump's performance. Once this diagnosis was complete, quality improvement teams were organized to find a solution to the trouble areas.

Pareto Diagrams

The results gathered in the check sheets are often displayed as Pareto diagrams, which are simple bar charts used to display defect types in descending order of occurrence. Pareto charts help to distinguish those defects that are important and ought to be studied from those faults that are trivial or random. For example, a large insurance company carried out a survey that quantified service performance levels within the insurance industry by comparing customers' expectations of services offered with actual customers' assessments of how well the company fulfilled those expectations. The tabulated results revealed gaps between expectations and assessments. The "width" of each "gap" represented the extent of a service problem within each service area. A Pareto diagram displayed each measured service delivery problem in descending order of occurrence or importance, from wider gaps (representing greater problems) to narrower gaps (showing less important problems).

Company strengths included physical facilities and equipment, technical expertise, confidentiality, and the personalized care provided by the customer contact personnel. The areas for improvement included soliciting customer feedback, pricing, system response time, communications, training, publications, operating hours, and responsiveness to ad hoc requests. Armed with knowledge of specific strengths and weaknesses, the company was able to address the most important issues first.

Cause-and-Effect Diagrams and Process Analysis

Once the most important defects have been identified, the possible causes (and causes of causes) of the defects must be mapped out by those familiar with the production or office administration process: technicians, engineers, foremen, secretaries, and office managers. The resulting diagram is known as a *fishbone chart*, because the lines of cause and effect converge in a pattern similar to that of the bones of a fish.

A related tool is process analysis. This involves techniques that help problem-solving groups understand the interrelationships between tasks and procedures. Process analysis is useful to employees who are trying to solve customer-value problems because it focuses their attention on understanding the *system* that produces a result rather than on criticizing the people who have to operate within the system.

As discussed in Chapter 3, a process is any set of conditions, causes, or inputs that work to produce a given result or output. The inputs to a process can be categorized into several groups: the *materials* that are to be transformed by the process, the *machines* or technology used to do so, the *methods* used, and the *skill levels* and training of the people involved. A process itself is the systematic series of steps, or tasks, that are used to accomplish the output. Process analysis teaches employees how to map the specific steps of the process in order to understand the relationship of the steps to one another. All processes have a built-in capability for performance. Describing and measuring process capability is an important method for discovering ways to improve the process.

The support services group within AT&T is a good example of a department that used quality improvement problem-solving tools to improve its service delivery, specifically in the area of word processing and reprographic accuracy and efficiency. A problem-solving team was convened. All administrative processes and how they linked to each other were illustrated by a flow chart that simplified the organization of the workflow. Next, cause-and-effect analyses were performed to identify sources of waste and rework. These efforts helped AT&T improve typing accuracy fivefold and reduce its reprographic turnaround time by half.

The fishbone and process-analysis charts can focus discussion on the key steps in the process, but such charts are often only the first step toward further investigation. Four other helpful tools are histograms, stratification charts, scatter diagrams, and control charts.

Histograms

Bar charts show the distribution of data within a population, by summarizing, for example, the variation in the magnitude of the defect (what size of crack is most common, for instance). A histogram can also be applied in a service measurement situation. For example, a supplier of maintenance and repair support services might use a histogram to measure a problem such as frequency and/or length of repair time. A histogram would illustrate the duration of each repair or maintenance occurrence, and also whether one aspect of repair service (such as a service representative not having correct parts or not having the expertise to fix the problem) is most common.

Stratification Charts

Histograms themselves can be further split into stratification charts, by plotting spreads evident in the histograms against other factors such as production lines (to see whether certain components have a tendency to produce more defects than others) or raw material batches (to determine whether material provided by one supplier has a greater propensity to produce defective items). Again, using the supplier of maintenance and repair support services example, a stratification chart could expand upon the histogram. For instance, if the histogram indicated that faulty parts were the cause of frequent and/or lengthy repair times, a stratification chart would indicate whether a specific supplier was responsible for poorly made components.

Scatter Diagrams

If there are important variables in the production process, such as oven temperatures, then defects can be plotted against temperature to see if these (or perhaps even defects of a certain type) tend to cluster at higher or lower temperatures. For example, at the Casting Division of Ford

Motor Company, quality is measured by what the company refers to as first-time capability or FTC, which is the percentage of castings or forgings processed without rejection or rework. Several variables affect the production process, one being the temperature of the molten metal. By adjusting this variable, Ford was able to improve the FTC rate for castings from 98.8 to 99.4 percent, a significant and cost-saving improvement.

Control Charts

The fluctuating factors tested in scatter diagrams can also be examined for their degree of variation over time, to determine whether the control (or lack of control) of oven temperature, for example, is coincidental with greater or fewer defects. The Cummins Engine Company, a designer and manufacturer of diesel engines, lowered its warranty costs following a reevaluation of its warranty processing system. The installation of process controls using control charts streamlined the procedures, including post-warranty service. The control charts used data from warranty reports that indicated performance over time and identified "normal and special causes of variance," such as type of engine failure, type of vehicle using the engine, difficulty of repair, quality of parts used, and so forth. This way, each process in the warranty system is monitored for unusually high failure rates, since causes of poor performance can vary over time.

LEARNING HOW TO DIG OUT AND SOLVE PROBLEMS

Whether you are creating a quality product from scratch, improving an existing one, measuring costs of quality, or even trying to get the glitches out of an operational process, problems are always inevitable. At some point, you may need to partake in some group-consensus problem-solving processes. Albert Einstein once said, "Imagination is more important than knowledge." With that in mind, your team of employees can be the best source of creative solutions. Traditionally, though, North American employee training has focused on the technical competence necessary for individuals to perform their functions. More businesses are now learning, however, that team collaboration—rather than working in isolation—is vital for value-creation success. Techniques that can facilitate this should be taught to employees from the shop floor to the executive suite.

These techniques are:

- Brainstorming
- Force-field analysis
- Effective management presentations

Brainstorming

This is an unrestrained and creative process for generating ideas and suggestions by all members of a group for solutions, especially nontraditional ones, to customer satisfaction problems. To optimize the process and get the greatest number of solutions possible, it is essential that the first rule of brainstorming—no-judgment—be followed. That means employees must refrain from either criticizing the ideas of others or defending their own until after the generation and synthesis steps. Criticism of ideas or defense of one's own ideas is the best way to stifle the most creative solutions. Brainstorming techniques stimulate creativity and provide for consensus on the best ideas for implementation. Employee teams can generate a wide variety of ideas and encourage each team member to build on the ideas of others.

Effective brainstorming consists of the following steps: First, the session leader defines the scope and direction of the issues to be discussed. Group members are then given time to write down their ideas, after which each person is called upon to contribute one idea. The process is repeated until all ideas have been heard. The group leader simply records the ideas on a flip chart or blackboard; evaluation or criticism is not allowed at this stage. Once the ideas have been listed, the discussion is opened up to generate and record new thoughts. The group should be encouraged to produce quantity, not quality. "Wild" ideas often spark insights into practical solutions that would not otherwise be uncovered. After the idea-generation process is complete, the group sets evaluation and priority criteria for assessing which ideas are most useful. Criteria might include, for example, the ideas' potential for success, cost savings, cost of implementation, effective use of resources, ability to be implemented within a specific time frame, and so forth.

Another problem-solving process that can be used is known as nominal group technique (NGT). This method begins the same way as brainstorming does, generating and combining ideas. The surviving ideas are numbered for identification, then each member privately ranks the top five ideas. The rankings are compiled from each person's rating to form a collective score for each idea. (The supervisor's vote is taken last to avoid prejudicing of the group.) The winning idea emerges from the voting.

At the Casting Division of Ford Motor Company mentioned previously, employees use brainstorming sessions to solve problems and facilitate teamwork. In one case, employees worked together to improve the percentage of castings or forgings processed without rejection or rework. The group identified all process variables that might be relevant to the problem, listing 42 factors. The list was then trimmed through a group voting procedure to the most relevant seven items. By using brainstorming and group problem solving, the team is able to gain the benefit of insights from all members and build a consensus on the critical issues that need to be addressed.

Force-Field Analysis

Force-field analysis was developed by the organizational researcher Kurt Lewin. This approach identifies those forces that both help and hinder you from closing the gap between where you are now and where you want to be. This method enables the organizing of perceptions together with impacts so that group discussion can uncover important relationships between drivers and barriers. The steps to carrying out a force-field analysis are as follows:

Draw a line down the center of a flip chart page. This represents the "as-is" situation—what currently exists. At the right edge of the sheet, draw a second vertical line parallel to the first. This represents the situation as it should be—the desired state. After using one or more of the tools for generating and collecting information, identify and list the helping forces to the left of the center line, the hindering forces to the right of the center line. These forces are often shown as arrows with the helping forces pushing toward the "should-be" state and the hindering forces pushing away from it, as shown in Figure 6–1.

It's often helpful to assess the relative strengths of both helping and hindering forces. Some groups use a scale (e.g., 5 = very strong, 4 = strong, 3 = medium, 2 = low, 1 = weak) to evaluate the relative impact of the forces. For graphic representation, proportionately sized arrows show relative strengths.

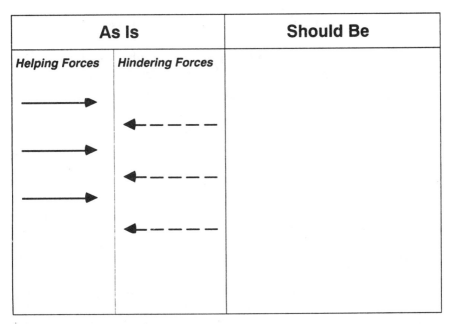

Figure 6–1. Force-Field Analysis

Once the analysis is complete, your group can use this information to generate potential solutions. For example:

- How to increase the number or strength of the helping forces
- How to decrease the number or strength of the hindering forces

Force-field analysis is simple to do and helps employees to feel more in control of their jobs. For example, a group of customer service representatives met to discuss a problem defined as "How can we increase the contribution of the customer service department to improve customer satisfaction?" After considerable discussion, the working group identified the following helping forces:

- Top management was increasing the budget and resources available for service department activities.
- Morale in the department was good.
- There was growing recognition within the company of the importance of good service in keeping customers happy.

However, there were a number of hindering forces:

- Service representatives had no customer-feedback mechanism for tracking their performance and effectiveness.
- The sales department did not think that the service department was very important; sales executives were not cooperative with the service staff.
- Customer service representatives had little training in "self-management" techniques; they did not know how to effectively take the initiative necessary to improve the functioning of their department.

As a result of the insights gained through the force-field analysis, the customer service group decided to take a number of action steps. First, they developed and implemented a customer service survey to collect data on their effectiveness as perceived by customers. Next, the service department initiated a series of meetings with the sales group to identify ways to improve cooperation between the two departments. As well, the supervisor of the customer service department took advantage of top management's interest in service to gain additional funding for increased training for customer service representatives. Thus, force-field analysis helped the customer service department to pragmatically identify problems that needed to be addressed and to capitalize on opportunities for moving the group towards its goal of increasing customer satisfaction.

Effective Management Presentations

One of the most important skills that a group working to improve customer value needs to learn is how to present its ideas for improvement in a way that will secure the support of senior management. This will require skills in preparing written reports and presentation materials, and, most importantly, in making oral presentations. Presentations to management help to improve communication between management and front-line employees, encourage management's active involvement in customer satisfaction problem solving, foster good relationships among the team members, and provide an opportunity whereby team members can be recognized for their efforts.

Effective presentations by customer satisfaction and value improvement teams have the following characteristics:

- The presentations are limited to 20 to 30 minutes.
- All members are called upon by the leader; the leader closes the session by answering questions.
- All members participate in the presentation.
- The data collected are used in the problem-solving analyses, such as histograms, Pareto diagrams, and cause-and-effect diagrams.
- Visual aids are employed to strengthen the effectiveness of the presentation.
- Cost savings, or other benefits to be achieved by the recommended action, are discussed.
- An outline is prepared for the presentation, perhaps with a booklet or paper that provides supporting details.
- All interested parties are invited and are given sufficient advance notice so that they can plan to attend.

In summary, to facilitate the flow of problem-solving ideas, employees should be trained to use these and other tools that will empower them to solve customer-value-improvement problems.

QUALITY FUNCTION DEPLOYMENT: DESIGNING QUALITY INTO YOUR PRODUCTS AND SERVICES

As mentioned earlier, true quality improvement incorporates customer feedback into the very earliest phase of the product and process design. After all, a superior quality reputation starts with a product or service definition that is clearly focused on customer needs and expectations. These expectations must then be transferred pragmatically into the production processes that can most readily deliver the required product or service characteristics.

Such was the case for IBM. The computer hardware giant declared 1987 the "year of the customer." It would be the year when the company, notoriously secretive about its new products, would finally break with tradition and swing open its lab doors to invite users right into the company to participate in the design and planning stages of its new minicomputer, the AS/400. Among the many suggestions customers made was that the new machine should easily run the same programs that ran on AS/400s' predecessors, the System 36 and the System 38. Potential buyers also tested 1,700 more prototype computers, and IBM responded to their ensuing criticisms by making further changes. Then the system was tuned to foreign markets, with the development of over 1,000 software packages that ran in 12 foreign languages including French, Japanese, and Chinese. The result was what in 1989 IBM called "the most successful product launch in its history."

Like IBM, auto giant General Motors was also jolted into the realization that it would have to incorporate customer feedback into product design. This was especially apparent after the flop of the "short Caddy" of 1984, a two-foot-shorter version of GM's traditional top-of-the-line car. It was clear GM had to rethink the way they designed the automobile. Their revised strategy put the customer in the "driver's seat" from the beginning. For three years, the company met with owners of Cadillacs and other models and let them fiddle with everything from the seat belts to the bells and whistles of the control panel as engineers carefully took note. The resulting products, the DeVille and Fleetwood, were rolled out in 1988; and Cadillac sales began growing for the first time in five years.

Quality function deployment, known popularly as QFD, is a "translation" tool that can help your company in the steps between defining customer requirements and incorporating them into the design of products and services. In its broadest applications, QFD can be used to create a common focus on quality and customer satisfaction across all functions in your company. In their book *The Customer Driven Company* William Eureka and Nancy Ryan define QFD as "a system for translating customer requirements into appropriate company requirements at each stage of the product (or service) development cycle, from research and development to engineering, manufacturing, marketing, sales and distribution." Simply, QFD is a system for designing a product or service based on customer demands and involving all members of the producer or supplier organization.

Quality function deployment is sometimes referred to as the "house of quality" because its primary technique is the use of a visual planning matrix that resembles the blueprint for a dwelling, as shown in Figure 6–2. The house-of-quality matrix links customer requirements, design requirements, target values, and competitive performance into one easy-to-read chart. Through completion of the matrix, marketing, engineering, and production executives learn to discuss, as a group, exactly what customers want and how this can be achieved through product design and operational processes. Consequently, quality and customer value can be built-in early on rather than dealt with later in the design, production, or selling phases of a new product or service when problems might occur.

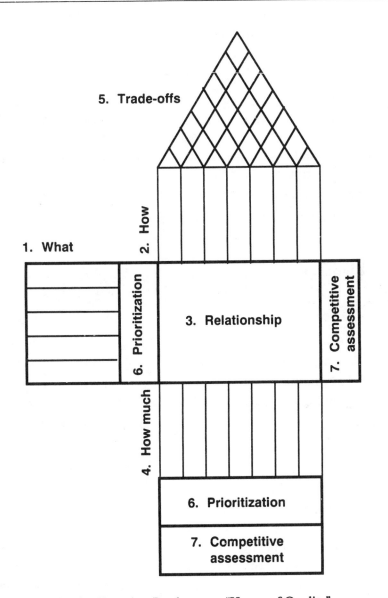

Figure 6–2. Quality Function Deployment "House of Quality"

Writing in the newsletter *Customer Focus*, Richard Huot, a consultant with The Coopers & Lybrand Consulting Group in Toronto, has summarized a typical QFD process using the development of the design for a personal computer as an example. The steps are described in the following paragraphs.

Customer Requirements

The critical focus of a QFD exercise is to start with customer expectations as the foundation for the product design and manufacturing process. This may be defined as the "what" that needs to be accomplished. The various methods for identifying customer requirements could include:

- Market research (personal interviews, telephone interviews, focus groups, mail questionnaires)
- Brainstorming sessions with sales staff
- Consultations with customer service staff
- Analysis of customer complaints

Once buyer expectations have been identified, they must be listed. In the case of personal computers, the features desired by customers might include:

- Ease of use
- Portability
- Quality of graphics
- Affordability
- Speed

Product or Service Requirements

The next step is to translate each of these requirements into one or more practical design elements, moving from customer expectations that are sometimes loosely defined to more precise expressions of these customer requirements. Again, considering personal computers, the design and feature solutions for meeting customers' expectations might include:

- Menu-driven commands
- Open architecture
- Lightweight unit
- Compact size
- High-resolution screen
- Medium price
- Fast microchip

Relationship between Customer Expectations and Design Solutions

Now it's time to link expectation to product design features. Here's where the QFD matrix comes in. By identifying the relationship between the "what" and the "how," it is possible to pinpoint the relative importance of offering a specific feature or design characteristic.

Special symbols are often used to depict weak, medium, and strong relationships between customer requirements and design features. Triangles often represent weak relationships, circles represent medium relationships, and double circles indicate strong relationships. The matrix space is left blank if there is no relationship. Hence, blank rows or blank columns indicate areas where you may have to radically rethink your solutions to customer requirements. Either the problem has not been addressed or the present solution is not relevant to meeting a customer expectation.

In the case of the personal computer, you might discover the following:

- A strong relationship between "ease of use" and "menu-driven commands"
- A strong relationship between "portability" and "lightweight unit" and "compact size"

Making the links described previously helps to pinpoint which design features have the greatest potential for meeting customer requirements.

Product or Service Requirement Measures

The fourth step in the QFD process is to develop clear measures for each proposed design feature. This means assigning specific values to each design solution to ensure measurable targets that will provide an objective means for determining whether or not the design requirements have been met. These targets might be referred to as the "how much" values.

For example, the design features of a personal computer could be defined precisely as follows:

- *Lightweight unit*—less than 20 pounds
- *Compact size*—20" x 16" maximum outside dimensions

- *Medium price*—greater than \$3,000, but less than \$4,000 per unit

Trade-Offs between Product or Service Requirements

The next step in building a "house of quality" is to focus on possible trade-offs in your design due to the conflicting effects of proposed design features. Some solutions may have complementary effects, making the resulting design more attuned to customer requirements. For example, in the case of your personal computer design, a compact size might contribute to your goal of "lightweight." On the other hand, the need to offer a lightweight computer may limit the ability to provide extensive memory.

Product or service trade-off analysis using QFD is done by employing symbols to establish the nature of the correlation between each "how" element. Each correlation is rated either as positive, and therefore favorable; negative, meaning that a trade-off is necessary; or neutral, meaning that there is no effect. Strong positive correlations are identified by a double circle, positive correlations by a circle, negative correlations by a cross, and strong negative correlations by a double cross.

Key Product or Service Requirements

The next step consists of setting priorities for the design requirements. Priorities are set by rating and weighting each of the elements. First, you must rate each "what" element. In other words, based on your customer research, you must assign a relative importance to each customer expectation. Usually, this is done by rating each customer requirement using a five-point scale; the most important requirements are rated a "5," while the least important are rated a "1."

Next, the relationships between customers' requirements and design features, defined earlier, are assigned weights. The weights are given numerical values, where "9" represents a strong relationship, "3" a moderate relationship, and "1" a weak relationship.

The various design requirements can then be given a priority. The relative importance of a specific design element is calculated based on the sum of the respective customer-expectation ratings, multiplied by the relative weight of the requirement's relationship with the design feature. Hence, using this technique, you can conclude that the key design requirements for your new personal computer are, in order of priority:

- Menu-driven commands
- Compact size
- Lightweight unit
- Medium price
- Fast microchip

Competitor Evaluation

The final step in the QFD process is to evaluate your company's ability to meet customer expectations compared to the competition. For each "what" element and "how" feature, you must evaluate your products or services compared to other offerings in the marketplace. This final analysis will highlight areas that demand particular attention in addressing specific customer requirements. You may discover areas that are important to customers, but where your design solutions are weak compared to those of your competitors. Conversely, you may discover design solutions that will give you an important advantage in meeting customer requirements compared to competitors' offerings.

For example, you may learn that the personal computers now being made adequately address customer expectations with regard to portability, quality graphics, and speed; but your design is weak compared to that of competitors on the issues of affordability and menu-driven capabilities. Your future design efforts will, therefore, have to pay particular attention to these latter elements.

QFD techniques can also be used to systematically translate design elements into the necessary operational processes to produce them, and QFD can act as a catalyst to bring all appropriate functional groups together and to build customer-defined quality into your products, services, and management processes.

But all the tools and techniques of quality management are useless without a company culture that supports their application. The next chapter will focus on the real "value creators" in your company—people.

7

The Value Creators: People

What do we live for if not to make life less difficult for others?

Nurses' Alumnae Association, Chatham, Ontario

So much of what we call management consists in making it difficult for people to work.

Peter Drucker

If there is one dominating challenge facing business enterprises in the next decade, it can be summed up in a single word: *people*. As companies struggle to become more customer-focused, they often find that their organizational structure and their employees' attitudes, beliefs, and habits present the greatest barriers to success. Ironically, part of the problem is that while businesses are attempting to treat their external customers with more care and respect, they sometimes fail to put the same value on their *internal* customers: their employees. Enterprises that go out of their way to make life less difficult for their customers may have management systems and practices that make it difficult for people to work.

This scenario cannot last for long, however, since, as one consultant put it: "Employee relations equals customer relations. The two are inseparable." Furthermore, lackluster management of human resources will eventually start to take its financial toll. According to the Research Institute of America, better management of human resources may represent the single greatest source of profit growth well into the 1990s. Robert L. Desatnick, the consultant quoted previously, concurs: Research he has done suggests that

> Eighty percent of the opportunity for productivity and profitability improvement lies in effective management of the work force. A work force committed to excellence—internally and externally—will provide most of that opportunity.

Or, as another book on corporate culture has put it, "Your company's real existence lies not in the factory or at the store front, but in the hearts and minds of its employees."

Executives who are used to dealing with the "science of business" may be loath to come to grips with knotty "people" problems. However, unless a customer-oriented culture is embedded into the organization, all the carefully developed service and quality improvement plans in the world will be useless. It is vital that the human resources department within your company be recruited to join the campaign to create a more customer-responsive organization. And part of this campaign will be the reexamination of old assumptions. Job and role definition, employee training, performance appraisal and incentive systems, management roles, and organizational structure will all have to be reviewed and renewed in order to establish a value-creation culture and more customer-oriented attitudes among employees at all levels.

Cultural change and the reorganization that often comes with it have been key factors in the success of many companies that have revitalized their ability to create value for their customers. The classic example of this kind of renewal is the turnaround of Scandinavian Airlines System (SAS) in the early 1980s. When Jan Carlzon took over the company in 1981, it was in its second consecutive losing year. Carlzon revolutionized the way the company treated its employees, turning the organizational chart upside down and encouraging employees to take risks in order to deliver superior service. He also led by example, making customer service the top priority. He was known for personally confronting pilots of late flights to find out what went wrong; and he contacted the crews of "on-time" flights to find out what went right! The year after Carlzon took over, SAS was profitable, and two years later it won *Air Transport World's* Airline of the Year award.

ASSESSING THE CORPORATE CULTURE

Companies that cannot boast of such single-minded devotion to the interests of its customers should do some self-examination to see how they rate on the following points:

- Market and customer orientation
- Strategic focus
- Intracompany communication
- Conflict resolution approaches
- Attitude toward problem solving and change

Market and Customer Orientation

Market and customer orientation can be gauged by asking the following questions:

- Does your organization care about its customers?
- Does it take its direction from changes in the marketplace, or is it driven by internal concerns, standards and organizational politics?

If customer orientation and sensitivity are strong, employees focus their attention on resolving the systems and procedures problems that get in the way of serving customers better. If the culture is inward-looking, however, employees will be more motivated to adhere to regulations or win political points than to attend carefully to the needs of customers. Inward-looking companies will have to implement programs to change the attitudes of management and employees.

This type of attitude change took place at H. E. Vanatter Limited of Ontario, a supplier of dies and machined and finished parts to automobile manufacturers. In the early 1980s, competition for market share had increased dramatically, and auto manufacturers had raised the restrictions on acceptable machine-part tolerances. Customers were rejecting parts at a rate of over 10 percent; hence, zero defects became the new goal.

In 1984, Vanatter began a proactive, company-wide quality improvement program to increase productivity and improve communications with employees and customers. As part of this initiative, the company started to listen more closely to buyer needs by sending employees to seminars held on the premises of its automobile manufacturer customers. By taking a collaborative approach to dealing with the company's customers, employees started to learn buyers' needs better. Customer satisfaction has improved, and Vanatter is being considered as the sole supplier by several of its major buyers for certain products.

Strategic Focus

Companies with strong customer-value cultures also have a clear strategic focus; that is, there is a high degree of consensus among employees as to what the organization's goals and objectives are. When a company does not have strategic focus, the different parts of the company start to pursue their own separate agendas, and company goals are not met as easily—if at all.

Consultant Ron Zemke proposes a way of making the company's value creation strategy real to employees, especially to those on the front line, who might have reason to say, "The corporate service strategy is really a 'so what—this doesn't affect me.'" Zemke writes

> If you want front-line employees to provide consistently high-quality service—as their customers perceive it—it is critical that employees understand what the service strategy is for their department or unit, what promise their department makes to its customers, internal and external, and how that promise will be kept. . . . At a hotel, for example, does better service mean speedy electronic check-in and check-out, or spending a few extra moments giving departing guests that personal touch? . . . A department or unit-level service strategy, such as "To provide business travellers with consistently speedy and efficient check-in, check-out, and billing," tells front-line employees how to serve their customers in the best way possible.

The First National Bank of Chicago has succeeded in making its customer service strategy real to employees at all levels. In an environment that had become extremely competitive, the bank found a niche for itself by renewing its commitment to customer service. First it asked customers to respond to questions about service, quality, price, competitors, and innovation. Acting on the results of the survey, the company decentralized service delivery to improve responsiveness to customers. And as part of this program, front-line employees were given a say in how matters of quality service should be resolved. Service representative recognition programs were also set up to reinforce the importance of employee involvement in the bank's customer service strategy.

Intracompany Communication

Companies in which employees are committed to customer-satisfaction goals also have good upward and downward communication channels. They view communication as an essential process, since it is the means by which all members of the company are brought together for a common purpose.

Critical to this communication process is the dissemination of information that educates every employee about the company's markets, the needs of these markets, and how the company compares to its competition in meeting customer expectations. Victor Kiam, owner and president of the Remington Shaver Company (of "I liked the company so much I bought it" fame), believes communication is so important that he stops the company's production line to talk with employees about company results. Four times a year, he delivers a status report to his employees on the company's performance. The production line is closed for 15 minutes at a down time cost of $10,000. But, as Kiam observes, "You can't turn out good product if the people who make it don't have a stake in its success."

Conflict Resolution

Customer-driven organizations are also able to resolve conflicts more easily than other kinds of organizations can, because customer needs are paramount in the discussion of problems. Conflicts are further reduced because the roles of each department and employee are clearly spelled out in job descriptions, and the job descriptions themselves are smoothly dovetailed.

The style for conflict resolution in a company is established by senior management. Executives who approach negotiations between functions with an "I-win-you-lose" attitude obviously do not foster an atmosphere in which problems are resolved in a cooperative way, with customer satisfaction as the overriding goal.

Problem Solving and Change

Finally, in high-performance, customer-driven corporate cultures, problems are seen to be opportunities to improve the value delivered to buyers. These cultures reflect a philosophy of *continuous improvement,* which begins with the belief that competitive success will be achieved through many small improvements made every day. For this type of thinking to thrive, top managers must daily communicate the fact that they value the ideas and suggestions of their employees.

WALKING THE TALK

In fact, as we have already pointed out in Chapter 3, it is up to the senior managers of a company to both initiate and sustain processes that encourage employees to put the customer first. They must explain in detail the long-term vision of the company so that employees don't feel cast adrift. They must be consistent and persistent in articulating the value creation vision. And they have to disseminate dissatisfaction with the status quo; this lays the groundwork for the creative tension between the vision of the future and current reality.

Fortune magazine reports that "visionary leadership," rather than management skills, will be the most valued attribute of tomorrow's top executive officers. This trend was discovered in a survey that *Fortune* had asked the Graduate School of Business at Columbia University to conduct. In the survey, nearly 900 senior executives in 20 countries, including Japan, the United States, and countries in Western Europe and Latin America, were asked to identify the characteristics of today's CEO and the traits necessary for success in the year 2000. The results were as follows:

- Nearly 98 percent ranked vision as the top attribute for the CEO of tomorrow, but only 75 percent thought that "visioning" was being done well in their companies.

- Eighty-nine percent of respondents indicated that frequent communication with employees would be critical to future success, but only 59 percent believed that they, or their current CEOs, were communicating effectively with their employees.

- Communication with customers was also identified as a critical skill, with 78 percent of the executives surveyed saying this would be important for the year 2000. Only 41 percent thought that they were doing a good job in this area at the time of the study, however.

In their book *Leaders: The Strategies for Taking Charge,* Warren Bennis and Burt Nannus point out that the tools used by leaders are different from those used by managers. Leaders pay attention to the emotional and spiritual resources of their companies and recognize the importance of values, commitment, and aspirations. Leaders have a vision, and they focus their activities on making the vision a reality. They pull people along; they don't push them.

Managers, on the other hand, are more concerned with the here and now. They focus on the physical resources of their companies, worrying about raw materials, technology, and financial resources. They are concerned about "things" and about administering the activities of today.

This is not to say that leaders have their heads in the clouds. To successfully implement visionary change, leaders have to roll up their sleeves and show personal commitment to the program. And they have to learn how to pull the levers of cultural change. These include developing the value-creation vision, communicating that vision, stimulating innovation, and leading through the example of their own personal behavior. As Wayne Johnson, vice-president of Human Resources at Royal Trust, has put it, implementing the vision is like "putting a 'hard edge' on the dream."

Although the vision—and, more specifically, the vision statement— is created with input from all areas of the company, the company's leaders must consolidate it and put their full weight behind it. Leonard Berry, director of the Center for Retailing Studies at Texas A&M University, defines vision as "having a mental picture of tomorrow's organization, of what it will be, of its essential success factors, of its reason for being."

To effectively communicate this vision to all the nooks and crannies of the company, leaders must also be visible. Rather than exhorting employees to reach service and product quality goals, senior management must be held responsible for carrying out—not delegating—tasks related to the value-creation process. Only in this way will all members of the organization understand and believe in the customer-value-creation vision. *Fortune* writer Walter Kiechiel III has emphasized the importance of communication in carrying out strategy: "Virtually everyone who has studied the problem—executives, consultants and business school professors—agree that you have to share lots of information with employees if you hope to elicit their commitment."

Leaders also understand that change is required to realize their vision. They actively encourage change; they are entrepreneurial and do not believe in "business as usual." Continually trying out new ideas is critical to succeeding as a value-driven organization. Experimentation, pilot tests, and trials need to take place continually, and leaders should foster a spirit of experimentation.

Leaders who hope to motivate their employees to create value for their customers must also generate a spirit of excitement, pride, and *esprit de corps*. Companies with a strong, positive corporate culture have an almost tangible spirit of excitement. In these enterprises, employees know how to work together as a team toward the common aim of serving customers, and their pride comes from setting and meeting challenging goals. This kind of pride begins at the top of the organization.

Senior managers who want to bring about change within their company must finally "walk their talk." They must do, and be seen doing, the kind of activities that are expected in a customer-value-driven organization. As the American Society for Quality Control explains, "A quality system cannot succeed without the active, visible and continuous support of management." Only by demonstrating their commitment to value creation and customer satisfaction through their personal words and deeds can senior leaders expect employees to follow.

Thus, top management must "model" their commitment to value creation by having more visible contact with customers. When senior-level executives increase their customer contact frequency, it sends powerful signals to the rest of the organization. If top officers are seen to value and respect customers, lower-level employees will tend to copy this behavior. That is why McDonald's restaurant executives are required to spend one day per year working on site, serving the customers over the counter, preparing food, and cleaning up.

This kind of high-level involvement in front-line jobs is not a new invention. William Van Horne, the legendary nineteenth-century general manager of the Canadian Pacific Railway, could have given modern-day managers a lesson in leadership by example. Although his style may not be to everyone's taste, he had no fear of pitching in and showing how the job should be done. According to one account,

> Van Horne was [always] pushing, prodding and inspiring his crews to ever more herculean efforts. No place on the line was safe from his inspection. He frequently waded unbridged rivers, walked for miles

overland and once went two days without meals to personally look at a trouble spot. If an engineer refused to drive across a shaky trestle, Van Horne shouldered him aside and drove the engine across himself.... The men admired Van Horne's stamina, daring and eating capability, but what they liked best about him was the fact that he never put on airs. Once, when he'd fallen into a river and couldn't find any dry clothes to fit, he spent the rest of the day, to everyone's vast amusement, in a red flannel shirt and a pair of pants that were split down the back and held together by clothesline.

More than a hundred years later and thousands of miles to the east, the executives of the Odakyu Department Store in Tokyo showed a similar attention to detail and willingness to help out on the front lines—though their *modus operandi* was perhaps not as dramatic. An American couple purchased a compact disk player at the department store while visiting Japan. Upon returning to their hotel, they discovered that the machine was missing its inner components. But before the couple could phone the store to complain, an employee of the store appeared at their door, along with the store's vice-president. They had discovered the error, got in touch with the couple's family in the United States by using information from their credit card, and found out where the couple was staying in Japan. The vice-president apologized for the store's error and presented the flabbergasted buyers with a new compact disk player, a set of towels, a box of cake, and a compact disk!

At the highly successful University National Bank & Trust Company of Palo Alto, California, the same kind of attitude prevails. There are no waiting lines at UNB&T, since the branch manager, and sometimes even Chairman Carl Schmitt, will open another window if there is more than one customer waiting in line.

At Dallas-based Southwest Airlines, a similar approach is taken. For 16 consecutive years, the airline has turned a profit; and CEO Herb Kelleher and his management philosophy are two of the major reasons behind this success. Kelleher regularly serves meals on his flights, joking and talking with passengers. He is often available for employees, and his attitude about working in a service industry is communicated effectively to his employees by the visible difference he makes in the company's day-to-day operations. Passengers and employees feel important because Kelleher shows, in a visible way, that he feels it is important to be with them.

To succeed in turning employees into consistent value creators, there has to be visible commitment from the executive suite. Senior officers must have a vision, communicate the vision, and constantly reinforce their goals through daily words and deeds. Value creation leadership cannot be delegated—it is a fundamental responsibility of the chief executive officer and the management team.

KNOCKING DOWN THE SILOS

As companies examine themselves to find points at which employees fail to deliver value to their customers, they may discover that the employees themselves are not the problem so much as is the system in which they are required to work. While traditional hierarchical structures are still valid forms of organization, they sometimes degenerate into a complex of "vertical silos," or separate departments, in which information flows up and down but *not out* to other functional areas. One author calls this phenomenon "segmentalism." The segmentalist manager defines problems narrowly, ignores the overall organizational context, and tries to implement solutions independently of other affected departments— all of which may add up to massive roadblocks in the value delivery process.

Chaparral Steel of Midlothian, Texas, one of the early developers of mini-mill technology, has succeeded in eliminating the silos in its organization. If a customer has a problem with a product, Chaparral sends a superintendent and a salesperson or, perhaps, a production employee, to determine the cause of the problem. Exchanging information and ideas with customers and among all employee levels is encouraged. According to the company's founder, Gordon Forward, "everyone can help and share product quality and customer satisfaction. . . ." This statement is proven in the fact that everyone in the company is considered to be a member of the sales department; and, therefore, every person is given authority to handle and respond to customer problems. There are no functional barriers; engineers are even found on the mill floor, helping front-line workers solve problems and improve quality for customers.

To reduce or eliminate the segmentalism that is characteristic of so many North American firms, managers may find it useful to go back to the concept of the "internal customer" mentioned in Chapter 2. It was Kaoru Ishikawa who first introduced this idea in Japan in 1950. While working to reduce defects in a steel mill, he discovered what he called "sectionalism"—which was a lot like segmentalism and "silo-ism." He asked one department to talk to another about the problems it was having because it was receiving poor raw materials from the group just before it in the production line. The workers refused because they did not want to talk to their "enemies."

Many companies suffer from poor relations between internal departments. It is common for employees in different departments to be jealous of one another and to guard their particular area of expertise. Associated with this is the tendency to grab the interesting company projects and go solo, while dull, repetitive assignments get shoved to another, unsuspecting department. Conflicts and inefficiencies such as these can, and often do, affect the satisfaction of external customers.

If employees consider the next group on the production or service-delivery "line" to be their customers, however, they will make it their business to know those customers and to meet their needs. To facilitate this process, managers need to develop mechanisms and foster approaches that get groups talking to one another about their activities and requirements. This creates a common feeling of understanding, responsibility, and accountability—a sense of belonging to an *organizational community.* When this kind of teamwork is taking place on the inside—from sales, production, engineering, and marketing to the order desk and shipping—external customers will be happier too.

Broadly speaking, business functions can be divided into line and staff groups. The line departments perform activities directly related to adding value to the end product or service. These include, typically, design, purchasing, operations, marketing, and shipping. Staff departments deal with personnel, legal matters, and finance, for instance. Although this idea is unconventional, Ishikawa believes that staff groups should be defined to include the president and other members of top management, as well.

Much of the friction that sometimes arises between staff and line functions stems from the fact that staff departments operate on the erroneous assumption that they do, or should, operate the entire company and that the role of the line functions is to carry out their orders.

Ishikawa recommends that staff groups, such as top management, personnel, accounting, and engineering, should devote 70 percent of their time to their "true customers," the line departments and workers. In other words, the staff group has services to perform for the line functions, in order to ensure that the entire company effectively serves its external customers.

According to this view, the role of the accounting department, for instance, is to provide data to the line departments to enhance their work methods, their profit generation, and their cost control. The role of top management is to develop plans and programs that will guide the company effectively in the future. Staff and top management, in other words, are there to give the line functions good service so that the line functions, in turn, can give good service to the customers.

OPENING UP

Although front-line employees are the ultimate deliverers of quality products or services, they are, of course, not the only ones who should have extensive contact with external customers. In fact, all employees should be given the opportunity to see the company's products in action. Jobs should be redefined in order to broaden the base of employees who come in direct contact with customers. And all these customer contacts should be dedicated to buyer retention, service, and relationship building.

This principle applies to all levels of managers as well, including senior management. For senior management to be motivated to stay close to customers, however, organizational changes may be required. The size of corporate, or divisional, headquarters groups may have to be reduced drastically so that managers can be put in direct-customer-contact, or field, positions. Once this kind of organization is in place, managers will naturally be more motivated to achieve success in the marketplace than to fight their way up the corporate hierarchy.

In 1988, IBM CEO John Akers concluded that his monolithic organization should be reorganized along such lines. The core company was reorganized into seven autonomous operating units, while an eighth unit was set up to handle marketing for all the others. Twenty thousand staff and laboratory positions were moved to the sales force so that customer contact would be increased. The general managers of each unit have been given complete responsibility for the bottom line of that unit. Customer service and customer contact are also of paramount importance in this structure, which places managers in the field with their customers.

BLASTING THE BUREAUCRACY

Lord Beaverbrook, the Fleet Street publisher, had a sign on his desk in the 1930s that read: "Organization is the enemy of improvisation." T. D.

Rodgers, the founder of the Silicon Valley semiconductor manufacturer Cypress, would agree. In order to avoid having new ideas stagnate on their way through the corporate bureaucracy, he sets up a new company whenever a new product line appears. Like the "in-the-field" managers in IBM's new structure, Cypress's company presidents have a lot of autonomy. They can "change product design, build factories, issue stock, raise money, up wages, and hire and fire." All of which no doubt results in accelerated responses to the changing demands of the market, and higher levels of value creation and customer satisfaction.

If (unnecessary) organization is the enemy of improvisation, it is the enemy of value creation and delivery, too, because to serve customers best, employees must be given the chance to improvise. When creative solutions to problems are discouraged or choked off by cumbersome rules and policies or complex bureaucratic structures, customers most often go away fuming. Here's a case in point: When consultant Warren Evans went out for a simple lunch to a new local restaurant, he got caught in a web of bureaucracy that took away his appetite:

> For whatever reason, the hot dog plate from the children's menu appealed to me. I asked the waitress if I could have one, even though I'm obviously over 12 years old.
>
> The answer was a surprise. She said: "I don't see why not. I mean, how would the kitchen know?" This made sense to me. If they can cook and serve a hot dog to a 12-year-old at a profit, logic suggests that they can cook and serve the same hot dog, at the same profit, to a 16-year-old or a 60-year-old. Right?
>
> Wrong. Two minutes later, this poor lady came back to explain, with obvious embarrassment, that the boss said I couldn't have a hot dog, unless I had a letter from my doctor stating that I needed the hot dog for dietary health reasons.
>
> She did volunteer that the boss couldn't explain why, and it didn't make any sense to her either—it's just "the rules."
>
> Silly rules, petty regulations and unnecessary paperwork are like crabgrass: no one has to consciously plant them. And once in place, they will spread and flourish without any attention or nourishment.

Some organizations, it would appear, are set up in a way that only encourages bureaucratic crabgrass to grow.

Writing in the newsletter *Customer Focus* published by Coopers & Lybrand, Gregory Lloyd reports he has come to the conclusion that bureaucracy runs rampant throughout most organizations in North America, even though his clients say it is "the single largest barrier for companies seeking to become truly customer-focused." These companies are plagued by the following structures and strictures:

- Hierarchical relationships
- A high degree of specialization
- An acute use of rules to control all levels
- Impersonality and reduced interaction across lines of authority
- Strict codes of discipline
- Firmly entrenched career patterns

This kind of environment also breeds territorialism, unproductive political behavior, and risk aversion; and it frustrates and alienates suppliers, employees, and customers. This is why:

- *For suppliers:* Channels of communication become complex and time-consuming. Often, the real needs of the buyer are not clearly communicated due to mixed messages and missed signals.

- *For employees:* Typically, there are complaints such as "It takes so much effort and so much time to get anything done. I get in trouble when I don't go by the book. Often, going by the book doesn't get the tasks accomplished. It's a no-win situation, so I'll just go with the flow, and stay out of trouble." Rigid bureaucratic structures and systems frustrate and immobilize employees at each tier within an organization.

- *For customers:* They feel as though no one cares, and that they are powerless to effect change when things go wrong. Often, bureaucracy complicates and confuses information dissemination so that problems are heard but not responded to and customers are made to feel like temporary intruders.

The alienation problems posed by bureaucracies can be solved to some degree by giving front-line employees more authority and flexibility in interpreting rules, and by actively encouraging them to recognize and eliminate bureaucratic actions. However, these measures need to be supplemented by organizational changes that eliminate bureaucratic flab. Successful customer-focused organizations are typically more decentralized and have more connections with their customers, whether these connections are created by people or technology.

The difference between a bureaucratic organization and a customer-responsive one is like the difference between an elephant and a shrew. The elephant, which is relatively secure in its environment, has a small surface-area-to-bulk ratio, which makes it slow, cumbersome, and relatively impervious to external stimuli. The shrew has a large surface-area-to-bulk ratio, which makes it extremely sensitive and agile in responding to changes in its environment. The comparison is maybe not perfect, however, because the elephant has strength and weight going in its favor, whereas even the largest corporation cannot depend on this. All companies have to become more like the shrew—finely tuned to the environment.

STRIPPING AWAY THE LAYERS AND REVERSING THE PYRAMID

The bureaucratic stranglehold on a company's value-delivery system may be eliminated by (a) avoiding excessive layers of management, and (b) turning the management pyramid upside down.

Tom Peters believes that the number of layers in any organization should be limited to a maximum of five. He goes so far as to state that, for most single-business units, there is no need for more than three levels of management. This kind of organizational "flattening" is one step in the right direction, but it may also be necessary to turn the hierarchical pyramid upside down to ensure that the company is responsive to its customers' needs.

According to the old hierarchical model, the customers would appear at the bottom of the pyramid supporting the front-line personnel. The front-liners supported middle management, and the middle managers supported the senior executives. The "inverted pyramid" approach has senior management at the bottom supporting middle management, who, in turn support front-line personnel and the customers. Where Peters' proposal is a visible organizational change, the "inverted pyramid" represents a change in attitude, whereby managers and supervisors act more as coaches or counselors than commanders.

This is the approach taken at Maritime Travel (Group) Ltd. of Halifax, Nova Scotia, which was featured in a 1990 issue of *Canadian Business* as one of 50 Canadian firms with an unceasing commitment to their customers and employees. Co-owner and president Jim Smith says that "[h]ead office is seen as a support group for branch staff, who know the marketplace best."

Organizational changes such as these obviously have earth-shaking implications for middle managers and the way they carry out their jobs. For one thing, this kind of restructuring will greatly increase the span of control of the managers who remain after the organizational pyramid is flattened. At the same time, employees will become empowered to make decisions on their own. As Reginald H. Jones of General Electric has said,

> The old hierarchical pyramid based on command is vanishing. Now it's the team approach, you rely on tremendous cooperation. . . . Adjustment to this change is going to be the most difficult task in U.S. business history.

Part of the adjustment will consist of acquiring new management skills. While middle managers in the past were rule interpreters and protectors of the boundaries between departments, they will now have to be integrators and facilitators. As Robert Noyce, inventor of the silicon chip and founder of Fairchild Semiconductor and Intel has put it:

> I have adopted the view that the job of the manager is an enabling, not a directive, job . . . coaching and not direction is the first quality of leadership now. Get the barriers out of the way to let people do the things they do well.

Mike Walsh, CEO of Union Pacific Railroad, who is using technology to merge 10 dispatching centers into one in Omaha is facing all the challenges of the "flat organization." He says:

> I don't think the CEO of the 1990s [let alone the middle manager!] will get away with being a hot-house plant. A CEO will have to know how to work the valves and switches in the middle of the night.

A recent *Fortune* article on business trends in the 1990s pointed out that negotiating will become a much more important managerial skill in the years ahead, simply because managers will not have as much authority over their employees as in the past.

And what are the implications for employees? Their higher level of autonomy means that they will have to learn to make more judgments, use more initiative, and take risks.

Federal Express already gives its employees the latitude to operate independently. They are to act as "the company" when they are making deliveries, speaking on the phone, and particularly when they are faced with a customer service problem. One junior telecommunications expert in the company took this policy to its extreme—to good effect. He was left with no telephone service for several days after a blizzard in the California Sierras. He took it upon himself to rent a helicopter, fly to a mountaintop, walk three-quarters of a mile in deep snow, and fix the phone line so that Fed Ex service could resume.

At Nordstrom Inc. a similar attitude prevails. Its one-sentence policy manual says, "Use your own judgment at all times." The manual frees Nordstrom employees from a mountain of bureaucratic processes and allows them to get on with serving customers.

At 3M, manufacturing workers and marketing employees are given opportunities to improve quality, reduce costs, and offer ideas for product development. Management recognizes that the best ideas are often from those closest to the manufacturing process or the customer.

To stimulate an environment that encourages new ideas from everyone, 3M has long had a corporate expectation that 25 percent of its annual sales will come from products that were not on the market five years ago. This aspect of the corporate culture reinforces the need to be discontented with the status quo. Most important, however, a senior vice-president reports: "People must not be punished for trying out new ideas which subsequently fail. If you do that, you quickly extinguish your best source of new ideas—employees who are working closely with customers where they spot new opportunities."

TEAMWORK

As old organizational hierarchies break down and the authority of middle managers devolves onto the front lines, the empowerment of individual employees will fill only part of the vacuum. The other part will be filled by self-managed employee teams. Unlike the "quality circles" of the 1970s and 1980s, the self-managed employee team "arranges schedules, sets profit targets, . . . has a say in hiring and firing team members as well as managers . . . orders material and equipment . . . strokes customers, improves quality, and, in some cases, devises strategy." Some teams, as a 1990 *Fortune* article pointed out, are permanent, while others operate for a few months to tackle a specific problem or develop a new product.

The same *Fortune* writer did interviews with a number of teams in American companies and came up with the following observations:

- The more complex a problem or proposal is, the more suited it is to a teamwork approach.

- Teams sometimes have a higher commitment and set higher standards than managers would.

- If teams are given real authority, their work will result in productivity gains. (Unlike quality circles, which would most often be given the mandate to point out a problem but not work on its solution, self-managed teams that have enough authority can push through to a solution.)

- If teams are to be effective, they must be supported by both middle and top management. Middle managers—who sometimes feel threatened by the very existence of a team—must be "persuaded to lend their time, people, and resources to other functions for the good of the entire corporation," and senior management must show a real interest in the goings-on. James Watson, a vice-president of the semiconductor group at Texas Instruments, says, "The worst thing you can do to a team is to leave it alone in the dark. I guarantee that if you come across someone who says teams didn't work at his company, it's because management didn't take interest in them."

- Although teamwork is often considered to be rewarding in itself, some management experts feel that this approach can be abused and that team members who come up with money-saving ideas should be given generous financial rewards.

- In a time when advancement opportunities are becoming more limited, teamwork provides a different kind of reward. In the words of Harvard Business School professor Anne Donnellon, "People are adjusting to career-ladder shortening. If a team is operating well, I hear less talk about no opportunity for promotion and more about the product and the competition. They're focusing on getting the work done. After all, people want rewarding work."

Teams are sometimes formed to respond to major crises. In 1986, when American Airlines realized that it had to reduce costs yet maintain service to remain competitive, it asked its employees to organize themselves into seven-person teams for a three-month "InnovAAtions" campaign. Nearly 3,500 teams were formed; the company offered team members merchandise prizes based on the cash value of suggestions that were implemented.

The results were significant. More than 1,600 ideas were adopted, members of 535 employee teams received merchandise worth $4.7

million, and American realized more than $20 million in cost-saving and revenue-generating improvements. And the effort led to the establishment of a continuing employee involvement and feedback system.

At General Motors, teams were set up in an effort to move auto workers away from the role of "assembly-line jocks" to that of brainstorming partners with management. Workers who were once expected to shut up and follow orders are now encouraged to use their heads. A team of hourly and salaried employees figured out how to reduce from 52 to 30 the number of parts in the rear floors of Cadillacs and Oldsmobiles. This change reduced the number of stamping dies from 93 to 38 and the number of presses from 93 to 10, while trimming the weight from 117 pounds to 105. The result of this collaborative problem solving? An impressive saving of $52 million.

Membership on a team is not always restricted to employees. Customers are sometimes included as well. Now that textile manufacturer Milliken has found itself faced with increasing foreign competition, it has responded by creating more than a thousand "customer action teams," in partnership with existing customers, to identify new business opportunities. To launch a team, customers have to agree to supply team members and join with Milliken representatives from manufacturing, sales, finance, and marketing in seeking new markets and new ways to serve current markets.

In one case, the company launched a two-year Partners for Profit program with jeans maker Levi Strauss to focus on ways to improve the way they did business with each other. Milliken and Levi Strauss have worked out methods whereby first inspections of Milliken material can be skipped. Through the use of state-of-the-art data and telecommunications link-ups and Milliken's uncompromising quality control processes, goods are shipped directly to specific receiving docks at the Levi Strauss plants where they are needed. The material is taken off Milliken trucks and taken directly to the machine location where the garments will be cut and sewn. This new process has resulted in huge cost savings for Levi Strauss and a reduction in delivery time.

Teaching Team-Building and Problem-Solving Skills

As effective as the team approach can be, it is still an unknown quantity in many organizations; and efforts to introduce this way of working will not be successful unless employees and managers are trained in team skills. Even if self-managed teams are never set up in a company, teamwork is gaining importance as a way of doing business, since customer satisfaction and value creation issues cut across organizational boundaries and levels.

This type of training is necessary because employees are still not used to participative decision making. As Leonard Greenhalgh, professor of management at Dartmouth's Tuck School, has said, "Typically, a team lacks skills to build a strong consensus. One coalition tries to outvote the other or browbeat the dissenters." Needless to say, this can't really be called teamwork, in the true sense of the word. That is why it is important for employees to learn team problem-solving skills.

In their book *Solving Quality and Productivity Problems*, Goodmeasure, Inc., a consulting firm based in Washington, D.C., has identified the following steps in the "corrective action process":

Step 1. Problem identification. The first step in problem solving is to identify the critical customer-satisfaction issues that require attention. This can be achieved through measuring and collecting data, asking for feedback from customers and other employees, or actively looking for signals that suggest that customers are not being well served.

For example, Wal-Mart, the retailing giant and business growth phenomenon of the 1980s, has achieved its success in large part because of the company's ability to access the ideas of its employees about changing customer needs. CEO David Gloss believes that employee participation is the key to success. "We have no superstars at Wal-Mart," he says. "We have average people operating in an environment that encourages everyone to perform way above average."

Gloss and his fellow executives keep in close touch with the company's far-flung network of stores using everything from a channel satellite system to an 11-plane corporate air force. Gloss himself spends several days a week visiting stores. He says, "Our grass roots philosophy is that the best ideas come from people on the firing line."

Step 2. Problem classification. Next, problems need to be classified and prioritized. Usually, a few problems will be at the root of much of a company's inability to deliver value to customers. The team should therefore focus on the vital few problems whose solution will bring the greatest results.

Step 3. Assignment of responsibility. The third step in the problem-solving process is to assign accountability for fixing the problem or for obtaining more information about its extent and potential solutions. Often the team assigns this responsibility to itself.

Step 4. Application of problem-solving techniques. This step applies problem-solving techniques to better understand the nature and causes of the problem. This process will, of course, begin to suggest possible solutions. Some analytical processes and techniques most useful for customer-satisfaction problem solving were discussed in Chapter 6. Checklists, charts and graphs, Pareto analysis, process analysis, and cause-and-effect diagramming are powerful ways to unravel customer value creation issues.

For example, as part of its company-wide value creation effort, one of Canada's largest flour-milling companies convened its top 25 managers for a series of intensive problem-solving workshops. Those who attended were divided into three groups representing each key regional business unit. With the help of outside facilitators, the groups discussed the results of recently completed customer and employee surveys. The customer survey indicated that the company got high ratings from buyers for product quality and delivery performance—two critical success variables. However, the employee survey brought up concerns about communications blockages between senior management and front-line employees, and between business functions.

Based on this information, each workshop group used process-analysis flow charting to discover opportunities to improve value creation and solve problems. By using problem-solving tools, the groups quickly discovered that the majority of issues centered around cumbersome internal policies and procedures that contributed to the communication problems noted in the surveys. As a result, the problem-solving teams directed their improvement efforts at revamping the systems and procedures that had been identified as hindrances to the smooth flow of information within the company.

Step 5. Implementation. The final step is implementation. At this stage, the team's ideas, analyses, and solutions are turned into action. The team needs to establish implementation steps, assign accountabilities, and get results.

Problem-Solving Principles for Team Members

To function properly, team members must have a good understanding of the basic principles of effective group collaboration, and they need to understand their basic roles and responsibilities as members. These include the responsibilities of the team as a whole, of team members, of team leaders, and of managers.

The overall purpose of a problem-solving team should be to accomplish the following tasks:

- Develop a clear statement of the problem.
- Provide an estimate of the cost and impact of the problem.
- Undertake investigation of causes and solutions.
- Recommend the best solutions.
- Provide an estimate of the cost and activities required to implement the solutions.
- Present a written or oral report to more senior management, if the solutions lie outside the boundaries or resources available to the team members.

Individual members have a specific role to fulfill in order for the group to be effective. Individuals should:

- Accept responsibility for the success of the group
- Participate actively
- Carry out assigned responsibilities
- Attend team meetings
- Be involved and active participants

The team leader's role is different from that of the other participants and is most important to the smooth functioning of the group. The team leader:

- Sets the schedule for meetings
- Keeps the meetings on time
- Keeps the discussion on topic
- Encourages participation
- Ensures that the team makes clear decisions

The more senior managers in the company must also understand their role, to ensure that problem-solving teams work effectively. Their job is to:

- Give problem-solving teams a mandate
- Allow team members to cross organizational boundaries

- Allocate the necessary time and resources
- Keep up to date with team activities, plans and progress
- Provide rewards and recognition to teams and team members

Managing Teams

Once problem-solving teams have been set up, managers have several additional responsibilities. They must monitor progress, respond to the recommendations, coordinate the activities between teams, and communicate the results of team progress.

Monitoring the team's problem-solving progress will show its members that management is taking an interest in its activities. Monitoring will also help maintain the momentum of the project by encouraging the team to be accountable for its activities. This can be accomplished through several mechanisms, such as written reports, special meetings to review progress, informal discussions on a regular basis, and brief reports made at regularly scheduled department-wide meetings.

If, after arriving at its conclusion, a problem-solving team determines that the indicated action is outside its area of authority, it should forward its recommendations to its immediate supervisors. The supervisors and executives in the organization must then decide how to respond to the suggestions arising from the team's work.

If a clear response from the executive group is not given within a fairly short period of time, the momentum and enthusiasm of the team will quickly decline. For this reason, it is often advisable for the problem-solving team to take on the responsibility of overseeing the implementation of its recommendations, assign the implementation to other relevant groups, or implement the recommended actions itself.

Where several problem-solving teams are working at the same time, or team members come from various departments and functions, managers will have to give some thought to the best means of coordinating their activities. They will have to work to smooth the conflicting demands placed on team members, balance schedules, and sequence problem-solving efforts so that the organization does not become overloaded.

Finally, it is important that management develop mechanisms to communicate the findings and results of team progress to the rest of the organization. This will help allay fears among those not involved in the team activities by keeping them abreast of proposed changes and avoiding surprises.

BUILDING THE CUSTOMER-ORIENTED WORK FORCE

"In the end," says Chrysler's Lee Iacocca, "all business operations can be reduced to three words: people, product, and profits. People come first. Unless you've got a good team, you can't do much with the other two."

To build a good team, companies must begin at the beginning. Clear corporate beliefs and principles, which emphasize value creation, must be established right from the first interview; and recruitment must be directed to hiring people who share these attitudes. All the time, effort, and money that goes into hiring people who are truly dedicated to delivering value to customers make up an investment that will pay off in spades down the road.

Although employees respond to the work environment and to leadership from their supervisors, it helps to tilt the odds in favor of value-creation excellence when employees are properly selected in the first place. Companies that succeed in creating superior value for customers are nearly fanatical in their desire to recruit good "human raw material" into their organizations. They spend inordinate amounts of time and energy getting it right the first time in their hiring decisions. They involve their most senior-level people in the recruiting process because they know that these decisions can have the most far-reaching effects on company performance of any they will have to make.

Employee Selection

The ability to work in teams is perhaps the most critical characteristic to look for in selecting new employees. Since value-improvement efforts require cross-functional solutions, individuals who cannot join others in problem solving will act as barriers to improvement. At a General Electric plant in Bromont, Quebec, all hiring is done by committees of workers who will work with the applicant. All workers in the team are obviously interested in who is hired, and whether he or she will make a good team member.

A customer-oriented attitude is another important attribute to look for in selecting new recruits. Some people just cannot accept "being in service." They find the role demeaning. Companies that are intent on delivering value to their customers, however, need employees who can accept a role that gives customers the chief priority within the organization.

A regional vice-president for Nordstrom, the department store famous for its dedication to customer service, says that its main criterion in hiring sales staff is not previous retail experience, but whether prospective employees exhibit "friendliness." Retailer Luciano Benetton operates from a similar philosophy. He has been quoted as saying that he looks for the "right spirit" in selecting managers for his outlets. You can teach people technical skills, but teaching them to be nice is more difficult, if not impossible.

In *Managing to Keep the Customer*, consultant Robert L. Desatnick suggests a way of systematizing the selection process to "pinpoint the behaviors necessary for a person to succeed in the company." The "patterned interview," as he calls it, is based on "eight to ten specific behavioral characteristics for the particular position. Once the job-related behaviors are identified, three to five questions are developed for each, to determine whether the candidate possesses these characteristics and to what degree." Because the patterned interview ties in with the *behavior* as well as the skills of the prospective employee, and because it allows the interviewer to ask the same kinds of questions of each candidate, Desatnick judges that it has the following advantages:

1. Reduces the risk of poor selection decisions.
2. "Selects in" those who will share your values.
3. Saves training time and money.
4. Minimizes the risk of failure and performance problems.
5. Is judged to be legally defensible.
6. Saves the manager's time.

This is only one interview method among many; but, whatever method is used, it should allow the interviewer to discern the prospect's attitudes towards value creation, customer satisfaction, and the "serving" role.

Job Definition

If employees are expected to treat customers in a sensitive way, management must be clear about this expectation, both during the interview and after a person is hired. That is why it is important to develop a formal definition of job activities so that performance standards can be more effectively communicated to employees. At McDonald's, for instance, every employee has a written job description that includes standards for quality, customer service, and cleanliness. The descriptions are so exact (they're written in a step-by-step format) that it would be impossible for anyone who read them to miss the point.

Training

Companies that have succeeded by delivering value to their customers have not been shy about investing in training their employees—right after hiring, and on an ongoing basis. A survey undertaken by financial services monolith Citicorp found that the 17 companies it had chosen to assess (which were all judged to be customer service leaders) made major investments in ongoing training programs—often 1 or 2 percent of gross sales. Some experts predict that training expenditures of 3 to 5 percent of annual sales will be necessary to create and maintain superior work forces able to cope with a rapidly changing marketplace.

One wag made the point another way: "If you think education is expensive, try ignorance." Desatnick concurs:

> To emphasize the importance of training, let me tell you about . . . a large publishing and printing operation that built a very sophisticated and very expensive—$100 million plus—automated factory. Two years later the plant was running at less than 70 percent efficiency.

> On close inspection it was discovered that only $50 thousand had been allotted to training. Middle managers, supervisors, and employees were unable to cope with the multitude of changes in working relationships brought on by the new technology. The end result was that many customers did not get their magazines and newspapers on time. The training budget was increased to $250 thousand, and within six months 90 percent capacity had been achieved.

Training is especially important in the first few weeks of the job, since attitudes can be shaped most effectively then. The impression that new employees form during their early days on the job can have a critical influence on their attitudes later. Orientation activities should focus on giving new employees an overview of the purpose of the company and the ways in which the various parts function, and they should emphasize the customer-oriented attitudes that are important to the company.

Initial training should also be keyed to giving employees exactly the skills they need in order to be successful on their first assignments. This will ensure that they get off to a good start and contribute immediately to the organization. Emphasis should be placed on those skills that enable employees to deal effectively with customers if they are in customer contact positions, or to work smoothly with other departments if they have "behind-the-scenes" roles.

S&O Copiers Inc., a small Toronto company with a big commitment to customer satisfaction, uses front-line personnel training as a key tool for providing superior service. "We are building for the future here," says S&O President Sheni Fazal. "It is important to set up the right foundation to ensure that we are there for the customer now and into the future." Every new staff member hired at S&O must participate in a six-week training program of seminars and videos, to familiarize them with the company's corporate philosophy and moral and ethical code, and to provide them with the tools necessary for absolute customer satisfaction. The investment is apparently paying off. S&O offers telecommunications products for large and small businesses, and it is a major dealer for Mita, Northern Telecom, and Fujitsu. They guarantee up to 98 percent "up-time" for all their customers' equipment—an almost unheard-of commitment. From a staff of 12 in 1984, S&O has grown to 43 people and now has between 3,500 and 4,000 contented customers.

Walt Disney is a better-known example of an organization with a commitment to up-front training. New Disney employees are given a two-day "Traditions" orientation program, in which they learn the culture, values, and expectations of visitors to the theme park. They learn Disney lore, the Walt Disney vision, and even the names of all the "seven dwarfs." They also learn, indirectly, about good treatment and care, as they are given special attention and a comfortable space in which to learn. Instructors are aware that what takes place during these two days will affect the employees' perception of the company and their performance on the job.

Constant Retraining

The Citicorp survey of service and customer satisfaction excellence found that, in superior companies, just about everyone goes to "school" for at least a full week every year. These companies reinforce the behavioral traits that were taught during orientation and introduce new skills to equip employees to do their jobs better.

Among the companies that provide long-term career training are such leaders as IBM, Johnson & Johnson, Hewlett-Packard, Motorola, and John Deere. IBM Canada invests an average of 13 days' training per year for each of the 12,900 staff members employed. This training is related to particular jobs within the company or to more general skills and developments in the computer industry. Incoming marketing employees, for example, get 28 weeks of training before they are launched into their first job.

It may not always be easy to convince colleagues and superiors of the need for constant training, but the benefits are sure if the program is carried out in the right way. When the Canadian Urban Transit Association proposed a quarter-million-dollar-plus training program for its member transit systems, the idea might not have gone further than the nearest bus stop if the Association had not had the support of a number of general managers who were motivated to improve the image of their transit companies and to raise the profile of their service. When the program actually began, it had several things going for it:

- The program had been developed by an advisory group made up of representatives from six transit systems and using input from a group of bus and subway train drivers. It had also been tested during pilot programs with real operators, supervisors, and managers from transit systems across Canada.
- The necessary financial resources had been allocated to ensure that the program could be carried out effectively.
- It had the support of management.

Although every training program will be different—they must be tailored to the needs of the specific company, department, or group of employees—these three factors should guide the development of any program.

Teaching the Bosses New Tricks

Managers who sign the approvals for employees to trot off to training sessions from time to time are in just as much need of constant education. Although training at all levels focuses on creating value for customers, the focus of management training is, of course, unique. Desatnick has identified the following areas as those in which managers need special training—for at least a week a year, he recommends:

1. Selection interviewing for job related behaviors

2. Employee orientation

3. Group dynamics, how to run a successful meeting

4. Teaching and counselling

5. Progress reviews and feedback

6. One-on-one encounters as developmental opportunities

7. Rewards and recognition

8. Performance planning

9. Performance standards

10. Performance appraisal and feedback

11. Constructive discipline that motivates

12. Negotiation skills

13. Conflict management

14. Stress management

15. Time management

To reinforce the concept of manager as facilitator and coach, management training should also focus on the need to treat employees well and to recognize and reward them. After all, as we have said before, the condition of a company's *internal* market is revealed in its success in the *external* market.

Employees who feel taken advantage of can hardly be expected to express a positive attitude toward customers. If employees feel that management is concerned about their interests and their assessment of how well they are being treated, trust will be established and commitment to organizational goals will be strengthened. A manager who shows concern for his or her employees and who makes every effort to provide the resources and encouragement necessary for them to carry out their jobs will reap benefits in the form of employee loyalty and dedication.

This doesn't mean that managers have to go soft on their employees and tell everyone to go to the beach. Napoleon Bonaparte and the aforementioned William Van Horne both provided their "employees" with ample resources and neither of them could be called soft. Napoleon's formula for successful management boiled down to the aphorism, "An army marches on its stomach." In other words, if you treat your army well by feeding them well, they get moving for you. Van Horne took this principle to its extreme—especially when it came to giving his railway workers enough to eat. When his hapless chief purchasing agent,

Burdock, had the temerity to slash a crew's supply list by 30 percent in the summer of 1882, Van Horne got wind of it and

> Burdock was hauled before The Presence. In a booming monotone and amid threatening gesticulations Van Horne gave him until evening to pack up and ship out a huge load of delicacies to [the crew]. "You can come back at six o'clock and tell me you have shipped it, you understand, but if you have not, you need not come back at all, but just go back to wherever you came from."

He was no featherweight, but he knew that he had to provide his employees with the necessary resources if they were going to perform well.

Especially in a company that promises excellence and delivers value to satisfied customers, front-line employees may be subject to burn-out. To avoid this, managers must spend time nourishing their spirits. As one after-dinner speaker said, "You can't deliver excellent service until you care for and cherish your own employees."

One way of doing this is by rewarding and recognizing the accomplishments of employees. Managers need to "manage" less and lead, coach, counsel, and inspire more. Most of all, they need to learn how to provide personal recognition through daily acts of appreciation.

One supervisor at a Midwestern U.S. dairy has used this approach successfully. He has a glass office in the middle of the plant. He is available for anyone, and people stop by to see him when they have work problems. He regularly takes a small group of employees out for breakfast—a different group each time—and personally pays for the outing. He asks employees what the company can do to help them perform better, and asks for suggestions about how to make the company a better place to work.

Drew Dimond, president of the Dimond Hospitality Group, had a "praising" coupon program when he was regional manager for Holiday Inns in Tennessee. In order to gather information about good service, coupons were given to guests when they checked in. When a customer returned a coupon with the name of an employee who had provided especially good service, the general manager praised the employee for what he or she had done. As a result, employee absenteeism declined significantly, customer service improved, and Dimond's Inns are recognized as leaders in delivering value to their customers.

Laura Secord, the Canadian chocolate company, also began to recognize the relationship between treatment of employees and customer satisfaction when it began a turnaround in 1983 after some years of declining performance. Breakfast meetings were held at which executives communicated issues and problems directly to managers and employees. A "hotline" connected to the human resources office provided employees with an effective way of proposing new ideas to management. Formal and informal recognition programs and an employee job enrichment program were established to demonstrate the company's commitment to its employees. As a result of a determined effort to better understand customer expectations and to be responsive to employees' needs, Laura Secord now has a leading position in the Canadian candy market.

Obviously, good management means praising employees for their accomplishments regularly. When difficulties arise, however, the matter should be dealt with in private, in order to correct the person without shaming them. It is especially important to honor good work publicly. Egalitarian North America has made some managers afraid of discriminating among employees and of rewarding the worthy. For employees to be motivated, however, this kind of thinking has to be laid aside. It is even a good idea to identify "customer satisfaction heroes" to act as role models for the rest of the peer group.

This is how Emery Apparel Canada Inc. does it. Every year, employees and their families are invited to the employee "Oscar" awards—a formal banquet and awards presentation, followed by dancing to a live band. Ten trophies are awarded to employees who have been nominated by a committee of three production people and two managers.

For employees who may be turned off by a system that only recognizes end results, there should also be recognition of ongoing improvement and progress. McDonald's has incorporated this approach into its reward system. At the same time that the Employee of the Month is recognized, employees who have reached certain service goals but who did not qualify for the Employee of the Month award are also recognized and given some McDonald's McBucks.

All the celebrations and hoopla must also be backed by sincere appreciation and care for the welfare of employees. At one retailing organization that is well known for its excellent customer service, prizes were given out for certain employee accomplishments, and other incentive programs were in operation. However, some of that company's workers have now launched complaints about exploitation and long, uncompensated hours. In that context, the baubles and gadgets that were handed out in "recognition" of sacrificial service became a mockery. Sincere care for the welfare of employees is essential.

Formal Standards and Reward Systems

Although glamorous and day-to-day rewards play an important role in motivating employees to deliver value to the company's customers, these forms of recognition have to be undergirded by a formal reward and compensation system that takes value creation and customer satisfaction into account.

Some companies have strict performance standards based on customer-satisfaction principles. McDonald's, predictably, has a particularly systematic set of standards. Here's an excerpt from the performance standards document for a cashier taking a breakfast order:

Step 1: Greet the Customer.

Standards:
1. Wish the customer a pleasant "good morning" and do so with a cheerful smile.
2. When asking for the order do so courteously. Please give a friendly greeting to let your customers know you are there to help them.
3. Call regular customers by name. It says to them, "You are important." It adds the dimension of warmth to an otherwise cold business transaction.

Not all performance standards will need to be based on such a detailed analysis of the employee's movements and attitudes, but they should be specific, to the necessary degree.

Compensation must also be linked with the individual's contribution to value creation, if employees are to buy into the concept of serving and satisfying customers. Merit pay awards granted through the performance appraisal program are a logical place to start. Executive and management bonuses can be directly linked to the achievement of customer satisfaction goals. For many years, in most companies, sales compensation has been directly related to achieving sales goals. However, if a company tells its sales force to please customers while tying their commission to sales quotas alone, it is obvious which will get the attention.

Employee incentive programs such as productivity gainsharing can also be structured to take value creation goals into account—and they can be applied to nontraditional areas such as production and distribution, not just sales and executive personnel. In these programs, in which "incentive" pools are built up as groups of employees achieve predetermined goals, it will be important to incorporate goals that relate not only to production, but also to high-quality products delivered to satisfied customers. In the most successful programs of this nature, a penalty is charged against the gain-sharing pool when poor-quality goods are returned from customers.

When it comes time to assess performance, some new methods may also be used to reinforce value creation standards. The people who work for builder F. W. Sawatzky (Western) Ltd. of Winnipeg get bonuses for profits and individual performance, and employees participate in their own evaluations. "They rate themselves, we rate them, then we talk about it," says President Lorne Evans. In other organizations, customer ratings of employee performance are factored into the appraisal process.

In Chapters 4 to 7, we have looked at the different ways in which marketing, operations, and human resources have solved their pieces of the value creation puzzle. Each area has an important contribution to make to the total picture. But, if real value is to be created and delivered to customers, all the puzzle pieces have to be put together; that is, the business enterprise has to take an integrated, strategic approach to creating value—and the initiative has to start right at the top of the corporate ladder.

This kind of initiative is easier described than done. Before effective change can be brought about, senior-level managers need to be familiar with the classic steps for implementing company-wide change, and they need to know what kinds of obstacles they are likely to meet on the way. That is why we have devoted the last three chapters to outlining a practical, no-nonsense method for transforming a rigid corporate structure into a flexible, market-driven organization.

8

Preparing for Change

No matter how full a reservoir of maxims one may possess, and no matter how good one's sentiments may be, if [one has] not taken advantage of every concrete opportunity to act, one's character may remain entirely unaffected for the better. With mere good intentions, hell is proverbially paved.

William James

The concept of value creation is not a difficult one to accept and believe in. It makes good, common business sense. The real difficulty comes when the concept is put to work. How does your business develop and implement value creation processes that will transform good intentions into concrete action?

Successful companies have discovered that there are a number of logical steps in formulating and implementing a value-creation strategy and its processes. Typically, these companies have a vision of a market-driven company that they would like to achieve, but they are caught in a reality that is far from their ideal.

VISION TO REALITY: CLOSING THE GAP

A series of gaps must be closed to make the vision of excellence a reality. These are the steps you will have to climb to close the gaps (they are also illustrated in Figure 8–1):

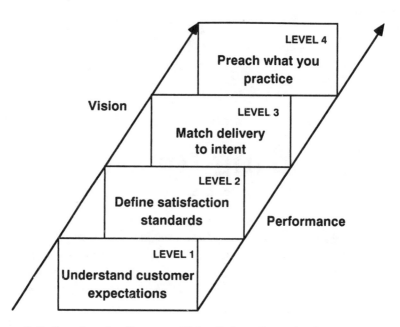

Figure 8–1. Creating the Customer-Value-Driven Organization

1. Understand customer expectations.
2. Define satisfaction standards.
3. Match delivery to intent.
4. Preach what you practice.

Step 1: Understand Customer Expectations

Your value-creation process must be based on a thorough knowledge of your customers' requirements. Your company must ask itself if it is currently *measuring the wants, needs, and expectations of its customers* and, if it is gathering information, how it is using the results. If you are not gathering customer data, you lack an understanding of how well you are able to satisfy your customers.

All aspects of the business should be measured, including:

- Pre-sales communication
- Product quality and design
- Sales representation

- Delivery
- Credit and invoicing policies
- After-sales service, including follow-up and problem resolution

As mentioned in Chapter 4, these measurements can be gathered in a number of ways: through focus groups, surveys, customer comment cards, or through a combination of methods. The specific information you should collect may include:

- Usage levels
- Preference ratings
- Overall satisfaction
- Ratings of satisfaction with specific departments or functional units of the company
- Measures of performance against competitors
- Future purchase intent
- Willingness to recommend the business to others

The type of information gathered and the method used to collect the data will vary according to the type of business. However, in most cases, it is desirable to interview both customers and your own front-line employees about each of the issues previously identified.

Step 2: Define Satisfaction Standards

The second step in the process is to *translate customer requirements into company standards of operation*, using input from each of the company's functional departments and educating employees in the implications of value creation for each department. Then, a visioning workshop should be conducted to set the ultimate goals and standards of performance. Subsequent workshops can be held to develop shorter-term (one-year) objectives and an action plan based on the vision. The visioning step is a critical event in establishing the employees' readiness and their emotional commitment to change. For the change process to begin and sustain itself, it is essential that all affected departments and closely related support groups participate in a significant way. They must invest sweat equity in the visioning and planning process. Senior management leadership will be truly tested through this critical step, but the payback can be many times greater than the investment of effort. To ensure maximum results at this initial step of the change process, the visioning workshop process should be outlined and conducted by a professional who has a good track record in value creation or customer satisfaction.

By setting satisfaction standards, you will be letting both your employees and your customers know what you consider to be the criteria for value creation and delivery. Standards should be set for all variables that affect the customer's interaction with your business—including product (or service) quality, pre-sales activities, delivery, and after-sales support.

This process of standards setting begins with the senior management team, which may include executives from marketing and market research, manufacturing/operations, logistics, human resources, and administration. The team should complete the following five activities during its visioning work sessions:

- Review the data collected in Step 1 to identify strengths and weaknesses as perceived by customers.
- Develop a blueprint of organizational activities to identify opportunities for improving value creation and customer satisfaction.
- Develop a value-creation mission statement.
- Define measurable standards linked to value creation for tracking results.
- Select an appropriate strategy for change, and commit the necessary resources to the process.

Step 3: Match Delivery to Intent

Your value-creation vision must now be turned into reality. *Implementation* will consist of several stages, each of which must be completed before the process can move to Step 4. Following are some of the stages you may go through:

- Introducing employees to the program
- Establishing a value-creation training program for employees
- Changing, or realigning, existing departments to enhance value creation

- Changing product or service features and quality
- Establishing a functional unit responsible for monitoring value creation
- Changing compensation and reward systems to encourage superior value
- Redefining advertising and marketing strategies
- Changing product delivery and transportation systems

As these changes are made, it will be essential to collect and analyze customer feedback regularly (some companies do it weekly). Customers must be encouraged to tell the company how well it is achieving the goals of the process. Staff members must be kept informed of the extent to which they are meeting their individual or department goals.

Step 4: Preach What You Practice

The value-creation mission you developed in Step 2 becomes the basis of the company's advertising and promotion. By *telling customers what to expect,* you are assuring them that you understand their expectations. You are also defining the standards by which customers should judge your firm and its offerings in the future.

The development of a customer-value-creation process takes time and effort. In order to ensure that this effort continues to pay off for the company, there must be an ongoing review to determine how well the process is helping the enterprise meet the expectations of customers. This is done, typically, through an annual customer satisfaction audit in which customers and employees are surveyed and management is involved in a detailed review of the strengths and weaknesses of the process. This process is applied to all aspects of the business, with the goal of identifying new opportunities for improving value creation and increasing customer satisfaction levels.

BARRIERS TO CHANGE

In moving from organizational stagnation to transformation, you will run into a number of barriers. During the last half of the 1980s, for instance, West German-based Siemens AG went through a major corporate restructuring. Commenting on this transformation, executive vice-president Hermann Franz has stated that "it is difficult to change a culture in a company of 350,000 people . . . it's a long-term process." The aim is to create a more customer-oriented company through reorganization, but Siemens realizes that the change will not come overnight.

The following are some of the reactions that you will likely encounter when you start talking about transformation:

• Fear of loss of control:	Change requires people to go from being on top of things to being unsure and out of control. They go through a *disillusioned learner* phase, during which they will need extra support from skilled coaches.
• Too much uncertainty:	The future is not obvious and it feels as if you are about to walk off a cliff every day. Many want to see all the details of the plan and want to examine all contingencies. Watch out for "paralysis by analysis."
• Too many surprises:	We like novelty, but hate surprises. Early warning is critical, since it is frightening to learn about changes at the last minute.
• We love our habits:	Habits are efficient, effective, and mindless. Changing to new ways of doing things is uncomfortable.
• Need for familiarity:	We like the familiar. We go back to places we know. Paint the walls, change buildings, and people become upset.
• New things mean more work:	This is often true, especially in the beginning.

- Concern for competence: People often question their ability to master new skills, particularly if training and ongoing support are not provided or are viewed with scepticism.

- Lack of skills: New ways require people to learn skills that they do not have. These are sometimes perceived as being difficult to acquire.

- Time to adjust: Saying "do it differently" is not enough. It takes time for new skills and a sense of comfort to develop. Rushing leads to disruption, sabotage, resistance, and poor performance.

BUILDING THE COMMITMENT TO CHANGE

Despite the many barriers managers will encounter as they introduce the value-creation process, there are many methods available to ease the transition. These are some of the methods used by companies that have transformed their corporate cultures.

- Involve as many people as you can in the change-planning process. Participation leads to ownership and enthusiasm.

- Communicate clearly, and often, what you are trying to achieve. Provide the firm's staff with as much detail as you can.

- Divide the implementation of change into manageable, comprehensible steps. Make the steps as familiar as possible. Keep the first steps small and easy, and make sure they are guaranteed successes.

- Allow no surprises. Communicate constantly.

- Let commitment grow. Do not ask for a pledge of allegiance to new, untried ways.

- Make clear what will be expected of people after the change. Carefully and fully communicate standards and requirements.

- Reward achievement and effort. When people try the new ways, reward them. When people succeed at the new ways, reward them. Reward progress, but do not expect perfection.

- Early on in the change process, seek out those who have learned and succeeded at the new ways. Compliment these people on their successes. Acknowledge their successes publicly. Use them as role models.

- Provide the extra resources people need to adapt to something new. Change takes extra time, extra energy, extra support. Make it available. Drive out fear. A failure is a treasure—a target for new learning.

- Anticipate the fact that some people will feel they will be losing stature through the change process. Compensate them for their loss. Keep the losses from being too obvious to others.

- Celebrate the past. Allow time for expressions of grief, nostalgia, loss. Bury the past with honor. Then build a sense of excitement and anticipation about the future.

PRACTICING PRACTICAL POLITICS

Transforming your company into a more customer-focused organization also requires *leadership*. To become a change leader, you must find the best way to communicate a vision of a more effective future for your organization. You will have to convince others in your company that creating customer value and satisfaction are the firm's most important goals.

Since changing people's attitudes, beliefs, and behavior is essentially a political process revolving around organizational persuasion and power, we can borrow from the methods used by successful politicians and military leaders in designing a strategy for change. Your selection of a change strategy will hinge upon two variables: how fast change must be accomplished and where the leadership for change is situated within the organization. Consider these four change strategies, each of which has specific advantages and risks:

- Annexation
- *Perestroika*
- Guerrilla campaign
- Palace coup

Annexation

Through the *annexation strategy*, you gradually convince your company, department by department, to adopt value creation as its primary goal. The move to a stronger customer focus can proceed through this type of evolutionary approach if the pace of change required is moderate and senior executives are the change leaders. Using this strategy, senior executives look for the parts of the organization that are most willing to adopt the desired behavior. As success in specific departments is achieved, the resulting momentum can be used to branch out and address the more reactionary parts of the organization.

The transformation of Toronto's *Globe & Mail* newspaper from a mass-circulation publication covering all types of news, to one with a definite focus on business events, was brought about partly through a strategy of annexation. Publisher Roy Megarry, who has been at the helm since 1978, has personally redefined the corporate mission of the paper, working with one department at a time.

First, to better serve readers from Canada's business community, Megarry revamped the business section of the paper by expanding its coverage, adding special supplements, and launching the monthly *Report on Business* magazine. Other sections of the paper have followed suit. New columnists have been featured in the front news section, for instance, to reflect the sharper focus on business affairs.

The annexation strategy is attractive because it minimizes disruption by allowing new attitudes to gradually work their way through the organization. The pace of this approach, however, may be too slow to meet the fast-changing needs of the marketplace. And there is the risk that the effort toward change may stall out when it runs up against organizational inertia.

Perestroika

When the restructuring required is great and must be carried out quickly, top management can emulate Mikhail Gorbachev by leading the change process with vigor and high visibility. That's why this strategy is called *perestroika*. Perhaps the best-known example of this style of leadership in the business world is the high-profile approach Lee Iacocca used to bring Chrysler back from the brink of bankruptcy. When he first took over the ailing operation, he ran a newspaper ad that asked, "Would America be better off without Chrysler?" The ads, which carried his signature, were his way of saying, "I'm here, I'm real, and I'm responsible for this company. And to show that I mean it, I'm signing on the dotted line." The impact of Iacocca's declaration was twofold. He told his employees and customers of his intention to transform the company, and he told them he was fully committed to leading the change.

The *perestroika* strategy allows for a fast pace of change, clear expression of top management's intent, and appropriate allocation of resources to the change process, since senior executives are spearheading the efforts. The risks are higher than with the annexation strategy, however, especially for the senior executives taking the lead. If the organization is pushed too far too fast, an employee backlash may develop that can derail the effort.

Guerrilla Campaign

Those who are most aware of their company's need to become more customer-driven are often not in the senior executive ranks. Marketing or sales managers in a large corporation may be more in touch with the market than is the CEO. Although they may see the need for change, they do not have the managerial clout to fully commit their organization to the battle.

If you are in this position, you may wish to consider a *guerrilla campaign*. Under this strategy, you search for selective opportunities to improve your company's customer responsiveness. Gradually, as success becomes apparent, you can persuade top management to take a more active role and commit more resources to the change effort.

Successful examples of this approach are difficult to find because good guerrilla leaders know how to remain in protective camouflage within their organizations. However, executives at Dow Chemical report that this type of process took place as the company adopted its "quality-first" philosophy in the mid-1980s.

Struggling to reduce costs to respond to the global demand slump experienced in the early part of the decade, senior management at Dow focused its attention on productivity improvement. Middle management, however, became convinced that superior quality and customer satisfaction were going to be the keys to success in the 1990s. Gradually, the middle management group was able to convince Dow's senior executives that quality improvement and customer satisfaction go hand-in-hand with achieving productivity gains. Today, Dow is one of the world leaders in its commitment to quality, having adopted "contributing to customer success" as its key business goal.

The most attractive feature of the guerrilla strategy is that you can unilaterally appoint yourself a leader and seize the best opportunities as you see fit. On the other side, there is the risk that the change process will be too slow, or incremental, to make any visible difference to customers. Without formal organizational sanction, your guerrilla campaign can fall victim to the tyranny of the status quo.

Palace Coup

Where the need for change is urgent and leadership from the top is lacking, you can elect to become a true revolutionary. According to this strategy, you seize the initiative and attempt to *gain control of key organizational positions* to carry out your plans. A bold move like this obviously places change leaders at great risk if the bid for power fails. However, when the need for change is so pressing that organizational survival is at stake, perhaps only new leadership can save the day.

For example, Tiffany, once considered *the* retailer from which to purchase diamonds and other luxury jewelry items, began to lose ground in the early 1980s to its arch-rival, Cartier. Tiffany management, seeing its customers' new preference for Cartier, concluded that the cause lay with the management strategies of Avon Products, which had bought Tiffany in 1979 and had introduced mass merchandising concepts into the store, with results disastrous for Tiffany. An internal management group led by William R. Chaney was so alarmed at the drop in sales and the exodus of Tiffany's select clientele that it took control and bought Tiffany from Avon in 1984.

To woo back its old customers, and, as *Fortune* magazine describes it, to "regain lost prestige," Tiffany has tripled advertising expenditures, begun a program to create exclusive lines of merchandise, and even hired a famous jewelry designer to assemble "image-setting pieces," a trade term for jewelry priced above $100,000. The new management team has aggressively shifted the company's focus to one that serves a select group of affluent customers, with the goal of being "the world's finest purveyor of jewelry and luxury products."

The type of political strategy you choose will depend on the extent to which your company is customer-focused, the receptiveness of your colleagues and superiors to change, and your own position within the organization. One of these strategies will likely have to be used, however, since change does not occur on its own.

CONFRONTING THE EXCUSES FOR NOT GETTING STARTED

Transforming your company into a more customer-focused organization is not an easy task. It requires commitment, a clear operating philosophy and strong management. It also requires the ability to get people to take the first step on the long journey toward progress. As you contemplate how to begin your value creation process, you should anticipate some of the excuses people offer for not getting started.

Excuse #1: Customers Don't Know What They Want

Yes, it is true that customers often cannot articulate their needs very well. They are sometimes shy, elusive creatures who become loyal patrons only after long and delicate coaxing. However, customers do know how they *feel.* They have a pretty clear view of who they like to do business with.

Since customers' perceptions define their reality, value-creation programs must start with understanding how customers feel about your company. If you bother to ask, on a regular and systematic basis, it really is not too difficult to ascertain customer perceptions of your organization. This is an important first step in pinpointing opportunities for improvement.

Johnson & Johnson is one company that continuously monitors its customers' perceptions of its products and uses the information obtained to improve existing products or to develop new ones. For example, working with the Toronto-based product-development company, Product Initiatives, Johnson & Johnson conducted consumer research through *consumer innovation groups*, which, unlike traditional focus groups, allow more creativity from the respondents.

A brainstorming approach featuring *action-building workshops* was then used to develop new-product concepts. The consumer innovation groups verified consumers' perceptions that Johnson & Johnson was a "sincere" company, offering safe and dependable family-oriented products. The action-building workshops developed a new product based on input from the consumer innovation groups, a liquid laundry soap for cleaning baby clothes, as an alternative to powdered baby soaps. Consumer reaction to the detergent has been positive, and the product has become especially popular with customers already using the company's other baby products.

Excuse #2: Even if Customers Know What They Want, We'd Have to Do Market Research to Find Out What That Is

Companies that are determined to create value for their customers also believe in actually going out and talking to them. They realize that you cannot manage what you cannot measure. They invest heavily in the customer satisfaction data collection methods that will keep them closely attuned to customer requirements. They keep score on how well they meet customer satisfaction criteria, and they share this information widely within their organization so that everyone knows how well the company is doing.

Many of the customer-satisfaction research tools currently in use were described in Chapter 4. But new research methods are always emerging, including an innovative one developed by the New Product Store in Toronto. At this "store," inventors can showcase their new products and prototypes and learn how to improve them through the market research the store can provide. Store employees conduct customer opinion polls and collect customer profile information.

The opportunities for the inventor to network with distributors, retailers, and potential buyers, and the information provided by the customer research, are often invaluable in refining product designs or packaging concepts. The whole process allows real customer needs and expectations to be communicated directly to the originator of the product, at a cost much lower than traditional market research approaches.

Excuse #3: Customers Don't Know How Hard It Is

Keeping customers satisfied *is* hard work. Customers enter into a transaction with your organization precisely because they have problems to be resolved or needs to be met. They are not interested in how your company is organized or what your costs are. That is what they pay your company to worry about.

Successful customer satisfaction initiatives are built on the premise that it is the vendor who must assume the primary responsibility for keeping customers satisfied. If you do it well, they will reward you with higher prices, greater loyalty, and positive word-of-mouth referrals.

If there's one company whose owners don't complain about how hard it is, it is Dell Computer, which launched its personal computer mail-order business out of Austin, Texas, in 1984 and has since become a leader in this ruthlessly competitive market. As Bruce Sinclair, president of Dell in Canada, puts it, the company's " . . . business strategy focuses on customer service and support [and] service is the biggest reason for Dell's success." No bellyaching about hard work there.

Dell differs from its competitors by allowing customers to design their own computers using components from separate systems rather than relying on prepackaged hardware. Free on-site service is provided for the first year. Staff members make follow-up contacts to ensure that everything is to the customer's satisfaction. An electronic mail network connecting all of Dell's offices provides buyers with instant information, technical tips, news, and product updates. Bilingual (English and French) employees are available to serve Canadian customers. Obviously, all this adds up to more work and more expenses, but who's complaining? Dell's decision to take complete responsibility for customer satisfaction has clearly been successful, inasmuch as 50 percent of the firm's sales now come from repeat customers.

Excuse #4: Middle Management Will Block the Program

If you are a senior manager, you may have noticed that your pronouncements to front-line personnel about the importance of happy customers are somehow stymied by inertia at the middle-management level. Some senior executives are naïve about the realities of communication within a large organization; the reality is that messages tend to get watered down as they filter through the company.

In planning for and implementing value-creation processes, ample allowance must be made to involve and "sell into" the middle management group. Without their active support, there is little hope that the value-creation message will reach the front-line employee.

At the Canadian Imperial Bank of Commerce, a recently launched value-creation program, "Project Delta," has been used to successfully rally middle-management and front-line employee support for the bank's new emphasis on servicing personal banking accounts in a bid to attract customers away from its competitors. The bank has succeeded in its efforts because it believes that financial institutions run by middle-management teams do better than those run from the chairman's office. By decentralizing the decision-making process, concentrating resources on staff retraining, and actively involving its middle-management group, the Commerce is well on its way to becoming a more market-driven organization.

Excuse #5: Employees Are Too Cynical to Change

Many observers believe the quality of treatment that customers receive is a reflection of how employees themselves are treated. But programs to improve the quality of work life are sometimes viewed cynically by employees and managers who have been burned in the past by lip-service quality programs. Even with the most effective program, change may come slowly if the negative attitudes of front-line employees towards customers have been entrenched for years. These important cultural and organizational climate problems have to be diagnosed before customer-value-creation initiatives are launched. Organizational "readiness" has to be evaluated.

AT&T, which has a history and reputation as a slow-moving bureaucracy, is making a concerted effort to encourage staff to take more responsibility in decision-making. Curtis J. Crawford, vice-president of National Sales at AT&T, tells his sales force that " . . . they are in charge of making this business successful [and should] be impatient with the organization if it gets in their way." The company recognizes that to be successful it must not only market effectively to customers; employees, too, must be the target of a well planned communications program.

Excuse #6: Top Management Will Soon Lose Interest Anyway

Customer-value-improvement initiatives require strong leadership from the highest levels of the organization, and this leadership must be consistent and continuous. Only by showing personal commitment and by tackling the difficulties of a long-term value-creation process will top management gain credibility in the eyes of its employees.

The Canadian Imperial Bank of Commerce, mentioned earlier, was once considered the most conservative member of Canada's financial industry. But now, thanks to the efforts of chairman Donald Fullerton, the bank is on its way to becoming a leading financial retailer. Fullerton introduced a new corporate vision in 1983 with the intention of transforming the bank from an autocratic institution to a customer-friendly financial organization. Since that time, Fullerton has personally carried to employees the message about the need to improve quality of customer service; and each year he has doubled the staff retraining budgets required to meet that goal. Although Fullerton is a supporter of management teamwork, the direction for the bank's "master plan" has come straight from his office, lending credibility and momentum to the bank's service-quality-improvement program.

Excuse #7: It Costs Too Much

Becoming more customer-oriented takes commitment. It is also becoming more obvious that it is not free. Although the exact price is not known, the costs of value-creation efforts should be on a par with the investments you make for other major business ventures. One observer calculates that medium-sized organizations can expect to make six-figure investments spread over several years. Large corporations are looking at multimillion-dollar commitments if they are truly willing to meet the value creation challenge.

For example, in 1982, the Southern California Gas Company decided to implement a customer relations training program for its customer service employees. The program covers a variety of topics in 10 sessions and is attended by the company's more than 750 customer service representatives. Over the five years since the program began, the utility has spent a total of $727,000. The price of training in the first year alone was $192,000.

Excuse #8: There's Not Enough Time

Some executives have one critical blind spot when they look at the possibility of initiating a value-creation program. They fail to recognize that a key lever in the battle for customer responsiveness is a "turned-on" corporate culture. Cultural change means modifying attitudes and beliefs—a complicated process, which does not happen overnight. New management directives, posters, and pep rallies are not enough to develop the true organizational commitment necessary to make a difference in creating and delivering value to customers.

One company that has devised a long-term strategy for corporate culture change is British Telecom, England's formerly government-run telephone company, which was privatized in 1984. Its current mandate is to overcome the deep-rooted problems of bureaucracy and lack of customer sensitivity that prevailed before privatization.

Senior management at British Telecom recognizes that reinventing the organization's culture cannot occur overnight. To speed up the process, they have worked hard to define what the new corporate culture must be—an entrepreneurial one, which depends on individual innovation and creativity, but which is also characterized by team-oriented management practices. By making the new values clear, management hopes they will be adopted more quickly.

Excuse #9: We Don't Know Where We're Going

A commitment to value creation takes leadership. Leaders who aspire to greatness in this area must clearly articulate a customer focus that sets action guidelines for the rest of the organization. They must be willing to live with difficult choices. Senior management must show the courage of its conviction by making decisions consistently in favor of customer value when trade-offs against costs, efficiency, and convenience have to be made.

For example, Dow Chemical has made it very clear to all employees what its priorities are for the 1990s. In the company's strategy statement, entitled *Vision and Strategy for the Nineties*, president and CEO Frank Popoff writes that Dow will become, by the year 2000, "a premier global company . . . dedicated to growth . . . driven by quality performance and innovation . . . and committed to maintaining our customers' successes. . . ." The vision statement concludes with a quotation from H.H. Dow, founder of the company: "If you can't do it better, why do it?"

Excuse #10: The Chances of Success Are Pretty Low

Gaining competitive advantage by creating superior value for customers is difficult. But it is precisely for this reason that great opportunities exist for companies with the stamina to make the journey up the mountain. Only a few will stand at the peak. But to these companies will go the rewards denied to those who opted for excuses instead of excellence.

At American Express, whose CEO James Robinson has said, "Quality is the only patent we've got," the journey up the mountain began in the late 1970s. At that time the Travel Related Services operating unit of the company, known for its travelers checks and travel products and services, was experiencing dramatic growth. Top management, however, recognized the need for a formal quality assurance program in order to maintain high levels of customer service, which could otherwise have been compromised by the rapid growth.

The firm carried out extensive market research on its products and services and on customer communications. Among the results of this research in the credit card business, it was shown clearly that customers depended on the timeliness, accuracy, and responsiveness of American Express service. Using these results as guidelines, the company set performance standards for all areas of customer interaction and transformed employee attitudes and behavior. Central to this transformation was the use of formal recognition programs for employees. Within three years of introducing the Quality Assurance program, service delivery quality had improved by 78 percent, and expenses per transaction were down by 21 percent. They're still heading up the mountain, but their chances of continuing success look good!

Once the excuses and psychological barriers to change have been broken and the value-creation strategy has been clearly developed by senior management, you'll be ready to start on the next phase—developing your action program.

9

Developing Your Action Program

Dream a little and work a lot.

Donald Jackson, champion figure skater

As in skating or any other sport, so in the business of value creation. The most inspiring vision of corporate change will never get off the ground without dedication, hard work, and a clear framework for implementation. After years of working with clients on value-creation processes in a wide range of industries, The Coopers & Lybrand Consulting Group in Toronto has established and developed an implementation framework, shown as Figure 9–1, that was initially based on the ideas of customer service expert Karl Albrecht. This framework consists of six phases:

Phase I: Establish the current baseline

Phase II: Clarify the business strategy and build the vision

Phase III: Train and communicate with the organization

Phase IV: Implement front-line improvements

Phase V: Lock in continuous improvements

Phase VI: Monitor and review

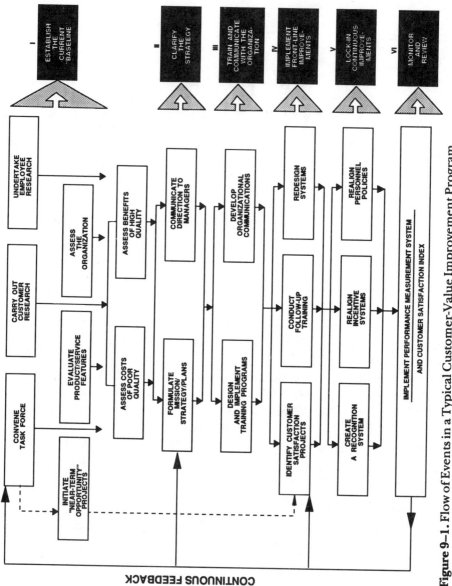

Figure 9–1. Flow of Events in a Typical Customer-Value Improvement Program

PHASE I: ESTABLISH THE CURRENT BASELINE

Your first task in launching a value-creation process is to establish your current position. This will require you to do not only customer and employee research, but also to tally the losses your company is sustaining as a result of poor-quality products or services. These and other *baseline assessment* tasks are shown below, in the approximate order in which they should be carried out:

- Convene a customer-value-creation task force.
- Do customer research.
- Do employee research.
- Assess organizational structure and procedures.
- Evaluate product and service features and quality.
- Assess the company's costs of poor quality.
- Assess the potential benefits of high quality.
- Initiate "near-term opportunity" projects.

Convene a Customer-Value-Creation Task Force

The customer-value-creation task force should be made up of all the senior executives of the company, from all functional areas, and it should be chaired by the chief executive officer. This task force will be the engine of change in the company and a clearinghouse for ideas and projects related to the value-creation process. It will formulate strategies and oversee implementation projects. Often, an outside facilitator can help the group function more smoothly.

The participation of top-level executives in the task force is essential if value-creation implementation initiatives are to succeed, since, as we mentioned in Chapter 3, high-profile leadership gives the value-creation process credibility and momentum. Senior executives must *not* delegate their responsibility to work on the task force or on customer-value-improvement project teams. Dr. Joseph Juran, one of the deans of quality management, notes that it is common for senior managers to look for ways to delegate involvement in and responsibility for these processes. The traditional approach is simply to exhort employees to reach quality and customer satisfaction goals. This goes against the whole philosophy of value creation. As Dr. Juran has said, managers must be "leaders, not cheerleaders." Senior management must realize that the effort to create value is not just a program but a never-ending process that requires their constant leadership.

Therefore, when implementing value-creation processes, senior managers must be held responsible for carrying out—not delegating— the following essential tasks:

- Serve on the customer-value-creation task force.
- Approve strategic value-creation goals.
- Allocate resources.
- Review progress.
- Recognize and reward appropriate behavior.
- Serve on customer-value-improvement project teams.
- Revise the employee evaluation system to better recognize value-creation priorities.
- Incorporate value-creation goals into the strategic business plan.
- Connect value creation to the financial growth of the business.

Some companies find that the best way to mobilize and promote the customer-value-creation task force is to launch a *program* that helps to focus the committee's effort. One major industrial textile producer, for example, launched a program called "C-QUEST" to establish a value creation culture. The initiative began when the company discovered, through customer research, that it was in danger of losing its dominant market position because of poor service and product quality. At the same time, issues of poor quality and late deliveries could not be dealt with efficiently because they crossed departmental boundaries and there was no mechanism to encourage department heads to work together.

To remedy the problem, a newly appointed general manager organized a Customer Value and Satisfaction Council to deal with the rising number of customer complaints. The council, composed of the general manager and the managers of manufacturing, marketing, sales, and technical development, initiated a series of meetings with employees throughout the company to elicit ideas on how to improve buyer satisfaction. Hundreds of ideas were generated. The council screened the list of ideas to identify the most critical issues and opportunities.

Through the discussions with employees, the council realized that it needed a mechanism to coordinate its efforts for remedying identified problems. That's where the C-QUEST program came in. It was designed to promote customer awareness and a service mentality—as its name implied. The name is an acronym standing for the following principles:

- **C**ustomers are first
- **Q**uality in products, service, and people
- **U**nderstanding customers' needs
- **E**xcellence in everything we do
- **S**ervice means survival
- **T**eamwork guarantees success

The C-QUEST program succeeded because senior executives participated actively in it. And the Customer Value and Satisfaction Council, which provided the initial momentum for the program, continued to act as a forum for improved cross-functional cooperation and problem solving.

Do Customer Research

Your next task will be to understand your customers better by commissioning *customer satisfaction research* to obtain objective data about how customers perceive the company compared to its competitors. In Chapter 4, we outlined the many different kinds of customer satisfaction research methods currently being used by businesses and professional market researchers, so we will not go into detail about them here. In general, however, you should seize every opportunity to bring customers and employees together, using approaches such as the following:

- *Video:* filming customers talking about how they perceived the service and value they received.
- *Customer visits:* inviting customers to meet shop-floor employees in the plant to discuss customer satisfaction, service and quality issues.
- *Employee visits to customers' premises:* sending employees out to meet their customers and report back to their colleagues.
- *Supplier visits:* promoting the interchange between shop-floor and front-line employees and their peers in supplier companies.

Chapter 4 also covers the key questions that should be asked in formal customer satisfaction research, but here, again, are three of the most important ones:

- What are the most critical factors that create satisfaction from the customer's point of view?
- Which are we doing well/badl by comparison with the competition?
- Which could we most easily improve upon, in comparison with the competition?

Do Employee Research

In addition to customer research, *survey employees.* Determine their perceptions of what customers want, and discover their opinions about company policies and practices that may stand in the way of customer satisfaction.

A major Canadian chemicals company that hired a management consulting group to conduct customer satisfaction analysis followed this advice and had the consultant interview company employees as well as customers about product and service quality. The employees were also asked to identify factors that affected their relationships with customers. Findings from this research indicated that front-line customer contact employees had a good appreciation for customer expectations but that internal administration groups were less understanding of buyer needs. This prompted the company to begin an internal education program to help all employees better understand what customers expected from the company.

Assess Organizational Structure and Procedures

Your next task is to *review company and administrative procedures, incentives, performance measures, organizational structures, and information flows.* Look for blockages in the system that limit the company's responsiveness to the customer.

Value analysis is a technique recommended by Wayne Peasgood, consultant with The Coopers & Lybrand Consulting Group. He has successfully applied this technique within financial institutions to improve service quality and reduce costs at the same time. The approach is based on value-engineering techniques that have evolved over the past 40 years and have been used to ensure that the design of new products, or the redesign of existing products, meets or exceeds quality and functional characteristics at minimal cost.

Value analysis relates the quality, importance, and cost of a function to its essential purpose or to an organization's mission. In doing so, it offers a means of quantifying these relationships and indicating to management where operational and/or quality improvements might be made.

In particular, value analysis will provide insights into

- Where customers' needs are not being satisfied
- Where important functions are not being performed adequately
- Where necessary functions or activities are not being carried out
- Where operational waste is occurring
- The impact of functional and service level changes on profitability

Value analysis simplifies organizational complexities by classifying functions within an organizational unit into basic and supporting activities, assigning costs to them and establishing their respective degrees of importance and quality. Once a value-analysis exercise is complete, management can make rational choices about how it should operate in the future to increase quality and productivity.

This technique is useful to managers in a wide range of departments and at various levels of the organization. It can be used to help managers make decisions about strategy setting; the allocation of resources; the integration, elimination, enhancement or simplification of specific functions; the evaluation of both front-line and back-office services; and overall performance improvement.

Evaluate Product and Service Features and Quality

The next task to be completed is to *identify the value of the product and service features* that your company offers, compared to those offered by the competition. To clearly establish whether your service is designed and produced to the highest quality standards, you will have to carry out competitive benchmarking studies. Benchmarking techniques will be discussed in more detail in the next chapter. For the moment, let us just look at one company that has become famous for its development of competitive benchmarking techniques.

Xerox Corporation began developing competitive benchmarking techniques as early as 1979, and by 1981 was using them in every division.

By the late 1980s, the company had so improved its business performance that it won major awards in both the United States and Canada: the Malcolm Baldrige National Quality Award and the Canada Award for Business Excellence.

According to the *DataQuest Research Newsletter*, "Xerox's Benchmarking Program deserve[d] the lion's share of the credit for the company's turnaround in recent years. A whole new way of doing business was inaugurated with the start of this program. Every group, product and system was dissected as Xerox searched for ways to become more competitive." Other companies now look at Xerox as a model of how to use benchmarking to maintain leadership in their industry.

In Xerox's electronics division, for example, benchmarking is used to improve engineering efficiency. Although the division's mandate is to "provide high-quality, cost-effective electronics designs that meet customer requirements and industry benchmarks," Xerox perceived at one time that European manufacturers of high technology were the leaders in engineering efficiency.

As the first step in seeking out ideas for improving its performance, the division prepared a list of companies against which to benchmark its performance. From this investigation, it discovered that there was increased market pressure for additional product performance at lower cost. The division's research then focused on ways to improve the quality, cost, and delivery of its electronic designs.

The investigators reviewed the overall design process, from inception through initial manufacturing activities, and broke down the typical design and development cycle into measurable factors such as:

- Overall design cycle time
- Resource requirements
- Manpower utilization
- Staffing structure
- Efficiency of the process in transferring new technology from the research laboratory to the engineering design laboratory

Using this list of factors, the investigators analyzed the design development process of 10 top European electronics companies and discovered that Xerox needed to make a number of changes to improve efficiency. The company reorganized its product design teams and introduced a training program to increase the knowledge and skills of its design engineers beyond their own narrow areas of expertise. New design tools and techniques were also introduced to improve turn-around time.

Assess the Company's Costs of Poor Quality

There are several ways of looking at *costs of poor quality*, which really means the "costs of unquality," or not "doing things right the first time." Surveys by the American Society for Quality Control (ASQC) suggest that many companies think their cost of quality is only about 5 percent of revenue. However, the Conference Board, a business think tank, reports that its members say the cost of quality is 20 to 30 percent of revenues.

The costs of poor quality, and resulting customer dissatisfaction, are really the costs associated with *waste*. Any activity that does not build value for the customer can be considered waste and, therefore, a cost that should be eliminated. John M. Groocock reports in *The Chain of Quality* that quality costs are particularly important to managers because they are so large, and yet they are relatively controllable compared to other costs.

If a typical manufacturer reviewed quality costs in relation to total costs, he would find that, out of each sales dollar, 50 cents would go to pay for purchased materials, components, subassemblies and so forth; another 20 cents would cover the value-adding manufacturing costs of labor and overhead; and the remaining gross margin of 30 cents would pay for research and development, marketing, administrative costs, interest, and profit.

If the costs of poor quality, or waste, directly associated with manufacturing activities were 5 percent of revenues (which is not an uncommon figure), then they would represent a major opportunity for cost reduction. Comparing the cost of quality to the manufactured value-adding costs—the 20 percent of revenues defined earlier—the cost of quality would be 25 percent of total value-adding costs (5 percent divided by 20 percent). In other words, over one-quarter of the value-adding costs are costs associated with poor quality practices.

Waste can be found in many parts of any organization, but conventional accounting and financial reporting systems do not make these costs easy to detect. As was pointed out in Chapter 6, to identify the costs associated with not producing a high-quality product or service "the first time," the following areas need to be looked at:

- Reworking defective output
- Carrying out warranty and field service
- Carrying excess inventories
- Scrapping defective output
- Incurring excess overtime
- Appraising, inspecting, and testing for defects

Another way of looking at the costs of poor quality is by assessing the *market damage* it causes; that is, the amount of business lost because of dissatisfied customers. Market damage can be calculated using the following equation:

$$\begin{matrix} \text{Profit lost per year} \\ \text{due to unhappy customers} \end{matrix} = \begin{matrix} \text{Lost sales} \times \text{Average expected} \\ \text{profit per sale} \end{matrix}$$

To develop a market damage estimate, the following information is needed:

- Average profit per sale
- Period of customer loyalty
- Repeat purchase rate during the period of loyalty
- Number of customers
- Percentage of customers experiencing problems
- Repeat purchase intentions for satisfied customers, for those who complain, and for those who are dissatisfied but do not complain
- Number of people told about the experience by satisfied customers, by customers who complain, and by those who are dissatisfied but do not complain

In other words, the value of lost profit is represented by the number of potential customers who do not buy because of negative word-of-mouth remarks from dissatisfied customers, multiplied by the average repeat purchase rate of a loyal customer.

Armed with these data, the manager can calculate the return on investment of embarking on customer-value-improvement programs. Ted Marra, a customer service consultant, says that improving customer satisfaction has demonstrable profit improvement effects. His studies show dramatic returns on investment from attacking the customer satisfaction problem through, for example, setting up effective complaint management systems. He indicates the following levels of return on investment have been achieved, in a variety of industries, through upgrading complaint management processes:

- Packaged goods   15 to 20 percent
- Banking   50 to 170 percent
- Gas utilities   20 to 150 percent
- Consumer durable goods 100 percent
- Electronic products   50 percent
- Retailing   35 to 400 percent
- Automobile service   100 percent

Assess the Potential Benefits of High Quality

In addition to compiling data on the losses associated with poor quality, you should investigate the potential benefits of improving the quality of your company's products or services. The magnitude of the benefits will be different for different companies and for different areas of a company's operations, but the kinds of benefits are common to all business enterprises. In *The PIMS Principles*, Robert Buzzell and Bradley Gale have identified a number of benefits that arise from delivering superior value for customers:

- *Stronger customer loyalty and more repeat business.* Companies that deliver higher perceived quality than their competitors achieve higher customer satisfaction levels and, in turn, higher repeat purchase rates. This lowers marketing costs and boosts profitability by reducing customer attrition. Royal Bank president John Cleghorn is aware of the value of customer loyalty. In a speech he gave in Toronto, he cited research indicating that, in the auto industry, a customer who continues to have his car serviced at a company dealership represents about $150,000 in revenues during his lifetime. "In the supermarket business," he went on, "a lifetime customer is worth $260,000 in sales. And in my business, the loyal, long-term customer is literally the engine that drives our bank. . . ."

- *Reduced vulnerability in price wars.* High customer loyalty reduces the chance that customers will switch to the competition during periodic price battles.

- *Ability to command higher prices without affecting market share.* In almost every industry, there is a leading company that is able to command a premium price from customers. These companies obviously have a greater chance to be highly profitable.

- *Lower marketing costs.* Companies that deliver high-quality products and service spend less money replacing their customer base and benefit more from referrals and word-of-mouth recommendations.

- *Growth in market share.* High levels of customer satisfaction create a positive cycle of success, which results in high repeat purchase levels, more efficient marketing expenditures, and a growing customer base. This provides for economies of scale and superior margins, which in turn provide the resources to launch new initiatives to build market share.

The following are additional benefits associated with high quality:

- *One-stop shopping.* Customers who are happy dealing with one part of your company are more likely to buy other products and services from you. It usually costs less for your company to supply single, bundled orders; and it is less costly for the customer to receive such orders than to split the business among many suppliers.

- *Less chance of surprises in the marketplace.* Businesses that have the customers' interests at heart keep in close touch with them and are seldom blindsided by new customer requirements. By receiving early signals about emerging customer needs, you can better anticipate market demand shifts and make the necessary transitions smoothly.

- *Positive word-of-mouth recommendations and enhanced image.* Satisfied customers tell their friends about their positive experiences, and this, of course, creates new customers for your company. This is particularly important where the purchaser perceives a high degree of risk from the purchase.

- *Successful innovations.* Satisfied customers are more open to sharing their experiences on the use of your products or services. They will let suppliers into their places of work, will work on collaborative development projects with your company, and will suggest improvements. The results of these joint efforts are new products and services that address real customer needs and are therefore more likely to achieve success in the marketplace.

All of these benefits will be important for your company. By describing them as they relate to your business, you will have concrete evidence that can be used to argue the case for initiating a value-creation process.

Initiate "Near-Term Opportunity" Projects

While you are awaiting the results of the research into quality status and customer satisfaction, initiate several immediate projects to tackle the most obvious value-creation opportunities. This will give momentum to the customer-value-creation task force and demonstrate to employees that senior management is serious about its commitment to change.

An important byproduct of tackling improvement projects quickly is that it gives senior management firsthand experience in the challenge of unraveling value-creation, quality, service, and customer satisfaction problems. Management will quickly learn that apparently simple problems can be more complex and difficult to resolve than they first appear.

This was the experience of a major food ingredients company that organized a customer satisfaction council to launch its value-creation process. The council's first task was to commission market and employee research on the company's position. While they were waiting for the results of the research to come in, the council members decided to tackle several early opportunity projects to gain experience in cross-functional problem solving and to demonstrate to employees senior management's commitment to customer satisfaction.

Using the help of an outside consultant, the council brainstormed to generate ideas for improving customer satisfaction. The council members then screened their ideas and came up with a "short list." The selected ideas for improvement had to pass two tests: (1) They had to be clearly visible to customers, and (2) they had to be capable of implementation within 90 days. Three opportunities were identified:

- Improved time lines and courtesy in responding to customer telephone orders and inquiries
- Improved appearance and cleanliness of delivery trucks
- Improved responsiveness to customer complaints

A vice-president was assigned to each project and asked to form a subcommittee of employees to analyze the issue and recommend solutions. Within a month, each vice-president reported that what appeared to be simple issues were, in fact, quite complex and represented the tip of the iceberg of related problems.

For example, the executive in charge of improving the company's telephone manner discovered several significant problems. First, employees managing the customer order desks had never been given telephone courtesy training. Second, and more important, the company's telephone equipment was grossly inadequate for handling the volume of customer calls coming in. Successive company programs to cut costs and improve efficiency had left the organization with obsolete technology. As a result, even well intentioned employees could not handle customer inquiries effectively.

The vice-president responsible for making sure that the company's trucks were clean and presented a good image to customers learned that the trucks and their drivers were supplied by an outside contracting firm. The need for clean trucks and neat, professional-appearing truck drivers had never been communicated to the contractor. In order to cut costs, this firm had cut down the number of times the trucks were washed.

The problem was solved by having a company employee take an office on the contractor's premises to develop quality and appearance guidelines and monitor results. Ultimately, the contract for managing the truck fleet had to be renegotiated; and the food company realized it needed to take a more active role with its transportation supplier to ensure that its image for quality and cleanliness was maintained with customers.

The final project, improving the complaint management process, also proved to be complex. Analysis showed that complaints were viewed within the company as evidence of wrongdoing. Therefore, many complaints were, in fact, never entered into the system. In addition, each internal department used complaints to blame the other departments for problems. No one was held accountable for a customer inquiry, so customers waited weeks to have their problems resolved. As a result of these findings, an interdepartmental task force was set up to improve cooperation in handling customer problems. Conflicts between departments were so intense, however, that it was difficult for the task force members to agree on solutions.

By the time each of these early opportunity projects was completed, the senior executives on the council gained firsthand experience in trying to solve customer problems; and they also gained a much more realistic view of the challenges they were asking their employees to tackle.

PHASE II: CLARIFY THE BUSINESS STRATEGY AND BUILD THE VISION

Once your company has established its current position with respect to value creation, you need to turn towards the future. A *value-creation strategy* should be formulated, followed by a program to communicate the strategy to the middle management group in order to gain their commitment to and suggestions for improving the strategy.

Formulate Value-Creation Mission, Strategy, and Plans

A written *mission, or vision, statement* must be prepared, stating what the company wishes to stand for in the minds of customers. A clear strategy for becoming distinctively better than competitors in areas critical to buyers should be defined.

The Maytag Corporation, which has for years been known for the quality of its products and its high levels of customer satisfaction, developed a value-based mission the hard way—by learning that poor quality doesn't pay. In the early years of its operation, Maytag made farm equipment, and one of the company's products was an attachment for threshing machines. Unfortunately, the attachment did not work well and farmers often discarded it and did the job by hand.

Maytag CEO Daniel J. Krumm reports that

> Mr. Maytag was disturbed by the sight of Iowa farms littered with his faulty feeders, but he was even more disturbed when harvest time came and the farmers refused to pay for them. So he issued an edict—"We will never again sell a bad piece of equipment"—which is the basis of our definition of quality: A product that works properly and dependably for a significant portion of its expected life.

Thus, product dependability has long been part of Maytag's mission and a principle by which it has distinguished itself in the marketplace.

A clear, well communicated strategy for value creation is critical to getting employees to develop the attitudes necessary for superior performance. "Peak performers are made, not born," says Charles A. Garfield, CEO of The Charles Garfield Group, Redwood City, California. "Give people an objective, not jobs." He notes that, at IBM, for instance, the mission is to provide the "best customer service in the world," and everyone in the company understands that. He goes on to suggest that the more specific the mission, the easier it is for employees to relate to. He cites one that couldn't be much more specific: "The mission of Bugs Burger Bug Killers is 'Get all the bugs.' Employees may or may not know that their job is to provide superior service, but they know [that] 99 percent is not good enough, they have to get all the bugs."

To develop a value-creation mission statement and supporting plans, it is often a good idea to convene an executive retreat away from the office. As you formulate the strategy, you should test it against these criteria, which Karl Albrecht has identified as the cornerstones of a customer satisfaction strategy:

- Is it non-trivial? Does it have weight? Your strategy must be more than simply a "motherhood" statement or slogan. It must be concrete and action-oriented.

- Does it convey a concept or mission which people in the organization can understand, relate to and put into action?

- Does it offer or relate to a critical benefit promise that is important to the customer? Does it focus on something the customer is willing to pay for?

- Does it differentiate the organization in some meaningful way from its competitors in the eyes of the customer?

- Is the strategy simple, unitary, easy to put into words and easy to explain to the customer?

Communicate Direction to Managers

After the senior management group has established a direction, a *communications strategy* must be formulated to make the new priorities clear to the middle management group. Your middle managers deserve an intensive development process tailored to their needs as potential leaders and advocates of the value-creation process. In fact, especially in cases where the strategy includes self-managed teams and the concomitant reduction in middle-management control, it is important to get middle managers to buy into the process before you take the process to the front line. Otherwise, middle management will justifiably feel bypassed and threatened, and some managers may therefore try to stall or sabotage improvement efforts.

The communications program for middle-level executives should include training seminars, meetings with top management to go over process objectives, and planning workshops where senior executives and their subordinates work together to develop implementation plans. You will also need to convene frequent review meetings and replanning sessions to help sustain the momentum with the middle management group and build ownership for the process.

David Clutterbuck, of the ITEM Group, suggests the following guidelines for getting a "customer care" program, as he calls it, underway. The same rules may be applied to the broader sweep of the value-creation process:

- *Insist on adequate resources.* Customer care is not cheap at first, but the payoff is better than for any other investment top management is likely to make.

- *Identify the key opinion leaders below top management.* Aim to get them on your side as committed insiders before the program begins, preferably through participation on steering groups.

- *Conduct customer research.* This will provide the facts, figures, and comments needed to get the message across to employees at all levels.

- *Schedule a continuous program of activities that will develop intensity.* In particular, aim to have at least one activity show rapid results to build early momentum.

- *Monitor and review frequently.* Every stage in the customer care awareness process has to be regularly reviewed. Meetings at which people can air grievances, as well as discuss their achievements, are essential. Everyone has to know what is happening. Customers and employees need to be kept up to date on new developments.

PHASE III: TRAIN AND COMMUNICATE WITH THE ORGANIZATION

In the third phase of the value-creation process, you will *communicate the new priorities* to front-line employees and *begin the training programs* necessary to help them develop new skills.

Develop Organizational Communications

First, a *communications* plan for front-line employees must be formulated. Reaching out to the "internal market" is just as important as communicating with the external customer market. For example, Air Canada has recently launched a multimillion-dollar internal marketing campaign to communicate to its 23,000 employees the importance of treating customers as top priority. The company's "Customer Care Campaign" is disseminating the company's customer care ideology through all company communications, including the airline's newspaper, 32 different newsletters, a news summary for executives, and computer updates transmitted through its reservation computer terminals. The company also held a "Customer Care Conference" at which employees discussed the need for better customer service.

Design and Implement Training Programs

As we mentioned in Chapter 7, your company must ensure that employees develop the skills necessary to produce quality goods and services, and to improve their responsiveness to customers. Especially important is *training employees in the basic problem-solving methods* they will need to resolve customer satisfaction issues at the front line.

Ken Blanchard, coauthor of *The One Minute Manager* series, believes that customer relationships mirror management/employee relationships. He notes that

> In the short and long runs, it is only through good management practices that good customer service can be achieved. By attending to what their employees need to stand on their own two feet and feel a sense of responsibility for their work, managers can establish effective relationships with them. These characteristics of help and support to employees are, in time, passed onto customers. They seldom go unnoticed.

Blanchard advises human resources practitioners to use training programs that help managers and front-line employees meet the following objectives:

- Pinpoint the characteristics of the working environment and the types of management behavior that facilitate the creation of a customer-satisfying organization.

- Identify the real nature of the company's business and who its customers are.
- Assess how the company's products are differentiated in the marketplace.
- Understand customer behavior and buying decisions.
- Determine key performance areas that will make the best impression on the customer.
- Learn management's role in a customer-value-driven company.

To inspire better attitudes among employees and regain a competitive market edge, companies are using a variety of techniques. For example, a noprofit medical facility in California requires all 3,200 of its employees to take a course on how to relate to patients and make them more comfortable during their stay in hospital. Patients are also provided with review cards so that they can comment on and commend especially courteous employees. The CEO follows up personally with each employee who receives a review card.

PHASE IV: IMPLEMENT FRONT-LINE IMPROVEMENTS

In the fourth phase of the process, you will organize the front-line employees in your organization to begin the process of *continuous improvement.* To support this effort, you will have to perform three tasks:

- Identify projects that will help create and deliver value to customers
- Redesign organizational systems
- Conduct follow-up training

Identify Customer Value Projects

Based on the data gathered during the first phase, and through employee brainstorming sessions, *specific value-creation projects* should be identified. Cross-functional employee task teams should set to work to identify the causes of problems and develop solutions. The customer-value-creation task force, described earlier, will oversee all these projects, set priorities, and provide the resources needed.

Value creation, quality, service, and customer satisfaction initiatives often fail because customer happiness is no one's functional responsibility. To combat this problem, some companies are taking a very pragmatic approach borrowed from the well known concept of quality circles. Value-creation project teams are formed throughout the company to look into and solve specific value-creation problems. By carrying a large number of value-creation projects to their successful conclusion, over time your company will be able to make tangible strides toward higher levels of performance.

Members of a value-creation project team should come from different departments and should include a mix of both junior and senior staff. Membership on the team should be determined by the nature of the opportunity or problem, not by traditional organizational relationships. Before the group can begin working effectively, team members will need training in group problem solving—as described in Chapters 6 and 7. Support from a trained facilitator will be vital during the first five or six meetings of the group.

The tasks of the value-creation project team are to discover the causes of customer dissatisfaction (which may include low levels of product or service quality) and to develop solutions to the problems identified. Team members will then find ways to prove out the effectiveness of their proposed remedies and to develop strategies for overcoming resistance to change within the organization. Finally, before disbanding, the group will develop control mechanisms to ensure that its improvements remain in effect.

BASF Corporation uses Quality Improvement Teams (QITs) to oversee its Quality Improvement Process (QIP). Each QIT, which consists of managers selected from each plant or business group, is responsible for identifying a problem, such as a recurring error. The QIT appoints a subcommittee to handle the problem. Subcommittee members introduce the necessary corrective action using skills they have been taught through BASF's "Quality Education System." The corrective action process includes identifying the original cause, implementing a solution, and devising a monitoring program. The subcommittee then evaluates the situation and follows up to prevent any possible recurrence of the problem.

The Metropolitan Life Insurance Company also uses QITs to ensure high levels of customer service and top-quality products. Each team is led by a manager and is responsible for developing a product or service according to certain performance standards. Quality improvement teams decide how to meet their own objectives and develop solutions to problems they might face, and they are encouraged to maintain an open dialogue with customers. One of the benefits of this communication with customers is the feedback they provide on the QIT's performance.

Redesign Organizational Systems

In addition to pinpointing specific problems, value-creation project teams will likely uncover procedures and organizational setups that hinder customer responsiveness. In such cases, whole *new policies and practices* must be developed, using value-creation principles as the basis of design. If the problems are systemic, solutions that do not include system changes will be no more than quick fixes, and quality will remain low. W. Edward Deming, the quality improvement consultant, has been widely quoted as pointing out, "Workers are never to blame for flaws in the process. Process design is management's responsibility."

Leonard L. Berry, best known for his research into how to improve the quality of service in financial institutions, suggests that managers

> [D]esign quality as a forethought into every form of support and technology your organization has. Whenever you do something new, whether implementing a new information system or other technology, you need to ask yourself: "Who is the customer for this new thing we are doing?" "What does this person expect, and how can we design the meaning of those expectations into this service?"

Customer satisfaction and, by extension, value creation can be improved dramatically by identifying and analyzing potential *fail points* in your company's relationships with customers. This is what the Richmond Metropolitan Blood Service of Richmond, Virginia, did when it examined its service quality. Project Coordinator Wendy M. Hosick says that the company found a critical fail point in the interpersonal relationship between blood donors and staff technicians. The people who drew blood had always been trained by the blood bank. They were technically qualified, she says, but many lacked the interpersonal skills needed to carry on a conversation with donors.

Hosick says that close analysis identified that donors valued the quality of the personal interaction with the blood technician more highly than technical quality. This knowledge led to a change in the way technicians were solicited in ads and evaluated in interviews. More emphasis was placed on the prospective employee's interpersonal skills than on his or her technical competence alone.

Conduct Follow-up Training

As improvement projects get underway, *additional employee training* will probably be needed to reinforce new skills. Since it takes time to learn new skills and reinforce new attitudes, your value-creation training strategy should include an ongoing program of activities to sustain momentum. Training that is not followed up regularly is a waste of time and money.

It is particularly useful to have work groups learn new methods by working together to solve real problems in their job environment. In this way, the training remains practical and employees stay enthusiastic because they can see the value of the new techniques as those innovations make their work more effective and rewarding.

At a General Electric plant in Bromont, Quebec, these work groups, or problem-solving teams, are part of an experiment the firm is conducting on autonomous work groups and employee committees. Hierarchical relationships have been minimized and employees are involved in the decision-making process. They spend an average of 35 percent of their time performing activities other than production work—including training courses and meetings. Despite the apparently large amount of time that employees spend away from "productive" work, teamwork and employee involvement has allowed GE and its employees to continuously improve their products and manufacturing processes.

PHASE V: LOCK IN CONTINUOUS IMPROVEMENT

The fifth phase of the value-creation process is extremely important. You need to *lock in the improvements* that have been initiated and provide the means to continually recognize and reward employees for demonstrating the new kinds of behavior you are seeking to foster within the company. You should:

- Create a recognition system
- Realign incentive systems
- Realign personnel policies

Create a Recognition System

The importance of *properly focused recognition systems* has already been discussed at length earlier in this book, but the power of recognition in creating a positive climate for change cannot be repeated too often. Informal recognition is also vital to reinforcing excellent performance. Catch people "doing something right," and make sure that customer-responsive behavior is recognized and communicated to other employees.

Vincent A. Sarni, Chairman and CEO of PPG, the Pittsburgh glass, paint, and chemical manufacturer, stresses that recognition is a key part of his company's quality improvement and customer satisfaction process.

> We have made an undeniable commitment. We've spent close to $15 million on quality programs and training materials designed to give employees a sense of ownership and authority. We say "thank you" a lot. We have Recognition Days. We give out awards—employees can get $150 a year in company stock just for signing up. I visit plants constantly. I get out there on the shop floor. I have lunch with the people who work there. What I am saying is [that] employees watch to see what top management does—not what it says.

The payoff from this recognition effort is evident in PPG employees' commitment to customer satisfaction. One PPG employee, for instance, noticed a hopper full of broken glass when he was making a delivery to an automotive plant. Although it was not PPG's glass, the PPG employee suggested ways to reduce breakage. His suggestions were implemented, and the customer was extremely grateful for his help. That is just one example of the "extra mile" mentality of PPG employees.

Realign Incentive Systems

While you examine your company's recognition programs, take a close look at *employee performance review policies*. Ensure that they reinforce behavior that supports the company's value-creation strategy. Performance review policies at Marriott hotels effectively link value creation with staff rewards and promotions. The hotel chain relies heavily on the "customer comment cards" filled out by customers during their stay. Both positive and negative customer remarks are recorded and used during an employee's performance appraisal. This system ensures that customer satisfaction remains a top priority with staff, it involves customers in the employee appraisal process, and it is an efficient way of rewarding or reprimanding a particular employee.

Bubbling Bath & Tub Works of Rockville, Maryland, has a brilliantly simple incentive policy that encourages top-quality work. The company, which was recognized by *INC.* magazine as one of the fastest-growing small businesses in the United States, provides superior repair service by attracting a top-caliber repair team, whose members are paid about three times the rate paid to repair technicians at competing firms. But to prevent costly callbacks, Bubbling Bath has a policy of not paying the technicians if they are called by customers within 30 days to fix the same problem. President Barry Fribush says that "Callbacks were a huge problem when we first started out. They were averaging 30 percent of all jobs. Since we have instituted this policy of not paying for them, they've just about been eliminated." Through this incentive program, Fribush is ensuring that the company provides what every customer wants—the job done right, the first time.

Realign Personnel Policies

To lock in continuous improvement, you will also have to make sure that *employee recruitment, training, and development programs are synchronized with the company's value-creation priorities.* IBM uses a rigorous but not-so-conventional method of recruiting and selecting new employees to ensure that they will fit in well with company philosophies. Instead of using professional recruiters, IBM gives the task to line managers. A single applicant could be interviewed by a marketing manager, a branch manager, and a regional vice-president. In this way, the people most knowledgeable about the job make the final selection.

Procter & Gamble, among other market-driven companies, has a comprehensive training and development program to ensure that employees deliver value in products and services. New P&G customer service representatives, for example, spend their first four to five weeks in a classroom learning how to solve problems and deal with the pressures of the job in a company-approved manner. By the time they are turned loose, they have the training they need to maintain smooth relationships with the company's customers.

PHASE VI: MONITOR AND REVIEW

In the final phase of the value-creation process, you should develop *measures to help track your progress.* This subject, which is discussed in more detail in the next chapter, includes the following key tasks:

- Develop performance measures
- Communicate performance information widely within the company
- Incorporate the review of performance measures during replanning

Develop Performance Measures

Your first task will be to *define internal operation measures* that are directly linked to the key variables associated with value creation. You must also establish means of regularly *monitoring customer* perceptions of your company's performance. Many companies have developed quantitative customer perception measures, known as customer satisfaction indexes, or "CSIs."

One such series of system-wide audits is used by the Marriott hotel chain to measure customer satisfaction. This "Guest Services Index" is based on an in-room survey distributed to each hotel customer to be filled out at the end of his or her stay. Through these surveys, Marriott is able to monitor its customer satisfaction performance constantly with up-to-date customer research data.

In *The Service Advantage,* Karl Albrecht has suggested a number of guidelines for designing an effective customer satisfaction measurement feedback system.

- *Start with your customer value-creation strategy.* Your performance measures should reflect the important elements that comprise your promise to customers. Federal Express promises "to deliver parcels by 10:30 A.M. the next day." The company's entire performance measurement system revolves around tracking the critical activities for achieving this goal.

- *Measure frequently.* The most effective measurement systems seem to be those that provide management and employees with monthly feedback. Longer intervals are not effective in creating a performance-enhancing feedback loop. Some companies even have weekly product and service quality and customer satisfaction systems.

•   *Ask customer-based questions.* The more specific and personal your questioning of customer perceptions, the more concrete will be the feedback you receive about the company's performance.

•   *Ask fair questions.* Track variables that are under the control of your organization. When devising the customer satisfaction measures for members of a specific work group or unit, focus these measures on elements of their jobs over which they can exercise some discretion.

•   *Collect both group and individual data.* Employees need to see not only how well they are performing, but also how their performance fits into the overall results for the work unit.

•   *Benchmark yourself.* Collect information on the sales, market share, and customer satisfaction achieved by your competitors, as well as by your own business.

•   *Collect both quantitative and qualitative information.* Your measurement system should collect numerical ratings that represent a broad cross-section of customer opinion. Actual customer comments are also useful because they help put the flesh on the bones of more abstract quantitative data.

•   *Make the results visible.* The displaying of results emphasizes their importance and stimulates employees to try to improve. At the Marriott hotels, front-desk results are posted where front-desk employees will see them, restaurant service results where kitchen and waiters will see them, and so on.

Communicate Performance Information

To communicate performance information throughout the company, you need to *develop mechanisms to circulate that information,* such a company videos, publications, bulletin board postings, management reports, and employee meetings. The most common mechanism by which employee performance measures are conveyed to all parts of the firm is the company newsletter. IBM, for example, puts out a company publication entitled *Think.* In one issue, a veteran employee who had been made a member of the Hundred Percent Club (the Club is for those who meet 100 percent of their sales and service targets) for the

30th consecutive year was profiled as a role model for younge employees.

In the retail trade, companies such as Sears display pictures of employees who have been selected as Employee of the Month or Year. Restaurants often proudly display employee awards and certificates of industry achievement in prominent locations, where they can be seen both by staff and by their clientele.

Incorporate the Review of Performance Measures during Replanning

As circumstances change—because of new markets, the introduction of new technology, or corporate growth, for example—*performance measures will need to be adapted to the new environment.* For this reason, the customer-value-creation task force should regularly review performance measures to stimulate refinements and improvements.

The Security Pacific National Bank uses a good system of ongoing measurement and replanning to evaluate branch service quality. Each branch manager receives a monthly report on his or her service performance. In order to obtain an adequate cross-section of opinion, that report is itself composed of a number of reports based on different methodologies. Among these are reports from "mystery shoppers," customer surveys, and the results of visits from bank quality-assurance officers.

The bank believes it is important to use multiple techniques to obtain different data for comparison. Each technique is important, but none stands alone. The monthly service quality review is used to track the effect of new service quality initiatives and to stimulate improvement if indicators show a decline.

Obviously, an effective value-creation process requires an integrated approach to implementation. The formation of the customer-value-creation task force, with the full participation of the most senior executives of the company, is the essential first step. But, after the value-creation strategy has been mapped out, you have to go company-wide with the process, getting employees at many levels and from all functional areas involved. Performance measures are a crucial part of the program—but not just for employees. The value-creation initiative itself must be rigorously assessed, which brings us to the final stage—tracking your performance.

10

Tracking Your Performance

Effective measurement . . . can't take the place of having a solid core product or service to begin with, nor is it a substitute for strategy, . . . but . . . lacking good measures, no company can assess its progress or adjust to changes in customer expectations.

William H. Davidow and Bro Uttal,
Total Customer Service: The Ultimate Weapon

Most managers are quite comfortable with the idea of using performance measures to monitor their businesses. Financial and cost measures, in particular, are a well developed and accepted part of managerial life; and your company probably has operations measures that it uses to keep track of the volume and efficiency of productive output. Even your sales organization keeps track of the number and types of sales calls made, sales expenses, and so forth. However, none of these indicators will help you keep track of the progress you are making in developing a competitive advantage through value creation. You need measures, or "metrics," as they are called, which are linked directly to the value-creation processes you have set up.

The Japanese have a term for the continuous and systematic effort to improve business performance: *"Kaizen." Kaizen* means gradual, unending improvement, doing "little things" better, setting and achieving ever higher standards. Masaaki Imai, in his book *Kaizen: The Key to Japan's Competitive Success*, explains that

> [T]he essence of *Kaizen* is simple and straightforward: *Kaizen* means improvement; moreover, *Kaizen* means ongoing improvement involving everyone, including both managers and workers. The *Kaizen* philosophy assumes our way of life—be it our working life, our social life or our home life—deserves to be constantly improved.

Part of that ongoing improvement effort consists of continuous performance measurement.

ESTABLISHING EFFECTIVE MEASURES

The Conference Board recently completed a survey of more than 150 companies in the United States, which examined how these organizations were tracking the success of their value-creation efforts. A wide range of methods was identified, as was the fact that increasing attention was being paid to the subject of measurement and performance tracking. The following customer satisfaction and quality indicators were reported:

- *Customer perceptions:* 57 percent of those surveyed analyze customer surveys, customer feedback, focus group reports, customer complaint statistics, and billing adjustments.

- *Profitability:* 42 percent evaluate the costs of poor quality (such as scrap, waste, and rework), as well as profit margins, cash flow, ratio analyses, and cost–benefit analyses.

- *Productivity:* 42 percent track yields, volume, efficiency, inventory turnover, overhead trends, ratio of production costs to revenue, down time, schedule compliance, and per-employee output.

- *Employee morale:* 38 percent monitor employee attitudes through surveys, focus groups, personal interviews, absenteeism, turnover, and complaints.

- *Market position:* 24 percent compare performance in the marketplace through industry statistics, market analyses, and consultants' studies.

Frank A. J. Gonsalves, of the management consulting firm Price Waterhouse, believes that effective performance measures are critical to managing a value-creation strategy. "Performance measures," he says, "should be derived from specific objectives and strategies. Feedback from performance measures will cause management to focus on improving performance as it relates to the organization's goals and objectives."

However, Gonsalves points out, most companies usually pay the most attention to internal, cost-focused measures of such things as manufacturing costs, material costs, and distribution costs. To assess value creation, you need to use a more wide-ranging set of indicators, including internal, non-cost-oriented ones such as percent of on-time delivery, number of new products, and design cycle time. You also need to measure your relative cost position using external benchmarks such as competitive cost position, relative R&D expenditures, supplier cost position, and relative labor costs. Finally, and perhaps most important, external, non-cost-focused measures of value creation should be made, including items such as the number of repeat buyers, the number of customer complaints, market share, and product image among target customers.

In other words, to effectively manage your company's value-creation strategies and programs, you will need *both* internal and external performance measures. In *Total Customer Service: The Ultimate Weapon,* William H. Davidow and Bro Uttal suggest three different internal and external metrics that are most useful: process measures, product measures, and satisfaction measures.

Process Measures

These are the common indicators used by most businesses. They are used to help control the process by which a product or service is created. However, these measures may never have been validated for their usefulness in tracking output variables that are important to external customers. Davidow and Uttal observe that companies that are well known for product and service quality excellence "balance . . . measures that keep employees' eyes fixed on the customer. They strive to ensure that measures used for process and product are not self-defeating, poorly structured or unrelated to customer needs and expectations."

Consider, for example, the Campbell Soup Company and its instant frozen breakfasts. The company successfully overcame production process problems that made for rubbery English muffins and blueberries that "bled" through the rest of the breakfast. But the company made the error of focusing too much on internal process measures at the expense of truly understanding customer expectations. Had the company done better marketing research, it would have foreseen slow consumer acceptance of the product and could have saved itself the effort of perfecting the frozen breakfast concept, which it later dropped.

Product Measures

These focus on the conformance of a product or service to the specifications or standards set for it or to the relative performance after purchase and use by the customer. As useful as good product metrics are, they can suffer from the same weaknesses as process measures do. The standards you develop risk not being clearly linked to customer expectations. You must guard against using measures that are convenient for your business but are out of touch with your buyers.

This kind of inappropriate measure was used by one financial services company when it adopted a standard response time to customer inquiries of 14 to 21 days. That might sound like an acceptable standard, but it wasn't: 60 percent of customers expected responses within seven days. A utility company made the same type of error when it set a standard of meeting 92 percent of repair appointments, even though this meant that more than 3,000 customers a month would be angered by repair people who showed up late, or not at all.

Satisfaction Measures

These use feedback collected directly from customers about their perception of your company's quality and service. Usually, these types of measures are taken through regular surveys. Analysis of complaints, periodic focus groups, toll-free telephone lines, customer comment cards, and management visits to customers will serve the same purpose. By using measures such as these, you can determine whether the good intentions embodied in your company's value-creation program are actually resulting in improved customer attitudes, acceptance, and repurchase behavior.

Companies that use customer satisfaction measures may be found in a variety of industries, collecting different types of data for different purposes. One research and development company, for example, used the data from customer satisfaction measures to design an internal performance model. That model is now used by each department to meet customers' needs and expectations with products superior to those of the competition. Managers and staff also used it to define performance standards from the customer's perspective and to work more closely with clients in accurately plotting the strengths and weaknesses of the company's service and products.

At the Dow Chemical Company, customer service revolves around helping customers handle hazardous products safely. The company's customer satisfaction measurement surveys have an unusual twist. For example, to perform an industrial hygiene survey, an industrial hygienist—at Dow's expense—takes air samples at the customer's plant, returns them to the Dow labs for analysis, and then sends a formal report back to the client's management. By providing this kind of survey, Dow determines whether or not the chemicals it sells are being used safely and properly; and thus it indirectly ensures that the client is satisfied with the product.

Developing a Measurement Program

The management cliche "you can't manage what you can't measure" really does apply to value-creation strategies. Without relevant performance indicators, you have no way of gauging your progress. Follow these guidelines to ensure that your measurement program is effective and accepted by employees:

• *Make sure the measurement activities have top management support.* Quality consultant Philip Crosby stresses the importance of top management commitment to measurement activities. "The organization," he says, "has to have clear goals and objectives that the employees can respect. . . . The management has to be consistently dedicated to having everyone understand and be able to meet the performance requirements . . . to reach those goals and objectives."

• *Involve employees in the development of customer satisfaction measures.* One major Canadian insurance company followed this advice by holding a series of employee workshops to debate proposed service measures and standards. As a result, improvements were made to the measures themselves and employees accepted them more readily when they were ultimately introduced, because they had personally contributed to their development.

- *Ensure that the measures used are relevant to managers and employees in performing their day-to-day jobs.* The Amway Grand Plaza Hotel has ensured that measures are relevant by asking employees to set their own service standards. Not only do employees have good ideas about what measures are most useful, but staff-developed standards are often more demanding than what management would recommend.

- *Make sure there is a feedback loop that links customer satisfaction measures to manager and employee performance appraisal.* For example, at Herman Miller, the Michigan manufacturer of furniture systems, the decision to award a bonus check to an employee depends on his or her contribution to the quality of service, and especially on how highly clients have rated the level of quality.

If your company's value creation process is to be implemented effectively, you will have to develop new measures of performance. Balance your internal, cost-based measures with process and product metrics that are closely linked to variables affecting external customer requirements. Most important, make sure that you are getting regular feedback directly from customers about their perceptions of your performance.

EFFECTIVE COMPLAINT MANAGEMENT

It takes courage to keep in touch with customers. Some of their feedback will include complaints, but customer complaints are not always merely a source of grief. By responding effectively to customer complaints in a timely and productive way, you can build up a lot of customer good will. An effective complaint monitoring and management system can also be a powerful tool for keeping in touch with customers and responding to their future needs and expectations.

Most businesses know instinctively that customers who complain are doing them a favor. First, complaints give your company the opportunity to win customers back and keep their business. Second, it is better to have buyers complain to you—instead of to other potential customers. By receiving a complaint, your company is, in effect, getting a second chance to win the customer's good will.

Statistics show that over half the customers who complain about major problems will buy from the offending company again—if the complaint is resolved. Better yet, if the company responds quickly, as many as 95 percent will remain loyal and continue to buy the firm's products regularly.

Unfortunately, many customers with problems never complain. As we mentioned in Chapter 1, for every unhappy customer you hear from, as many as 26 other customers with similar problems, and possibly customers with serious problems, never call at all. This means that the trends you identify, and the problems you fix today, can have an impact far beyond the number of people you hear from on a day-to-day basis. These noncomplainers are the group least likely to buy from your company again. Studies show that between 65 and 95 percent of noncomplaining customers have been lost forever. It is critical, therefore, that you encourage customers to give you a second chance, which will allow you to correct the problems they have encountered.

General Electric has invested millions of dollars in turning customer complaints into business opportunities. The company's Answer Center, located in Louisville, Kentucky, receives customer inquiries 24 hours a day, 365 days a year and handles 15,000 calls a day from people having problems or considering making a purchase of a GE product. There are more than 650,000 possible answers to customer inquiries stored in the company's computerized database, which is available to customer service representatives at the touch of a button. This ensures a fast, knowledgeable response to almost any inquiry. N. Powell Taylor, manager of the Center, says that GE's investment in managing customer inquiries is just as important to the company as investments in production capacity, technology, and personnel. "Every contact with the customer gives us a chance to enhance brand loyalty," he says.

In addition to building better customer relationships, General Electric has derived other benefits from operating the Center. GE designers and engineers sometimes bring new products to the Center to get reactions from the service representatives. Ideas for new products and improvements and modifications of existing products are also developed by analyzing the types of complaints received. Taylor notes that:

> Our people talk to 20,000 customers a year, so if they have been here for three years, which is about average, and you get ten of them in a room, you indirectly have about 500,000 to 600,000 customers represented. It is a powerful tool for understanding what needs to be fixed and what does not, and for expressing consumers' emotions about features and preferences.

According to Dick Berry and Carol Suprenant of the Department of Business and Management at the University of Wisconsin—Extension, a comprehensive policy for complaints and inquiries should encompass a number of activities, described in the following sections.

Define Responsibility

Many companies have no *clear guidelines for responsibility and accountability* for responding to complaints. In one major food ingredients firm, for example, complaints, or "investigation requests," are routed throughout the company without ever landing on the desk of anyone who is accountable for resolving the problem. As a result, an investigation request turns into a finger-pointing exercise in which each internal department tries to lay blame on another. In the meantime, the customer's problem may never be resolved.

You need to clarify which individual or group is responsible for receiving, processing, and resolving complaints, and who is responsible for handling inquiries. Owens-Illinois Glass Container, a glass manufacturer, did this when it reorganized its system of responding to monetary claims submitted by commercial customers who had suffered a financial loss due to an incorrect or late delivery of product. The responsibility for investigating and resolving all complaints was moved from an accounting function in the sales administration department to the quality assurance department. The company has also streamlined its decision-making process to make settlements more timely, sensible, and fair to all concerned.

Spell Out Authority

Who has the *authority and resources* in your company to resolve a customer problem? One of the biggest complaints that customers have about complaint handling is their inability to find someone with enough knowledge and authority to take action on their problems. Employees are often handcuffed by procedures and red tape that prevent them from making obvious adjustments for customers that would settle matters quickly and build good will for the future. A great deal of this authority can be effectively delegated to field or front-line personnel, although clear limits must be defined.

Armco Steel is one company that has moved to employer front-line employees to resolve customer complaints. The enterprise intentionally works at keeping upper management out of complaints investigations, and instead approaches problem solving from the bottom up. As General Sales Manager Jerry Judd explains, some clients try to involve management in the complaint process by circumventing the front-line employees (in this case, service and mill representatives). But Armco consistently brings the problem back down to the product center level, where "ninety-nine out of 100 cases are settled. . . ."

Set Up Procedures

Clear processes and procedures for routing complaints and inquiries will ensure that all those who need to know are kept informed and that proper record keeping and analysis can be undertaken. If the complaints you receive are not properly documented and evaluated to establish the patterns they form, you will be missing out on an important source of ongoing market information. Leading companies track complaints carefully, breaking them down into specific categories which can be used to discern both volume and category trends over time. This allows them to reduce the number of complaints category by category and to respond quickly if a sudden upward spike in one complaint category becomes apparent.

Winnebago Industries uses this type of categorization method. Each complaint it receives about recreational vehicles or motor homes is coded by product, service, or part, along with relevant information indicating why the problem exists. Then it is added to a computer bank. Information may be retrieved in a variety of combinations, such as service complaints according to dealer, vehicle complaints according to model, complaints according to service district, and each dealer's percentage of complaints as related to retail sales activity. This system keeps the company aware of the number and types of complaints it receives, and quickly brings any problem areas to its attention.

Set Time Standards

There are few things more annoying to a complaining customer than delays in resolving the problems. It is therefore essential to *incorporate time standards* into your complaint management procedure. One study undertaken by *Sales & Marketing Management* found that the average response time to complaint letters was 23 days, with a spread of five to 72 days. Companies committed to value creation are moving aggressively to resolve customer problems more quickly than this. They also monitor the time it takes to resolve a problem, not merely the response time for a letter or phone call. Your standards should focus on how long it takes to actually rectify a customer's problem, because this is the standard by which customers will judge you.

Strict time standards govern complaint handling at *USA Today's* National Customer Service Center, as mentioned in Chapter 5. Employees are required to adhere to the following standards: Respond to each customer request with one phone call and spend no more than two minutes per customer call; take only 20 seconds or four rings to answer each incoming call; answer all incoming letters within 48 hours; and resolve all complaints within five days.

Establish Follow-up Procedures

Follow-up procedures are probably the most important part of your company's complaint management process, since, without them, you will have no way of ensuring that complaints and inquiries are brought to a successful conclusion. You may have to establish a priority system whereby problems involving actual damage or injury are handled first. Next in line may come situations in which the product is not working, followed by cases in which the product is still functional, but requires some repair.

Mediacom, Canada's largest outdoor advertising company, which operates thousands of outdoor billboards, illuminated shopping mall posters, and transit shelter signs, has a quick-reflex follow-up procedure to handle complaints about the appearance of transit shelter signs that are especially prone to damage, dirt, and vandalism. Within 24 hours of receiving a complaint from a customer (who has already been provided with a toll-free complaint number), the customer is called back and told what was done to fix the problem. This feedback loop has been very effective in building customer good will. Kevin O'Leary, vice-president of the company, says that

> At first, customers were amazed that we actively solicited their complaints. But the follow-up calls earned us even more good will. People like to know we take action on their recommendations. As well, another benefit of the follow-up calls was that it became obvious to all

our major customers that we were committed to high quality and service and our competitors were not.

Complaint management is not a cost to be avoided within your company. Complaints are a valuable way to stay in touch with the needs and expectations of your customers and an investment in customer good will that will strengthen your business position for the future.

BENCHMARKING YOUR PERFORMANCE

Benchmarking, as we mentioned in Chapter 9, is an effective tool for measuring your performance against that of your competitors. With good data on competitive performance, you will be in a better position to exploit competitor weaknesses and build on your own strengths. Benchmarking studies can be undertaken to measure your performance against the leaders in other industries as well. In this way, you can compare your achievement against those of the best performers, regardless of business sector, to determine whether your company is doing its utmost to become a customer-satisfying business.

For example, IBM, a leader in the use of benchmarking techniques, compares itself to DEC in the work stations business, Canon in the photocopier market, L. L. Bean in warehouse operations, John Deere in service parts logistics systems, and Ford in assembly automation processes. The company has even studied the Federal Reserve's bill-scanning procedures and Citicorp's document-processing activity to learn better methods for performing these tasks.

Benefits of Benchmarking

Xerox Corporation, as mentioned in the previous chapter, is another leader in the development and application of benchmarking research. David T. Kearns, chief executive officer of Xerox, defines benchmarking as follows: "Benchmarking is the continuous process of measuring products, services and practices against the toughest competitors or those companies recognized as industry leaders." Other major players in North American business have also begun benchmarking programs during the last five years: Ford, Eastman Kodak, GTE, General Motors, Motorola, AT&T, Du Pont, Corning, and NYNEX. The experience of these companies, and others, suggests that the following benefits can be gained by including benchmarking activities in your value-creation process:

•   *Improved ability to meet customer requirements.* By gathering data about customer needs, how well you meet these needs, and how you compare to the competition, your company can more easily make necessary improvements or changes that will allow your company to go the extra mile in creating value for customers.

•   *Assurance that company goals reflect external realities.* Rather than setting targets based on internally developed standards, or on the extrapolation of past achievement, benchmark data force a company to look at external standards of performance.

•   *Improved measures of productivity.* By continuous studies of customer requirements and the best industry practices, it is possible to isolate and solve the most important business problems in your company. Through this process, your resources are applied most effectively, thereby enhancing productivity.

•   *Enhanced competitive position.* With a deeper understanding of competitors, effective business strategies for outperforming them can be developed.

•   *Greater awareness of the industry's best practices.* Benchmarking will help you find better business methods more quickly, sparing you the painful process of having to discover these on your own.

Benchmarking was a vital part of the GTE Service Corporation's strategy to create and deliver value for its customers. In 1982, the company launched a competitor comparison program, called "BEST," which was designed to discover what it would take for GTE to be the best in all facets of production and service.

Under the BEST Program, all staff, functional groups, and major business units were asked to define their key competitors and to compare their own performance in relevant areas. This helped GTE establish a quality-improvement policy, define more clearly the needs of customers and their expectations, and reinforce the need for quality leadership. As a result of the program, GTE redefined internal measurements of quality, improved internal management processes, and upgraded the quality of products and services purchased from suppliers.

While there are several ways to apply benchmarking concepts, a typical analysis will fall into one of three categories: strategic benchmarking, operational benchmarking, and business management benchmarking.

Strategic Benchmarking

In *strategic benchmarking* studies, researchers compare different business strategies and determine whether these strategies lead to marketplace success. Lawrence S. Pryor, vice-president of Kaiser Associates, of Vienna, Virginia, writes in the *Journal of Business Strategy* that the following issues should be addressed in a strategic benchmarking study:

- Which segments of the market is the competition focusing on?
- Is the competitor pursuing a commodity (low-cost) strategy, or a specialty (value-added) strategy?
- What level of investment is the competitor making in the market, and in what areas are those investments being made (R&D, factory automation, sales, and marketing)?
- From which functional areas is the competitor deriving its true strength and competitive advantage?

Strategic benchmarking can yield valuable insights. For example, some industry observers believe that AT&T's failure in the computer industry was due to a lack of strategic insight into the key success factors for the industry. The company seemed poised for success when it entered the computer market. It had world-class research and development capability and expertise in high-technology products.

However, had the company carried out strategic benchmarking studies, it would have discovered that its own strengths were not relevant to the needs of the market. By the end of the 1980s, when AT&T entered the market, anybody could make a computer; what was important to most users was not advanced technology, but responsive sales support and reliable service. A high-quality, experienced sales and service force, which IBM had already developed, was the key to success. Consequently, AT&T was forced to withdraw from the market.

Woodward's, the department store chain that dominated the western Canadian market for decades, would also have benefited from a strategic benchmarking study. The company built its success on offering modestly priced merchandise to the "average Canadian family" and sold everything from gasoline to household pets. But the company's performance has recently faltered by trying to satisfy all price segments of the market by offering, for example, dining room tables priced from $100 to $5,000. Trying to compete in all price ranges resulted in mediocre products and services in each category, making the store an easy prey for its newer competitors, specialty shops.

Operational Benchmarking

Operational benchmarks are most often used to help a company understand and attempt to exceed "best-in-class" companies in a specific activity or function. To make the most of operational benchmarking, you need to determine which function has the greatest strategic leverage in your industry. In other words, which area would most improve your strategic position if you could meet or exceed best-in-class performance? Operational benchmarking should therefore be focused on improving your relative cost position or discovering ways to increase market differentiation.

Cost benchmarking is the most common form of operational benchmarking. Data are gathered about other companies to discover how these firms operate specific functions at less cost and/or with fewer people than your company does. These data can be very helpful in challenging traditional ways of thinking within your firm about its level of efficiency and the real potential for improvement.

Business consultant Timothy R. Furey cites a case study of a firm he refers to as "Company X," whose plastic components were being underpriced by a smaller regional manufacturer. Using the benchmarking technique, Company X identified four key cost performance measures: the price it paid for the major raw material used in the production of its products, the material yield, the number of man-hours required to produce 100 units, and the average wage rate.

Using these measures, the company compared itself not only to the regional competitor, but also against the leading national competitor. From the comparison, Company X discovered that the smaller competitor could afford to cut its prices because it was using a lower-quality and less expensive raw material. That raw material did not measure up to the product quality performance expected by Company X's customers, however, so Company X felt justified in charging its clients a premium price for its product. However, the comparison between Company X and its leading national competitor indicated that the latter's raw material yields and labor productivity were better, motivating Company

X to examine its manufacturing process and make productivity improvements.

In other operational benchmarking studies, researchers systematically assess how competitors (or leaders in other industries) achieve differentiation in the marketplace through product features, product quality, customer service, and brand image. One company in the electrical equipment market used the benchmarking process to verify what clients had perceived as the organization's lower level of technical support, compared to the service offered by competitors. By analyzing the differences in levels of service support within the various competing companies, the deficiencies in the company's technical support service became apparent. The firm then decided to narrow the service gap between itself and its competitors by increasing the number of technical support staff, devising a more attractive salary scale to retain a better caliber of employee, and offering stronger incentives to the company's dealers to carry and promote its products.

Business Management Benchmarking

Management benchmarking refers to analyses of the support functions within competing companies or other best-in-class performers. In this kind of study, "staff" and administrative functions, such as the human resources, research and development, order processing, and management information systems departments, are benchmarked. Because overhead costs are a key concern in many companies, the evaluation of the ways in which best-in-class performers handle these functions is becoming more and more important to many companies. Often, the value of such studies lies in the fact that they make support-function staff think more clearly about who their "customers" are within the company and how they might better meet the needs of those they serve.

When the internal legal group of one diversified company became concerned about its large size and increased costs, it benchmarked its activities against the legal departments of other conglomerates, as well as outside law firms. Using the benchmarking data, the legal group divided up its wide variety of functions into 24 different categories and determined which activities should be kept in-house and managed more efficiently. Other functions were contracted out to law firms, which resulted in an increase in quality in some of these activities, as well as reduced costs.

In another firm, an internal reprographics group benchmarked itself against outside suppliers and reprographics groups of other companies in an effort to better service its internal customers, who in some instances were sending work to small outside copy shops. Using the benchmarking process, the reprographics group concluded that improvements were necessary in its turnaround time for orders, that the pricing strategy for certain types of work was out of line with prevailing outside rates, and that both department management and staff were generally out of touch with the diverse needs of the company's users.

The Benchmarking Process

Robert C. Camp, in his book *Benchmarking: The Search for Industry Best Practices That Lead to Superior Performance,* describes the 10 steps that Xerox uses in carrying out its benchmarking programs:

- *Identify what is to be benchmarked.* You can benchmark any function of the business for which a "product," or output, can be defined. However, you should only attempt to benchmark key functions, which represent a high percentage of your total costs, or which play a key role in differentiating your company in the marketplace.

- *Identify comparative companies.* These should be the best-in-class, superior performers from whom you can learn the most. Included in this group could be direct competitors, potential competitors, or out-of-industry companies that have a superior level of performance.

- *Determine the data to be collected.* The method of investigation will vary with the type of performance variables you have chosen for comparison. These variables could include cost and overhead comparisons, customer satisfaction levels, quality levels, service levels, product line breadth, financial performance, market share, sales growth, and profitability. The most important information, however, is not the results that a particular company achieves, but an understanding of the operation of the business processes and practices used to achieve these results. Benchmarking investigations are usually completed through analyses of existing published information, interviews with industry observers and, where possible, visits to the companies being studied.

- *Determine the current performance "gap".* The next step is to measure your own performance and compare it to that of the benchmark partners. This can be difficult, since the data you collect is often incomplete. Nevertheless, even if the resulting comparisons are not exact, you can identify performance gaps that will point to improvement opportunities.

- *Project future performance levels.* Look at trend data to determine whether the gap between your company's performance and that of your benchmark partner is likely to close or continue to widen.

- *Communicate benchmark findings and gain acceptance.* A crucial test of the benchmarking process will be convincing the executives who are responsible for the functions being benchmarked that the findings are sound and based on credible analyses. Benchmark results need to be communicated to all parts of the organization that must support the changed practices.

- *Establish functional goals.* The next step is to translate the findings of the benchmarking analysis into a new set of operating goals, principles, and standards. The purpose of the benchmarking exercise is to determine new, externally based performance targets that the organization should strive to meet.

- *Develop action plans.* The crucial step during benchmarking is to develop action programs for improving your performance. These may include working harder to strengthen identified weaknesses, emulating the competition, or attempting to introduce practices that are superior to those being used by your business rivals.

- *Implement specific actions and monitor progress.* The action steps taken must include provision for specific milestones to be achieved and identification of who will be accountable. Results must be measured and communicated to those carrying out the action program so that they can adjust their activities as necessary.

- *Recalibrate benchmarks.* The final step is to recalibrate the benchmark performance targets periodically. Companies often forget that while they are improving their operations, competitors and other best-in-class performers are improving as well. Therefore, benchmarking is a dynamic process that requires a constant rechecking of the performance standards developed during the comparison process.

Benchmarking is a powerful technique for ensuring that your company steadily improves the value it delivers to customers. It will not only keep you alert to competitors' marketplace results but will also reveal the practices and processes they are using to build their businesses and keep their customers happy.

USING A CUSTOMER SATISFACTION INDEX TO MONITOR YOUR PERFORMANCE

Many companies have introduced *customer satisfaction indexes* to track their performance on an ongoing basis, since a good customer satisfaction rating usually indicates that customers are receiving value for their money. A customer satisfaction index, or CSI, is an overall measure of your company's or department's performance against selected product or service attributes that customers judge to be critical to their satisfaction. Examples of such attributes would include speed of delivery, order-filling, speed of complaint handling, meeting specs, ease of ordering, and so forth. CSIs should be recorded regularly; indeed, many companies use CSIs to grade their performance monthly.

Introducing a CSI is your company's best means of overcoming the difficulties associated with translating its corporate commitment to value creation into action. It offers managers a tangible measure of their customer satisfaction performance and will guide them in their efforts to improve. For example, Esso Chemical Canada uses a customer service index to measure customers' perceptions of its total "product/service/package offering" and to define which areas require improvement. The index quantifies for the company's marketing, distribution, and manufacturing executives the organization's performance in such areas as product quality, time and place of delivery, and form and accuracy of documentation.

Each CSI must be customized to address the specific needs of your company's target customers. Depending on the nature and number of variables being monitored, CSIs also vary in complexity. For example, the Financial Products Group, a Chicago-based consulting firm in the financial services industry, has developed a CSI for banks that consists of 20 attributes, including responsiveness, interest rates, friendliness, number of employees, parking convenience, service literature, and advertising. By contrast, DEC, the computer manufacturer, has a CSI comprising 55 component variables.

There are five major steps in developing and effectively using a CSI for your company:

- Define the scope to be addressed by the CSI
- Identify what criteria are associated with customer satisfaction
- Develop standard measures of performance
- Design a monitoring program
- Link the CSI to performance management

Define Scope

Before analyzing specific customer needs, you must clearly *establish the coverage and depth of customer satisfaction* which the CSI should monitor. A CSI whose objective is to measure overall corporate performance will take longer and cost more than one that focuses on a specific department or division's performance. Similarly, a detailed monitoring of 20 customer satisfaction variables for each department will require much more effort than a regular measure of only the top five criteria.

Identify Weightings for Criteria

The next step is to *identify and assign different weightings* to each of the key customer satisfaction criteria. Each criterion will, in turn, have to be broken down into more specific service or product performance attributes. For example, 3M's transportation department uses performance standards based on important factors such as the initial pick-up of the product, what happens to it while it is en route, the actual delivery, and, finally, the follow-up procedures. Among the key attributes assessed during the pick-up process is timing—whether pick-up was early, late, or missed altogether. While in transit, key attributes include whether or not there was a carrier breakdown, or notification of nondelivery if there was a problem. Key attributes during delivery include an early, late, or damaged delivery, and delivery to the wrong location. Follow-up-procedure attributes include incorrect or late billing and claims problems.

Focus groups are commonly used to identify customer satisfaction attributes, while surveys are typically used to establish the relative priorities for them. For example, your research might lead you to define the key influences on customer satisfaction, the specific attributes associated with each particular factor, and their relative importance, as shown on the next page.

Key Satisfaction Influences	Specific Attributes	Relative Weight
Product quality	Zero defects Meeting performance promises	30
After-sales service	Speed of response Trouble-free problem resolution Efficiency of after-sales support personnel	30
Dependability	Order-fill Meeting specified date of delivery	20
Ease of access	Emergency accessibility Ease of making contact Efficiency of contact personnel	15
Administration	Error-free invoicing	5
		100

Develop Performance Standards

After you have defined the key attributes that are important to customers, you must *define target standards of performance for each attribute.* These performance standards might include 48-hour service calls, 90 percent order-fill, and five-minute-long waiting lines. Standards can be developed based on any one or a combination of the following:

- Customer requirements as expressed in a survey of customers
- Benchmark comparisons with competitors
- Judgments based on the experience of company executives

The York Engineering Center, part of Philip Morris U.S.A.'s engineering department, which rebuilds cigarette-making and cigarette-packing machines for the Philip Morris factories, has developed five sets of measures to evaluate the quality, productivity, and timeliness of its service delivery. These measures include a machinery quality survey, a service assistance survey, a quality assurance audit for each machine, rebuild efficiency measures, and scheduled completion measurement.

To improve performance, the center has developed a five-year plan setting long-range goals for each category of measurement. Each group of measures is summarized to an index score yielding a point score of 1.0

for "poor" to 5.0 for "excellent." The machine quality survey and the service assistance survey achieved a rating of 3.0 for the first year of the program, but both were expected to receive a 5.0 rating by the end of the fifth year.

Design a Monitoring Program

The final step in developing the CSI involves the design of a regular monitoring program. Normally, it will be possible to track some performance variables internally by establishing appropriate monitoring mechanisms. For example, weekly reports on the percentage of service calls made within the 48-hour standard, or reports on the number of customer complaints received, can serve the monitoring process.

For variables that cannot be measured internally, a regular survey of customers will have to be undertaken. The survey, usually conducted by telephone or through a mailed questionnaire, should be short, focus on the key CSI variables, cover a representative sample of your customer base, and allow for a comparison of the company's performance relative to that of its competitors.

Ideally, these surveys should be conducted at predetermined, regular intervals. Some companies do them monthly, or every second month. Ratings achieved for each satisfaction attribute then need to be translated into relative scores based on each attribute's weighted contribution to the overall CSI. Adding up each score gives the CSI performance for that period.

The Financial Products Group, mentioned earlier, asks a random sample of people to evaluate bank, credit union, or thrift institutions on 20 attributes and scores for specific subcategories, such as facilities, operations, pricing, and staffing. This procedure allows a financial institution to see where its strengths and weaknesses are. A specific bank might, for example, receive an overall rating of 4.68 out of 6. Individual scores for facilities attributes might be 4.7; operations attributes, 4.79; pricing attributes, 4.51; and staffing attributes, 4.65.

Link to Performance Management

To use the CSI within your organization to the maximum benefit, you should follow these principles:

- The role and importance of the CSI should be communicated extensively throughout the company, at each operational level.
- Systems should be developed to link employee rewards to the CSI, reinforcing the importance of customer satisfaction as a company priority.
- Finally, follow-up mechanisms should be initiated to ensure that appropriate corrective action will be undertaken to improve overall performance.

Sherry Khan, a manager of Marketing Services at Esso Chemical Canada, says that the company's original CSI has broadened and evolved to the point that it may now be considered an "index of excellence." The index is now measuring performance in all areas of the company's business and has proven to be so effective that it is being adopted by other Esso affiliates around the world.

Chrysler began a CSI measurement program in 1980. It gives every one of its auto dealers an individual score based on its own customers' opinions of the service they received at the dealership. The program is designed to give dealers additional information that will help them be successful in the marketplace.

Each dealer's customer satisfaction index is developed from two surveys. The first survey is mailed to all of Chrysler's retail customers within three months of their purchase date. It focuses on the condition of the vehicle at delivery and, if customers have had need of service, their satisfaction with it. A second survey is mailed at the end of one year to every customer who has been to the dealer for warranty work. It focuses on the customer's overall satisfaction with the service at the dealership. Customers rate their satisfaction in a number of areas, on a scale of "1" (poor) to "4" (excellent).

To use the CSI to encourage better service at the dealership level, Chrysler devised a reward initiative called *America's Team*. Chuck Halsig, manager, Dealership Management Education, Service and Parts Operations, says that America's Team was designed to be a "continuously evolving system for rewarding improvements in our dealerships' service culture and their customers' satisfaction."

America's Team works as follows: At the beginning of each calendar quarter, Chrysler establishes a CSI improvement objective for each participating dealership. If the dealership meets the objective, everybody on the team, including everyone from the service manager to service technicians, shares equally in the rewards. The objective is based on the dealership's current CSI score plus an attainable improvement factor. The dealership pays half the cost of financial and merchandise rewards/bonuses, while Chrysler pays the other half.

Every team member has the opportunity to earn up to $2,000 per year in "satisfaction shares," which can be redeemed for prizes ranging from sporting goods and furs to travel and home electronics. Participants can even use their shares to purchase tools for use on the job. Chrysler worked out an agreement whereby technicians could redeem their shares, dollar for dollar, for Snap-On and Mac brand tools, the two leading suppliers of professional automobile repair tools.

To implement the necessary communications and training, Chrysler uses a group of dedicated field coordinators whose sole responsibility is America's Team. The company also provides in-dealership skill development sessions on such topics as team-building and listening techniques, which Chrysler believes have helped America's Team perform to expectations.

Measurement and feedback are important parts of the America's Team concept. Each dealer receives a monthly standings report indicating his or her scores for the latest three-month period, as well as cumulative scores for the last 12 months. An America's Team newsletter also keeps all participants up to date on details of America's Team activities. A series of training videos is distributed to further supplement the information provided.

Halsig believes that this integrated approach to the use of CSIs, in which the index measurements are coupled with training, rewards, and feedback, has been responsible for an improvement in the company's satisfaction scores. During one period, the scores improved for 45 straight months. Indeed, Chrysler often achieves the top ranking for customer satisfaction in surveys conducted by the independent research firm J. D. Power and Associates.

Well designed and thoughtfully applied CSIs such as these are useful tools for encouraging continuous improvement and measuring the progress you are making through your value-creation efforts.

ASSESSING THE EFFECTIVENESS OF YOUR CUSTOMER-VALUE-IMPROVEMENT PROCESS

Quality managers have developed techniques not only to evaluate the quality of their companies' products and services, but also to evaluate the system by which value is delivered. The tool for doing this is the quality system audit or review. Quality system audits identify the elements of the management system that must function properly in order to deliver the high-quality products and services that result in customer satisfaction.

One of the best-known examples of such audits is the Malcolm Baldrige National Quality Award audit (see Figure 10–1), which the

---

1.0   Leadership

The senior management's success in creating quality values and in building the values into the way the company operates.

2.0   Information and Analysis

The effectiveness of the company's collection and analysis of information for quality improvement and planning.

3.0   Strategic Quality Planning

The effectiveness of the company's integration of the customer's quality requirements into its business plan.

4.0   Human Resource Utilization

The success of the company's efforts to realize the full potential of the work force for quality.

5.0   Quality Assurance of Products and Services

The effectiveness of the company's systems for assuring quality control of all its operations and in integrating quality control with continuous quality improvement.

6.0   Quality Results

The company's improvements in quality and demonstration of quality excellence based upon quantitative measures.

7.0   Customer Satisfaction

The effectiveness of the company's systems to determine customer requirements and demonstrated success in meeting them.

Together, the seven Examination Categories address all major components of an integrated, prevention-based quality system built around continuous quality improvement.

Figure 10–1. Malcolm Baldrige National Quality Award Criteria

United States National Bureau of Standards uses to judge companies that have adopted effective quality and customer satisfaction management processes. By becoming familiar with the Baldrige criteria, you can develop your own set of evaluation guidelines for checking the health of your value-creation efforts. It is often useful to have a third party carry out the review, to keep it objective.

In the Baldrige Award audit, companies are judged in a number of categories and subcategories, each with a set of criteria and associated point values. A maximum of 1,000 points can be scored. The categories for evaluation are as follows:

- Leadership
- Information and analysis
- Strategic quality planning
- Human resource utilization
- Quality assurance of products and services
- Results from quality assurance of products and services
- Customer satisfaction

By reviewing each area within your company, your management team can focus quickly on where your value-creation system needs improvement. Furthermore, by doing an annual evaluation, you can see if the company's continuous improvement efforts are occurring quickly enough to meet corporate goals.

Leadership

Effective leadership is critical to successfully building a customer-focused organization. Are the most senior members of your company actively involved in your value-creation strategies and programs? Does your company have a formal value-creation plan for coordinating activities? Do you have a quality-improvement plan? Was it prepared by a multifunctional team that represented the views of all parts of the organization? Are there specific goals for the improvement of product and service quality in customer satisfaction? Are the goals and results tied to individual responsibilities and performance appraisals?

Behind successful value-creation processes, there is usually a chief executive officer who is visibly and actively involved. Stanley C. Gault is one such CEO, who has transformed a previously modestly successful

Rubbermaid into a powerhouse, largely through his obsession with quality, superb customer service, and designing attractive, useful products. Gault never stops being the company's chief quality controller. He visits stores several times a week to see how Rubbermaid products are displayed and inspects the quality of workmanship. If he finds anything that displeases him, he buys up the stock on the spot and brings it back to headquarters. There, senior staff are summoned for a lecture. He is known throughout the company to "get livid about defects."

This attention to quality and customer service has energized Rubbermaid's corporate culture. As a result, since 1980, company sales have quadrupled and earnings have risen eightfold. Rubbermaid has been rated by *Fortune* magazine among the top seven companies for five years running in the publication's annual report on "America's Most Admired Corporations."

Information and Analysis

You must be able to *control operations processes* effectively in order to consistently produce high-quality products and services. Does your company use statistical methods to control its operations processes? Do you have a training program to teach operators these methods? Are appropriate problem-solving methods used and reviewed regularly? Are indicators available that track problem identification and correction? Are these indicators widely circulated within the company? Are they understood and acted upon?

The BASF Corporation can answer yes to most of these questions, thanks to a quality improvement process program that includes both managers and employees. The company's quality education activities teach defect prevention by training individuals to recognize nonconformance to established standards and to solve the problems that led to the defect. The program emphasizes the need for quality improvement, teaches concepts of quality improvement, and sets down methods of establishing quality requirements, eliminating defects through teamwork and maintaining performance standards. As mentioned earlier, quality improvement teams (QITs), consisting of managers from each plant or business group, cooperate with the work force and upper management. Each QIT manages the program on a daily basis and has the authority to create a subcommittee to solve recurring errors.

In addition to process controls, the *quality of inputs* must be managed. Has your company developed formal supplier-quality-management guidelines? Do you have standards by which to designate "approved" suppliers? Do you measure conformance to these standards (incoming materials sampling or process control/capability indices from your suppliers)? Do you work with suppliers to help them meet your requirements?

Even if you do give careful attention to identifying and resolving quality problems early in the production process, you need to check the *final output*. Do you have methods to test finished products and to detect defects before the products are shipped to customers? Do you measure the defect rate, analyze the data to detect the causes of these defects, and take corrective action on a regular basis? Are the occurrence and recurrence of problems declining steadily? Does your defect level reflect a world-class standard?

Strategic Quality Planning

The Baldrige Award encourages *formal strategic planning and operational goal setting*. Do you have a strategic-planning function? Do you have a plan for value creation? For example, the GTE Service Corporation, mentioned earlier, incorporates value creation into its strategic-planning process. Each of the corporation's business units is asked to identify the role of quality in its strategy, define the elements of quality in its strategic program, outline long-range quality-related goals, and indicate how staff will meet these goals.

Telecommunications giant Northern Telecom Canada has defined quality in terms of "total customer satisfaction." The company's strategy includes a clear working definition of quality, a commitment to quality by all levels of management, quality maintenance through the product life cycle, and employee training and development programs to support the customer satisfaction improvement process. Northern Telecom recently received ISO 9000 certification—the highest international quality standard.

Human Resource Utilization

Your quality-improvement efforts will not succeed without the *active involvement of employees*. Does your quality system have an activ program of quality circles or similar problem-solving teams? Are team members trained in analyzing simple quality problems using such techniques as Pareto analysis, cause-and-effect analysis, and control charts?

In the early 1980s, the Bank of California began experimenting with a program of problem-solving teams to tap into the knowledge and experience of staff members as a way of resolving service quality issues. After a period of training in problem-solving methods, several employee quality circles set out to assess and recommend solutions for a number of identified concerns.

The Account Reconcilement Department decided to look at the problem of not being able to find an old check in the microfilm records whenever one was needed to balance a checkbook. The department met as a group and, using brainstorming techniques, developed uniform filing procedures. Group discussions also helped the staff that did the microfilming better understand the needs of personnel who used the microfilm in the course of their jobs. To solve the problem of disorganization and lack of space, the quality circle members decided to rearrange the work space and to recommend hiring temporary staff for peak loads for each month. Bank of California's experiment with group problem solving has been so successful that the number of quality circles has been greatly increased.

Some service quality and customer satisfaction issues are best resolved as these were—through the in-depth involvement of the staff members closest to the problem. However, employee involvement teams work effectively only if there is a mechanism for review and resource allocation at the senior management level. Does your company have a formal quality or customer satisfaction committee chaired by the most senior executive? Does the committee meet regularly to review quality improvement ideas? Do its members have enough signing authority to fund projects?

Quality Assurance of Products and Services

An important opportunity for improving quality and customer satisfaction lies in the *design of your products and services.* Do you regularly review designs to look for opportunities to increase their safety, reliability, dimensional tolerances, and so forth? Are specific, multifunctional projects under way to "design in" quality and customer value and satisfaction, rather than "inspecting it in?"

At Du Pont, a recently introduced successful product was designed with a high level of customer input. Although the company has supplied yarns to the carpet industry for many years, it spent three years working closely with retailers, textile mill operators, and other customers to discover how the new product would affect each group, and to define the most effective approach in pricing and promoting the product for long-term success. The result was StainMaster, a stain-resistant carpeting that has revived carpet sales for the company's customers and, of course, improved sales and profitability for Du Pont.

Sometimes, quality problems are caused by new products and services that have not been tested rigorously enough before being released for use on a commercial scale. Does your company have clear standards and procedures for determining when a new product or service is suitable for release to the market? Are products and services tested and passed before they are released to customers? If products are significantly changed in the design process, are they requalified before being marketed?

Results from Quality Assurance of Products and Services

As you implement your value-creation process, you must check to see if you are getting the *desired results*. Do you measure the results of your quality assurance and customer satisfaction efforts? For example, do you measure your quality costs regularly? Are there specific programs in place for reducing these costs? Do you track rejected products or services, complaints, warranty and field support work, and reductions in claims and litigation? Have you reduced your liability insurance costs?

AMP Inc., a large producer of electrical connecting devices, has adopted cost-of-quality measures and reported impressive cost savings. Its quality-improvement strategy is dedicated to measuring hundreds of variables across every function of the company. The effort spent in putting such a massive monitoring program in place has paid off. The company has trimmed its cost of quality from 16 percent of sales to 8 percent.

In addition to quality assurance, any value-creation system should also be set up to ensure that proper safety analyses and contingency procedures are in place. Are all labels, warnings, and instructions prepared to ensure proper product and service use and customer safety?

Customer Satisfaction

The most important group of criteria for the Baldrige Award consists of *customer satisfaction measures*; these account for up to 30 percent of the total points that can be earned. Unless you know what your customers actually think about your efforts to please them, you will not be able to focus those efforts for the best results.

Does your company take regular measurements of the quality of its products and services as perceived by customers? Do these measures include a comparison to your competition? Do you track product conformance to quality specifications? Are there specific, multifunctional project teams working on customer-value-improvement projects?

Ford, General Motors, and Chrysler all rely heavily on customer focus groups, surveys, and questionnaires to monitor customer satisfaction performance. At Xerox, a cross-section of customers is contacted every 90 days to give the company ongoing feedback about its standing with buyers. American Express supplements its elaborate service tracking measures with post-transaction customer interviews to make sure that the company's internal measures remain relevant to the way customers judge the organization. Through all these techniques, each of the companies mentioned makes sure that it gets direct feedback from the only group that can truly judge success—customers themselves.

It is only by taking measurements like these that businesses will understand what their customers want. And this understanding is the cornerstone of all the strategies and functions of a value-creating enterprise. The company that sets its goals beyond profit and market share and aims to profitably deliver value to its customers on an ongoing basis must first know what benefits its customers want. Then its senior executives and top-level managers can provide the leadership necessary to build a customer-value-driven business.

For such leadership to develop, managers can no longer operate in their separate departmental worlds; they must have a working knowledge of the quality assurance and customer satisfaction tools from all of the company's functional areas. As consultants Robert Hayes and William Abernathy have pointed out,

> The key to long-term success in business is what it has always been: to invest, to innovate, to lead, to create value where none existed before. Such determination, such striving to excel, requires leaders—the drive

trains of our corporations—not just controllers, market analysts and portfolio managers.

Create value for your customers, pay attention to meeting their needs and expectations, and you will also create value, and success, for your company.

Endnotes

Preface

vii   *"view an industry as a customer-satisfying process . . . ":*
Speech by Warren Evans, presented at the Total Service Action Plan Conference, Toronto, Ontario, July 5, 1988.

Chapter 1   Value Creation: The State of the Art

2   *In a recent* Fortune *article . . . :*
Thomas A. Stewart, "Westinghouse Gets Respect at Last," *Fortune,* July 3, 1989, p. 94.

2   *And Carl Arendt, marketing manager . . . :*
Thomas A. Stewart, "Westinghouse Gets Respect at Last," *Fortune,* July 3, 1989, p. 94.

2   *"You always put the interests of the customers first . . . ":*
Patricia Sellers, "What Customers Really Want," *Fortune,* June 4, 1990, p. 62.

2   *And in a recent survey conducted by* Canadian Business *. . . :*
Ian Allaby, "The Search for Quality," *Canadian Business,* May 1990, p. 31.

2–3   *However, this strategy, in the words of R.C. Inglis . . . :*
R. C. Inglis, "Good Service—Your Competitive Edge," *The Canadian Manufacturer,* January/February, 1986, p. 8.

3   *As William Davidow . . . rivalry among suppliers:*
William Davidow and Bro Uttal, *Total Customer Service: The Ultimate Weapon* (New York: Harper & Row, 1989), p. 13.

3   *Rushed two-career couples . . . conservative lifestyles:*
Peter A. Greene, "Customer Service in the Financial Services Industry: Thriving in the 90's," speech given at "Service Levels and Profitability: In Conflict or Complementary?" a strategic management event presented by The Coopers & Lybrand Consulting Group and TAMA (Toronto chapter of the American Marketing Association), February 24, 1989, Toronto, Ontario.

3   *"insist on making her own trade-offs . . .":*
Laurel Cutler, "Consumers Are Tougher Customers," *Fortune,* July 3, 1989, p. 76.

3   *As RJR Nabisco's chairman Louis Gerstner has said . . .*
Brian Dumaine, "What the Leaders of Tomorrow See," *Fortune,* July 3, 1989, p. 48.

6   *In the United States, 15 percent of the respondents . . . :*
Spencer Hutchens, Jr., senior vice-president, Intertek Services Corp., and president of the American Society for Quality Control, "What Customers Want: Results of ASQC/Gallup Survey," *Quality Progress,* February 1989, p. 33.

6   *According to the same survey . . . :*
Spencer Hutchens, Jr., senior vice-president, Intertek Services Corp., and president of the American Society for Quality Control, "What Customers Want: Results of ASQC/Gallup Survey," *Quality Progress,* February 1989, p. 34.

6   *These figures may not look bad at first glance . . . :*
Spencer Hutchens, Jr., senior vice-president, Intertek Services Corp., and president of the American Society for Quality Control, "What Customers Want: Results of ASQC/Gallup Survey," *Quality Progress,* February 1989, p. 34.

6   *In Canada, the Better Business Bureau reported in 1989 . . . :*
Paul Tuz, president, Better Business Bureau of Metropolitan Toronto Inc., speech given to Institute for International Research, April 26, 1989, Toronto, Ontario, p. 2.

6   *Reflecting the shift from a manufacturing-based economy . . . :*
Paul Tuz, president, Better Business Bureau of Metropolitan Toronto Inc., speech given to Institute for International Research, April 26, 1989, Toronto, Ontario, p. 3.

6   *The relatively low percentage of product complaints . . . :*
Paul Tuz, president, Better Business Bureau of Metropolitan Toronto Inc., speech given to Institute for International Research, April 26, 1989, Toronto, Ontario, p. 3.

7   *These were the kinds of things Toronto customers complained about . . . :*
Paul Tuz, president, Better Business Bureau of Metropolitan Toronto Inc., speech given to Institute for International Research, April 26, 1989, Toronto, Ontario, p. 4.

7–8   *[A]n overwhelming number . . . ". . . park your car," says Hall:*
Patricia Orwen, "Disappearance of 'Service with a Smile' Leaves Consumers Nostalgic and Angry," *The Toronto Star,* May 14, 1988, p. A8. Reprinted with permission, The Toronto Star Syndicate.

8   *"courtesy, promptness . . . ":*
     Spencer Hutchens, Jr., senior vice-president, Intertek Services Corp., and president of the American Society for Quality Control, "What Customers Want: Results of ASQC/Gallup Survey," *Quality Progress,* February 1989, pp. 34–35.

8   *"American consumers . . . ":*
     Spencer Hutchens, Jr., senior vice-president, Intertek Services Corp., and president of the American Society for Quality Control, "What Customers Want: Results of ASQC/Gallup Survey," *Quality Progress,* February 1989, p. 35.

8   *"if you make a better mousetrap . . . ":*
     Milind M. Lele, with Jagdish N. Sheth, *The Customer Is Key* (New York: John Wiley & Sons, 1987), p. 1.

8   *Although this philosophy . . . development alone:*
     Milind M. Lele, with Jagdish N. Sheth, *The Customer Is Key* (New York: John Wiley & Sons, 1987), p. 1.

8   *Government protection . . . regulations:*
     Milind M. Lele, with Jagdish N. Sheth, *The Customer Is Key* (New York: John Wiley & Sons, 1987), p. 2.

9   *Cutting back profits . . . services:*
     William Davidow and Bro Uttal, *Total Customer Service: The Ultimate Weapon* (New York: Harper & Row, 1989), p. 6.

9   *In other cases . . . quality service:*
     Laura A. Liswood, "A New System for Rating Service Quality," *The Journal of Business Strategy,* July/August 1989, p. 43.

9   *Short-term economics . . . long term:*
     William Davidow and Bro Uttal, *Total Customer Service: The Ultimate Weapon* (New York: Harper & Row, 1989), p. 7.

9   *Misapplied technology . . . at least:*
     William Davidow and Bro Uttal, *Total Customer Service: The Ultimate Weapon* (New York: Harper & Row, 1989), p. 8.

9   *Overzealous portfolio management . . . competitors:*
     G. Harlan Carothers, Jr., Richard D. Sanders, and Kenneth E. Kirby, "Management Leadership in the New Economic Age," *Survey of Business,* Summer 1989, p. 7. Reprinted by permission of *Survey of Business* and the Center for Business and Economic Research, The University of Tennessee, Knoxville.

9   *Management not sold . . . by the customer:*
     Karl Albrecht, *At America's Service: How Corporations Can Revolutionize the Way They Treat Their Customers* (Homewood, IL: Dow Jones-Irwin, 1988), p. 3.

9   *No solution . . . have identified:*
G. Harlan Carothers, Jr., Richard D. Sanders, and Kenneth E. Kirby, "Management Leadership in the New Economic Age," *Survey of Business*, Summer 1989, p. 11.

9   *Change is slow . . . structure:*
Karl Albrecht, *At America's Service: How Corporations Can Revolutionize the Way They Treat Their Customers* (Homewood, IL: Dow Jones-Irwin, 1988), pp. 4–5.

10   *John Goodman . . . lip service:*
John Goodman, president, Technical Assistance Research Program, "The Nature of Customer Satisfaction," *Quality Progress*, February 1989, p. 37.

10   *"doing it right . . . problem solving":*
John Goodman, president, Technical Assistance Research Program, "The Nature of Customer Satisfaction," *Quality Progress*, February 1989, p. 37.

10   *"spend 95% . . . begin with":*
John Goodman, president, Technical Assistance Research Program, "The Nature of Customer Satisfaction," *Quality Progress*, February 1989, p. 37.

10–11   *"I read . . . as customers":*
Ellen Roseman, "Portfolio: Another Sad Victim of American Express," *The Globe and Mail*, July 19, 1989, p. B15. Reprinted by permission of *The Globe and Mail*.

11   *According to one 18-month study . . . :*
"Companies Told That Poor Service Can Result In Huge Financial Losses," *Marketing News*, July 4, 1988, p. 8.

11   *Another survey, undertaken by Sandy Corp. . . . :*
"Rhetoric Contradicts Reality in Implementing Service Systems," *The Service Edge*, Volume 2, Number 4, April 1989, p. 2.

11–12   *Yet another study . . . " . . . completely satisfied":*
Theodore A. Marra, "Opening Remarks," speech delivered to the Institute for International Research Improved Customer Care and Service Conference, April 26 and 27, 1989, Toronto, pp. 8–9.

12   *According to customer service consultants . . . :*
Karl Albrecht and Ron Zemke, *Service America! Doing Business in the New Economy* (Homewood, IL: Dow Jones-Irwin, 1985), p. 6.

12–13   *John Cleghorn, president of the Royal Bank . . . :*
John E. Cleghorn, "Service Included?" speech delivered to the Vancouver Board of Trade, Vancouver, B.C., November 3, 1988, p. 7.

13   *And the network is a powerful one . . . 20 people:*
      Consumer Complaint Handling in America: An Update Study, Parts I, II
      and III. Study by Technical Assistance Research Program's Institute for
      the Consumer Affairs Council, United States Office of Consumer
      Affairs, September 30, 1985.

13   *The good news . . . they received:*
      Consumer Complaint Handling in America: An Update Study, Parts I, II
      and III. Study by Technical Assistance Research Program's Institute for
      the Consumer Affairs Council, United States Office of Consumer
      Affairs, September 30, 1985, pp. 42–43.

13   *This was borne out . . . ROS of 5 percent:*
      Robert D. Buzzell and Bradley T. Gale, *The PIMS Principles: Linking
      Strategy to Performance*, (New York: The Free Press, a division of Macmillan,
      Inc., 1987), p. 107.

14   *Walt Disney himself . . . start all over again:*
      Frank Wells, president, the Walt Disney Company, "Marketing
      Factors and Customer Satisfaction," *Quality Progress*, February 1989, p. 49.

14   Pinocchio . . . *more than $20 million:*
      Frank Wells, president, the Walt Disney Company, "Marketing
      Factors and Customer Satisfaction," *Quality Progress*, February 1989, p. 50.

14   *The Land's End mail-order . . . own momentum:*
      Patricia Sellers, "Getting Customers To Love You," *Fortune*, March
      13, 1989, p. 45.

15   *"imbued with . . . rigid control":*
      Carol J. Loomis, "Stars of the Service 500," *Fortune*, June 5, 1989,
      p. 55.

15   *"Whenever we . . . Big Volume":*
      Carol J. Loomis, "Stars of the Service 500," *Fortune*, June 5, 1989,
      p. 58.

15   *"Sell good merchandise . . . for more":*
      L. L. Bean. Christmas 1988 catalog.

16   *"continuous 'top-down' . . . considerations":*
      G. Harlan Carothers, Jr., Richard D. Sanders, and Kenneth E. Kirby,
      "Management Leadership in the New Economic Age," *Survey of Busi-
      ness*, Summer 1989, p. 7. Reprinted by permission of *Survey of Business*
      and the Center for Business and Economics Research, The University
      of Tennessee, Knoxville.

16   *"What's good . . . vice versa":*
      Arthur Johnson, "The World's Biggest Comeback," *The Globe and
      Mail Report on Business Magazine*, June 1989, p. 36.

16   *Consultant Tom Peters . . . " . . . lucky to have a job":*
Thomas J. Peters and Robert H. Waterman, Jr., *In Search of Excellence: Lessons from America's Best-Run Companies* (New York: Harper & Row, 1982), p. 32.

17   *"philosophy and practice . . . expense of quality":*
G. Harlan Carothers, Jr., Richard D. Sanders, and Kenneth E. Kirby, "Management Leadership in the New Economic Age," *Survey of Business*, Summer 1989, p. 7. Reprinted by permission of *Survey of Business* and the Center for Business and Economic Research, The University of Tennessee, Knoxville.

19   *Symbolic of . . . hire and fire:*
Brian Dumaine, "Who Needs a Boss?" *Fortune*, May 7, 1990, p. 52.

19   *"long-term . . . to society":*
James A. Belasco, *Teaching the Elephant to Dance: Empowering Change in Your Organization* (New York: Crown Publishers Inc., 1990), p. 102.

20   *"Wealth . . . a useful service":*
Henry Ford, as quoted in James A. Belasco, *Teaching the Elephant to Dance: Empowering Change in Your Organization* (New York: Crown Publishers Inc., 1990), p. 102.

20–21   *The creation . . . of operation:*
G. Harlan Carothers, Jr., Richard D. Sanders, and Kenneth E. Kirby, "Management Leadership in the New Economic Age," *Survey of Business*, Summer 1989, p. 7.

20–21   *Those firms . . . consumer goods:*
G. Harlan Carothers, Jr., Richard D. Sanders, and Kenneth E. Kirby, "Management Leadership in the New Economic Age," *Survey of Business*, Summer 1989, p. 7. This and previous quotation reprinted by permission of *Survey of Business* and the Center for Business and Economic Research, The University of Tennessee, Knoxville.

21   *"rigid organizations . . . performers":*
Robert O. Knorr, "Managing Resources for World-Class Performance," *The Journal of Business Strategy*, January/February 1990, p. 2.

Chapter 2   Know Your Customers—Know Yourself

23   *In a recent . . . basic product:*
Joel Dreyfuss, "Reinventing IBM," *Fortune*, August 17, 1989, p. 31.

23   *Akers has broken . . . " . . . needs of customers":*
Joel Dreyfuss, "Reinventing IBM," *Fortune*, August 17, 1989, p. 33.

23   *In fact . . . them satisfied:*
    William H. Davidow and Bro Uttal, *Total Customer Service: The Ultimate Weapon* (New York: Harper & Row, 1989), p. 44.

24   *The first two made the list of Canada's 50 . . . :*
    This list of the 50 best-managed private companies in Canada was compiled by Arthur Andersen & Co. for *Canadian Business* magazine and appeared in Ian Allaby, "The Search for Quality," *Canadian Business,* May 1990, pp. 31–42.

24   *When CEO Alex Starko . . . $12 million in 1989:*
    Ian Allaby, "The Search for Quality," *Canadian Business,* May 1990, pp. 34–35.

24   *Alderbrook Industries Ltd. . . . $18.4 million in 1988:*
    Ian Allaby, "The Search for Quality," *Canadian Business,* May 1990, p. 34.

25   *Richard Sharp, CEO . . . video cameras":*
    Brian Dumaine, "What the Leaders of Tomorrow See," *Fortune,* July 3, 1989, pp. 61–62.

25   *"The winners . . . same time":*
    Brian Dumaine, "What the Leaders of Tomorrow See," *Fortune,* July 3, 1989, pp. 61–62.

25   *A recent survey . . . personal care and respect:*
    John Oldland, "The Difficult Quest for Quality," speech delivered to The Coopers & Lybrand Consulting Group Winning Through Customer Satisfaction Conference, July 14, 1988, Toronto, p. 1.

26   *This principle . . . top 10 accounts:*
    Harvey B. Mackay, "Humanize Your Selling Strategy," *Harvard Business Review,* March/April, 1988, p. 2.

26   *When Gary Comer . . . " . . . not always easy, but we do it":*
    Patricia Sellers, "Getting Customers to Love You," *Fortune,* March 13, 1989, p. 44.

26   *"At $31 . . . our jobs: $29.50":*
    Patricia Sellers, "Getting Customers to Love You," *Fortune,* March 13, 1989, p. 44–45.

26   *The combination has worked . . . $30 million:*
    Patricia Sellers, "Getting Customers to Love You," *Fortune,* March 13, 1989, p. 44–45.

27   *One research company . . . decisions to buy:*
    David Climenhaga, "GM Improves Medium Truck Warranties," *The Globe and Mail,* Friday, May 19, 1989, p. B5.

27   *"But when you get . . . dollars in their pocket":*
David Climenhaga, "GM Improves Medium Truck Warranties," *The Globe and Mail,* Friday, May 19, 1989, p. B5.

27   *One Toronto building company . . . " . . . will adopt [the warranty]":*
Marion Stinson, "Bramalea Offers Its Buyers Twelve Months of Protection," *The Globe and Mail,* Wednesday, April 1, 1987, p. 84.

28   *[C]umbersome . . . products or services:*
Milind M. Lele, with Jagdish N. Sheth, *The Customer Is Key* (New York: John Wiley & Sons, 1987), p. 219.

28   *One analysis . . . becomes frantic:*
Milind M. Lele, with Jagdish N. Sheth, *The Customer Is Key* (New York: John Wiley & Sons, 1987), pp. 190–191.

28   *John Deere . . . anywhere in North America:*
"Marketing Strategies Must Integrate Systems To Support Services," *The Service Edge,* Volume 2, Number 4, April 1989, p. 2.

29   *When Henry Ford . . . has not caught up:*
Milind M. Lele, with Jagdish N. Sheth, *The Customer Is Key* (New York: John Wiley & Sons, 1987), pp. 21–22.

29–30   *Unless an ongoing effort . . . an American organization:*
Thomas C. Kaiser, "Strategies for Enhancing Services Quality," *The Journal of Services Marketing* (Summer 1988), Vol. 2, No. 3, p. 67.

30   *Beginning in the mid-1950s . . . problem too late:*
"Company Name Poisons Corporate Image," *The Globe and Mail,* Friday, August 19, 1989, p. B20.

30   *IBM's hegemony . . . on the benches:*
Joel Dreyfuss, "Reinventing IBM," *Fortune,* August 17, 1989, p. 38.

30–31   *"The FUD factor . . . effective support":*
F. Stewart DeBruicker and Gregory L. Summe, "Make Sure Your Customers Keep Coming Back," *Harvard Business Review* (January/February 1985), p. 95.

31   *Then, as customers . . . buying needs:*
F. Stewart DeBruicker and Gregory L. Summe, "Make Sure Your Customers Keep Coming Back," *Harvard Business Review* (January/February 1985), p. 95.

31   *When Corning . . . metal cookware market:*
Judith D. Schwartz, "How Corning Prevented Revere Ware From Going To Pot," *Adweek's Marketing Week,* October 23, 1989, p. 76.

31   *Another household products . . . businesses in North America:*
Tim Morawetz, "Rubbermaid Drums Up 'Unbeatable' Success," *Playback Strategy*, November 20, 1989, p. 13.

32   *Xerox has a strategy . . . has been delivered:*
Richard C. Whiteley and Michael E. Hepworth, "Creating Customer Focus," promotional flyer, The Forum Corporation, Boston, MA, p. 3.

33   *IAF BioChem International Inc. . . . R&D:*
IAF BioChem International Inc., *You're in Good Company: Winners of the 1989 Canada Awards for Business Excellence*, p. 36.

34   *When People Express . . . bankruptcy:*
Bernard C. Reimann, "Sustaining the Competitive Advantage," *Planning Review* (March/April 1989), p. 33.

34   *Every enterprise has to offer . . . expected product or service:*
Theodore Levitt, "Marketing Success Through Differentiation—of Anything," HBR Classic Reprinted From *Harvard Business Review*, January/February, 1980, p. 85.

34   *"In today's Baskin-Robbins' . . . marketplace":*
John Naisbitt, *Megatrends. Ten New Directions Transforming Our Lives* (New York: Warner Books Inc., 1982), p. 232.

34   *That's why some business thinkers . . . customers:*
Theodore Levitt, "Marketing Success Through Differentiation—of Anything," HBR Classic Reprinted From *Harvard Business Review*, January/February, 1980, p. 88.

35   *Austin Trumanns Steel . . . value of the order:*
"Delivery on the Dot—or a Refund," *Industrial Marketing Digest*, p. 46.

35   *Of course . . . before it advertises:*
D. Randall Brandt, "How Marketers Can Identify Value-Enhancing Service Elements," *Journal of Services Marketing* (Summer 1988), pp. 35–42.

35   *Efforts to improve . . . capabilities:*
William H. Davidow and Bro Uttal, *Total Customer Service: The Ultimate Weapon* (New York: Harper & Row, 1989), p. 43.

35   *Procter & Gamble . . . runs out of diapers:*
Brian Dumaine, "Marketing Rules," *Fortune*, November 6, 1989, p. 42.

36   *Dave Nichol, president of Loblaw International Merchants, . . . their own green lines:*
Jared Mitchell, "No Deals," *Globe and Mail Report on Business Magazine* (October 1989), p. 75.

37   *LSI Logic Corporation . . . competitors:*
B. Charles Ames and James D. Hlavacek, *Market Driven Management* (Homewood, IL: Dow Jones-Irwin, 1989), p. 71.

37–38   *Similarly, Ecusta . . . fine paper:*
"Companies To Watch," *Fortune,* June 5, 1989, p. 176.

38   *Glatfelter services different . . . values the most:*
"Companies To Watch," *Fortune,* June 5, 1989, p. 176.

38   *Customers can also be classified . . . :*
Barbara Bund Jackson, *Winning and Keeping Industrial Customers. The Dynamics of Customer Relationships* (Lexington, MA: D.C. Heath and Company, 1985), p. 43.

38   *At one end of the spectrum . . . company cars):*
"Customers Come First," *The Economist,* December 6, 1986, p. 79.

39   *the well-known Pareto Principle . . . :*
J. M. Juran, *Juran on Planning for Quality* (New York: The Free Press, 1988), p. 26.

39   *General Motors . . . drives down costs:*
Bernard C. Reimann, "Sustaining the Competitive Advantage," *Planning Review* (March/April 1989), p. 36.

39   *"1. Fulfill a need . . . simple":*
Quoted in Robert F. Mirvish, *Viewpoint from Honest Ed's* (1963). Reprinted in John Robert Colombo, *Colombo's New Canadian Quotations* (Edmonton: Hurtig, 1987), p. 45b.

39–40   *Those CEOs . . . competitive strengths:*
Brian Dumaine, "What the Leaders of Tomorrow See," *Fortune,* July 3, 1989, p. 50.

40   *When Frito-Lay . . . chip niche:*
William H. Davidow, "Service Companies: Focus or Falter," *Harvard Business Review,* July/August, 1989, p. 78.

40   *"This is what the Canadian Imperial Bank of Commerce did . . . likely become richer":*
Keith H. Sjogren, senior vice-president, private banking, Canadian Imperial Bank of Commerce, "A Private Banking Case," speech given at "Service Levels and Profitability: In Conflict or Complementary?" a strategic management event presented by The Coopers & Lybrand Consulting Group and TAMA (Toronto chapter of the American Marketing Association), February 24, 1989, Toronto, Ontario.

40–41   *In the case of another company . . . profit potential:*
Thomas V. Bonoma and Benson P. Shapiro, "Evaluating Market

Segmentation Approaches," *Industrial Marketing Management* (1984) 13, p. 261.

41   *H. B. Fuller, the St. Paul adhesives company . . . publicly owned glue factory:*
Patricia Sellers, "Getting Customers to Love You," *Fortune,* March 13, 1989, pp. 48–49.

41–42   *Coca-Cola Co. . . . had toward Campbell's:*
Cathryn Motherwell, "Truly Loyal Shoppers Can Be Fickle," *The Globe and Mail,* May 6, 1987, pp. B1–B2. Reprinted by permission of *The Globe and Mail.*

42   *excessive vertical integration . . . independent supplier:*
"Roger Smith's Troubled Second Act," *New York Times,* January 12, 1986, p. F-23. Quoted in Robert D. Buzzell and Bradley T. Gale, *The PIMS Principles: Linking Strategy to Performance* (New York: The Free Press, 1987), pp. 163–64.

42   *Even the venerable Hudson's Bay . . . in the long run:*
Rick Spence, "Try, Try Again," The Globe and Mail *Report on Business Magazine,* September 1989, pp. 87–94.

42–43   *Zellers, a deep-discount subsidiary . . . satisfaction and profits:*
Rick Spence, "How to Do It Right," The Globe and Mail *Report on Business Magazine,* September 1989, p. 89.

43   *A survey of large American manufacturers . . . own sales staff:*
"Customers Come First," *The Economist,* December 6, 1986, p. 79.

43   *If your customers . . . locking out the competition:*
Peter D. Moore, "New Ways to Reach Your Customers," *Fortune,*   ✗
November 6, 1989, p. 210.

43   *Citicorp, the financial services giant . . . less prominently displayed:*
Peter D. Moore, "New Ways to Reach Your Customers," *Fortune,* November 6, 1989, p. 210.

43–44   *Robert Sinclair . . . best in the industry:*
Patricia Sellers, "Getting Customers to Love You," *Fortune,* March 13, 1989, p. 48.

45   *By following the "product" . . . along the way:*
J. M. Juran, *Juran on Planning for Quality* (New York: The Free Press, 1988), p. 18.

45   *A supplier-to-customer chain . . . the ultimate user:*
"Service Journal," *The Service Edge,* Volume 2, Number 6, June 1989, p. 5.

45   *To improve internal customer relations . . . "internal service vision":*
James L. Heskett, "Lessons in the Service Sector," *Harvard Business Review*, March-April 1987, pp. 120–23.

45   *This kind of internal marketing campaign . . . special acknowledgment:*
Sybil F. Stershic, "Internal Marketing Campaign Reinforces Service Goals," *Marketing News*, July 31, 1989, p. 11.

45–46   *Air Canada uses such methods . . .* Horizons*:*
Michelle Gagne, "Air Canada Focuses on Customer Care," *Playback Strategy*, November 20, 1989, p. 32.

46   *In 1989, for example, . . . management had sought:*
John C. Wilcox, "How to Win Shareholder Loyalty," *The Journal of Business Strategy*, September/October, 1989, pp. 16–19.

46–47   *"Below you . . . would you jump into?":*
John Guaspari, *The Customer Connection: Quality for the Rest of Us* (New York: AMACOM, A division of American Management Association, 1988), p. 195.

Chapter 3   Upside Down and Inside Out: Creating the Customer-Value-Driven Culture

49   *When John C. Marous . . . breakthrough or conquest:*
Thomas A. Stewart, "Westinghouse Gets Respect at Last," *Fortune*, July 3, 1989, p. 98.

50   *From 1984 to 1989 . . . " . . . shareholder value":*
Thomas A. Stewart, "Westinghouse Gets Respect at Last," *Fortune*, July 3, 1989, p. 93.

50–51   *Customer satisfaction is the main . . . customer satisfaction:*
Milind M. Lele, with Jagdish N. Sheth, *The Customer Is Key* (New York: John Wiley & Sons, 1987), p. 45.

51   *The company sets for itself . . . service quality:*
Milind M. Lele, with Jagdish N. Sheth, *The Customer Is Key* (New York: John Wiley & Sons, 1987), p. 45.

51   *"If a company follows . . . long-run":*
Kaoru Ishikawa, *What Is Total Quality Control? The Japanese Way*, translated by David J. Lu (Englewood Cliffs, NJ: Prentice-Hall, 1985), p. 104. Reprinted by permission of the publisher, Prentice-Hall, Inc., Englewood Cliffs, New Jersey 07632.

51   *In practice, many companies . . . the Japanese:*
Kaoru Ishikawa, *What Is Total Quality Control? The Japanese Way*, translated by David J. Lu (Englewood Cliffs, NJ: Prentice-Hall, 1985),

p. 105. Reprinted by permission of the publisher, Prentice-Hall, Inc., Englewood Cliffs, New Jersey 07632.

51   *the company that is really interested . . . its customers:*
Milind M. Lele, with Jagdish N. Sheth, *The Customer Is Key* (New York: John Wiley & Sons, 1987), pp. 9–10.

52   *Proctor & Redfern Ltd. . . . " . . . involved in projects":*
Ian Allaby, "The Search for Quality," *Canadian Business,* May 1990, p. 40.

52   *Fergus Groundwater . . . $10.4 million in 1988:*
Ian Allaby, "The Search for Quality," *Canadian Business,* May 1990, p. 40.

52   *At the Four Seasons Hotels . . . one of the three:*
Patricia Sellers, "Getting Customers to Love You," *Fortune,* March 13, 1989, p. 40.

52–53   *Reuben Mark . . . " . . . You're never going . . . be the best.":*
Brian Dumaine, "What the Leaders of Tomorrow See," *Fortune,* July 3, 1989, p. 50.

53   *Mack Truck's stated vision . . . for customers":*
"Belief Systems," in *Case Studies in Service Quality: When America Does It Right,* ed. Jay W. Spechler (Norcross, GA: Industrial Engineering and Management Press, 1988), p. 587.

53   *"Valued for total commitment . . . of their work":*
Lintas Advertising vision statement.

54   *"Many upper managers . . . top priority":*
J. M. Juran, *Juran on Planning for Quality* (New York: The Free Press, 1988), pp. 248–49. Reprinted with permission of The Free Press, a Division of Macmillan, Inc., from *Juran on Planning for Quality* by Joseph M. Juran. Copyright © 1988 by Juran Institute Inc.

54   *If only one or two . . . caution is over:*
Kaoru Ishikawa, *What Is Total Quality Control? The Japanese Way,* translated by David J. Lu (Englewood Cliffs, NJ: Prentice-Hall, 1985), pp 122 and 128. Reprinted by permission of the publisher, Prentice-Hall, Inc., Englewood Cliffs, New Jersey 07632.

55   *the company's informal cultural values . . . business performance:*
Milind M. Lele, with Jagdish N. Sheth, *The Customer Is Key* (New York: John Wiley & Sons, 1987), p. 100.

55   *At the U.S. manufacturing operations of Honda . . . :*
Martin Mittelstaedt, "Strong Honda Performance Gives It New Clout in U.S.," *The Globe and Mail,* February 8, 1990, p. B1.

56   *"acquired taste . . .":*
Kaoru Ishikawa, *What Is Total Quality Control? The Japanese Way*, translated by David J. Lu (Englewood Cliffs, NJ: Prentice-Hall, 1985), p. 122.

56   *Armand V. Feigenbaum . . . mostly by QC specialists:*
Kaoru Ishikawa, *What Is Total Quality Control? The Japanese Way*, translated by David J. Lu (Englewood Cliffs, NJ: Prentice-Hall, 1985), p. 90.

56   *"on having . . . promoting QC":*
Kaoru Ishikawa, *What Is Total Quality Control? The Japanese Way*, translated by David J. Lu (Englewood Cliffs, NJ: Prentice-Hall, 1985), p. 90. Reprinted by permission of the publisher, Prentice-Hall, Inc., Englewood Cliffs, New Jersey 07632.

56   *It's not that the Japanese . . . " . . . promote QC":*
Kaoru Ishikawa, *What Is Total Quality Control? The Japanese Way*, translated by David J. Lu (Englewood Cliffs, NJ: Prentice-Hall, 1985), p. 91. Reprinted by permission of the publisher, Prentice-Hall, Inc., Englewood Cliffs, New Jersey 07632.

56–57   *Industry has strong . . . cross-function[al] management:*
Kaoru Ishikawa, *What Is Total Quality Control? The Japanese Way*, translated by David J. Lu (Englewood Cliffs, NJ: Prentice-Hall, 1985), p. 114. Reprinted by permission of the publisher, Prentice-Hall, Inc., Englewood Cliffs, New Jersey 07632.

57   *"is quite similar . . . goals at all levels":*
J. M. Juran, *Juran on Planning for Quality* (New York: The Free Press, 1988), pp. 244–45.

57   *New products . . . participation:*
J. M. Juran, *Juran on Planning for Quality* (New York: The Free Press, 1988), p. 247. Reprinted with permission of The Free Press, a Division of Macmillan, Inc., from *Juran on Planning for Quality* by Joseph M. Juran. Copyright © 1988 by Juran Institute Inc.

57   *"interfere . . . departmental goals":*
J. M. Juran, *Juran on Planning for Quality* (New York: The Free Press, 1988), p. 247.

58   *A planning department . . . two months:*
J. M. Juran, *Juran on Planning for Quality* (New York: The Free Press, 1988), p. 247.

58   *Another purpose . . . invasion of her turf:*
J. M. Juran, *Juran on Planning for Quality* (New York: The Free Press, 1988), p. 247.

58   *Consider the case of manager A saying to manager B . . . :*
      William J. McCabe, "Examining Processes Improves Operations,"
      Quality Progress (July 1989), pp. 31–32.

58   *Furthermore, as Dr. Juran . . . against goals:*
      J. M. Juran, *Juran on Planning for Quality* (New York: The Free Press,
      1988), p. 248.

58–59   *Once the company . . . are corporate officers:*
      J. M. Juran, *Juran on Planning for Quality* (New York: The Free Press,
      1988), p. 250. Reprinted with permission of The Free Press, a Division
      of Macmillan, Inc., from *Juran on Planning for Quality* by Joseph M. Juran.
      Copyright © 1988 by Juran Institute Inc.

59   *coordinate establishment . . . reward system:*
      J. M. Juran, *Juran on Planning for Quality* (New York: The Free Press,
      1988), p. 250.

59   *In cases where a vision statement . . . be delivered:*
      J. M. Juran, *Juran on Planning for Quality* (New York: The Free Press,
      1988), p. 251.

59   *In order to build these systems . . . :*
      Lynn W. Phillips and Michael J. Laning, *Building Market-Focused
      Organizations.* Brochure describing seminar, November 5–10, 1989,
      Monterey, California, p. 8.

59   *Divisional cross-functional teams . . . his or her staff:*
      J. M. Juran, *Juran on Planning for Quality* (New York: The Free Press,
      1988), p. 250.

59–60   *Some companies . . . interdivisional rivalries:*
      Kaoru Ishikawa, *What Is Total Quality Control? The Japanese Way,*
      translated by David J. Lu (Englewood Cliffs, NJ: Prentice-Hall, 1985),
      pp. 116–117. Reprinted by permission of the publisher, Prentice-Hall,
      Inc., Englewood Cliffs, New Jersey 07632.

62   *Jane Kingman-Brundage, a specialist . . . " . . . company's interests":*
      Jane Kingman-Brundage, *The ABC's of Service Blueprinting* (Chicago:
      American Marketing Association, 1989), p. 3.

63   *[A]ll processes . . . poor performance:*
      J. M. Juran, *Juran on Planning for Quality* (New York: The Free Press,
      1988), p. 272. Reprinted with permission of The Free Press, a Division
      of Macmillan, Inc., from *Juran on Planning for Quality* by Joseph M. Juran.
      Copyright © 1988 by Juran Institute Inc.

64–65   *Case in Point #1:*
      William J. McCabe, "Examining Processes Improves Operations,"
      Quality Progress (July 1989), pp. 30–31.

66   *Case in Point #2:*
Thomas A. Stewart, "Westinghouse Gets Respect at Last," *Fortune,*
July 3, 1989, pp. 94–96.

67–68   *Information on all important . . . strengths of each party:*
Reprinted by permission of *Harvard Business Review.*
An excerpt from "What the Hell Is 'Market Oriented'" by Benson P.
Shapiro (November/December 1988), pp. 120–122. Copyright © 1988
by the President and Fellows of Harvard College; all rights reserved.

68   *The kind of company-wide cooperation . . . made in time:*
Michelle Ramsay, "Esso Chemical Canada—In Search of PD Excellence," *Canadian Transportation and Distribution Management* (April 1984),
p. 31.

69   *One program, called "Count on Me," . . . :*
BellSouth Corporation, "What Can Customers Expect From the
People of BellSouth?" (Advertisement).

69   *In the early 1980s . . . a Motorola vice-president:*
John Hillkirk, "Top Quality is Behind Comeback," *USA Today,*
Tuesday, March 28, 1989, pp. 1–2B.

Chapter 4   Measuring Customer Satisfaction and Value Perception

Chapter-opening quotation: From David Garvin, *Managing Quality.* Quoted in
The Burke Institute, "Customer Satisfaction Research," seminar given in
Cincinnati, Ohio, March 6–7, 1989. © The Burke Institute, 800 Broadway,
Cincinnati, Ohio, 45202, p. 1.13.

Excerpts in this chapter from *The Service Edge: 101 Companies That Profit from
Customer Care* by Ron Zemke with Dick Schaaf. Copyright © 1989 by Ron
Zemke and Dick Schaaf. Reprinted by permission of the publisher, New
American Library, a division of Penguin Books U.S.A., Inc.

74   *"a product . . . theme":*
Allen Paison, president of Walker: Customer Satisfaction Measure-
ment, quoted in: George Dixon, "Keep 'Em Satisfied," *Marketing News,*
January 2, 1989, p. 1.

74   *"calls . . . research"; "customer . . . decision-making":*

George Dixon, "Keep 'Em Satisfied," *Marketing News,* January 2, 1989,
p. 1.

74–75   *Seemingly innocuous . . . business was well served":*
Tom Peters, *Thriving on Chaos: Handbook for a Management Revolution*
(New York: Alfred A. Knopf, 1987), pp. 102–103. Copyright © 1987 by

Excel, a California Limited Partnership. Reprinted by permission of Alfred A. Knopf, Inc.

76 *In* The Service Edge . . . *"'. . . think we are?'"*:
Ron Zemke, with Dick Schaaf, *The Service Edge: 101 Companies That Profit From Customer Care* (New York: New American Library, 1989), p. 51.

76 *The Battelle Memorial Institute . . . exceeded their expectations:*
Ron Zemke, with Dick Schaaf, *The Service Edge: 101 Companies That Profit From Customer Care* (New York: New American Library, 1989), p. 496.

76 *in a 1989 survey of the Canadian . . . competition:*
Stanley A. Brown and Marvin B. Martenfeld, *Creating the Service Culture: Strategies for Canadian Business* (Scarborough, Ont.: Prentice-Hall Canada, 1990), p. 64.

77 *A good example of top management . . . senior management:*
William A. Band, "Performance Metrics Keep Customer Satisfaction Programs on Track," *Marketing News,* May 28, 1990, p. 12.

77 *In* Creating the Service Culture *. . . to the competition:*
Stanley A. Brown and Marvin B. Martenfeld, *Creating the Service Culture: Strategies for Canadian Business* (Scarborough, Ont.: Prentice-Hall Canada, 1990), p. 39.

77 *American Express Canada . . . "'. . . each department'":*
Stanley A. Brown and Marvin B. Martenfeld, *Creating the Service Culture: Strategies for Canadian Business* (Scarborough, Ont.: Prentice-Hall Canada, 1990), p. 61.

77 *One major Canadian . . . recommend:*
William A. Band, "Performance Metrics Keep Customer Satisfaction Programs on Track," *Marketing News,* May 28, 1990, p. 12.

78 *Ron Zemke discovered . . . ". . . enough feedback":*
Ron Zemke, with Dick Schaaf, *The Service Edge: 101 Companies That Profit From Customer Care* (New York: New American Library, 1989), p. 54.

78 *As Marriott's . . . ". . . explain the numbers":*
Ron Zemke, with Dick Schaaf, *The Service Edge: 101 Companies That Profit From Customer Care* (New York: New American Library, 1989), p. 56.

78 *Questions in the survey . . . collect and record:*
Ron Zemke, with Dick Schaaf, *The Service Edge: 101 Companies That Profit From Customer Care* (New York: New American Library, 1989), p. 58.

78   *"A major problem . . . actionable statement:*
Arlene R. Malech, vice-president, Technical Assistance Research Programs, "How to Select and Work with a Customer Satisfaction Measurement Consultant," presentation given at AMA/ASQC Customer Satisfaction Measurement Conference, Atlanta, Georgia, February 28, 1989, p. 6.

79   *Equally problematical . . . situation:*
Ron Zemke, with Dick Schaaf, *The Service Edge: 101 Companies That Profit From Customer Care* (New York: New American Library, 1989), p. 57.

79   *In an interview with consultants . . . among other things:*
Stanley A. Brown and Marvin B. Martenfeld, *Creating the Service Culture: Strategies for Canadian Business* (Scarborough, Ont.: Prentice-Hall Canada, 1990), p. 47.

79   *Measurement for the sake of . . . value perception:*
J. W. Marr, "Letting the Customer be the Judge of Quality," *Quality Progress* (October 1986), p. 48.

79   *Product quality, including . . . design and packaging:*
William A. Band, "How to Measure Customer Satisfaction," *Sales & Marketing Management in Canada,* January 1989, p. 24.

79–80   *After-sales support . . . damaged goods:*
William A. Band, "How to Measure Customer Satisfaction," *Sales & Marketing Management in Canada,* January 1989, p. 24.

80   *The interaction between employees and customers . . . resolving problems:*
William A. Band, "How to Measure Customer Satisfaction," *Sales & Marketing Management in Canada,* January 1989, p. 24.

80   *as did the customer service division . . . was serving its customers:*
Jack Smith, "Quality in Computer Services: Maintenance Repair, and Support Services," in *Case Studies in Service Quality. When America Does It Right,* ed. Jay W. Spechler (Norcross, GA: Industrial Engineering and Management Press, 1988), p. 138.

80   *"the state in which customer needs . . . loyalty":*
Theodore R. Marra, president, TARP MidWest, speech given at "Improved Customer Care and Service Conference," Toronto, April 26, 1989.

81   *Advertising and marketing . . . being sold:*
The Burke Institute, "Customer Satisfaction Research," seminar given in Cincinnati, Ohio, March 6–7, 1989. © 1989. The Burke Institute, 800 Broadway, Cincinnati, Ohio 45202, p. 2.01.

81   *"A firm should not . . . less attractive":*
J. O'Shaughnessy, *Why People Buy* (New York: Oxford University Press, 1987), p. 184. Quoted in: The Burke Institute, "Customer Satisfaction Research," seminar given in Cincinnati, Ohio, March 6–7, 1989. © 1989. The Burke Institute, 800 Broadway, Cincinnati, Ohio 45202, p. 2.01.

82   *A general evaluation . . . service attributes:*
D. Randall Brandt, "How Service Marketers Can Identify Value-Enhancing Service Elements," *The Journal of Services Marketing*, Vol. 2, No. 3 (Summer 1988), p. 37.

85   *Improved internal response times . . . its service levels:*
Donald B. Berryman, "A New Commitment to the Customer," in *Case Studies in Service Quality. When America Does It Right*, ed. Jay W. Spechler (Norcross, GA: Industrial Engineering and Management Press Institute of Industrial Engineers, 1988), pp. 438–440.

91   *[T]ypes and frequency . . . management action:*
D. Randall Brandt, "How Service Marketers Can Identify Value-Enhancing Service Elements," *The Journal of Services Marketing*, Vol. 2, No. 3 (Summer 1988), p. 37.

91   *Some research instruments focus . . . dealt with:*
Based on: J. W. Marr, "Letting the Customer be the Judge of Quality," *Quality Progress* (October 1986), p. 49, point no. 10.

91   *The choice of research approach . . . collecting data:*
Based loosely on The Burke Institute comparison chart in: The Burke Institute, "Customer Satisfaction Research," seminar given in Cincinnati, Ohio, March 6–7, 1989. © 1989. The Burke Institute, 800 Broadway, Cincinnati, Ohio 45202, p. A4.13 to A4.17.

92   *J. W. Marr . . . and cost—problems:*
J. W. Marr, "Letting the Customer be the Judge of Quality," *Quality Progress* (October 1986), p. 48. Reprinted by permission of Marr, Walker: CSM.

93   *When Armstrong introduced . . . " . . . field sales people":*
Ron Zemke, with Dick Schaaf, *The Service Edge: 101 Companies That Profit From Customer Care* (New York: New American Library, 1989), pp. 467–68.

93   *"Some managers . . . guests in the hotel":*
Ron Zemke, with Dick Schaaf, *The Service Edge: 101 Companies That Profit From Customer Care* (New York: New American Library, 1989), p. 119.

93   *How seriously does the Marriott chain . . . month:*
Ron Zemke, with Dick Schaaf, *The Service Edge: 101 Companies That Profit From Customer Care* (New York: New American Library, 1989), p. 119.

93–94   *Another operation . . . gave the suggestion:*
Ron Zemke, with Dick Schaaf, *The Service Edge: 101 Companies That Profit From Customer Care* (New York: New American Library, 1989), p. 318.

94   *Carol Cherry . . . research for them:*
George Dixon, "Keep 'Em Satisfied," *Marketing News,* January 2, 1989, p. 1.

94   *Domino's Pizza . . . across the United States:*
Ron Zemke, with Dick Schaaf, *The Service Edge: 101 Companies That Profit From Customer Care* (New York: New American Library, 1989), pp. 302–303.

94   *Eleanor Holtzman . . . " . . . pad and pencil":*
Cynde Miller, "Roving Camera Captures Fresh Consumer Opinions," *Marketing News,* January 2, 1989, p. 8.

94–95   *Visual imagery profiling . . . that personality:*
Edward J. Vatza, "Get Accurate Views from Consumers by Giving Them the VIP Treatment," *Marketing News,* January 2, 1989, p. 34.

95   *Among the Service 101 . . . they maintain:*
Ron Zemke, with Dick Schaaf, *The Service Edge: 101 Companies That Profit From Customer Care* (New York: New American Library, 1989), pp. 53–54.

95   *The First Pennsylvania Bank . . . comment cards:*
Sara Wedeman, Tobi Schupack, and Shashi Rao, "Taking the Extra Step: The First Pennsylvania Approach to Service Quality Improvement," *Measuring and Monitoring Service Quality,* published by the Research and Planning Department, Bank Marketing Association, 1988, pp. 1–7.

95   *The Eastman Kodak Company . . . a telephone hotline:*
Thomas M. Hally and John R. Bauer, Jr., "Quality at Kodak's Parts Services: Evolving into a State of Mind," in *Case Studies in Service Quality. When America Does It Right,* ed. Jay W. Spechler (Norcross, GA: Industrial Engineering and Management Press, 1988), p. 398.

95   *Apple Canada Inc. . . . " . . . or the distributor, etc."*
Stanley A. Brown and Marvin B. Martenfeld, *Creating the Service Culture: Strategies for Canadian Business* (Scarborough, Ont.: Prentice-Hall Canada, 1990), p. 40.

95   *Burger King uses three measures . . . cleanliness:*
      Anthony L. Scherber and Warren G. Malkerson, "Service Quality at
      Pillsbury U.S. Foods Company," in *Case Studies in Service Quality. When
      America Does It Right*, ed. Jay W. Spechler (Norcross, GA: Industrial
      Engineering and Management Press Institute of Industrial Engineers,
      1988), p. 162.

95–96 *John Cleghorn . . . where do you think . . . ":*
      Stanley A. Brown and Marvin B. Martenfeld, *Creating the Service Cul-
      ture: Strategies for Canadian Business* (Scarborough, Ont.: Prentice-Hall
      Canada, 1990), pp. 58–59.

96   *The Body Shop . . . "'. . . a blast at us'":*
      Stanley A. Brown and Marvin B. Martenfeld, *Creating the Service Cul-
      ture: Strategies for Canadian Business* (Scarborough, Ont.: Prentice-Hall
      Canada, 1990), p. 51.

96   *In an American Management Association . . . feedback process:*
      American Management Association (AMA), "Close to the Cus-
      tomer," *AMACOM Briefings and Surveys* (New York: AMA Membership
      Publications Division, 1987), p. 15.

97–98 *Determining which . . . over time:*
      Kaiser Associates, Inc., "Improving Your Competitive Position
      Through Benchmarking," pamphlet issued by Kaiser Associates, Inc.,
      1595 Springhill Road, Suite 700, Vienna, Virginia.

98   *Air Canada . . . own thinking:*
      Stanley A. Brown and Marvin B. Martenfeld, *Creating the Service Cul-
      ture: Strategies for Canadian Business* (Scarborough, Ont.: Prentice-Hall
      Canada, 1990), p. 55.

98   *In another case . . . with its customers:*
      William A. Band, "Customer Satisfaction Studies Changing Market-
      ing Strategies," *Marketing News*, September 12, 1988, p. 14.

99–100 *The following questions . . . satisfaction?:*
      The Burke Institute, "Customer Satisfaction Research," seminar
      given in Cincinnati, Ohio, March 6–7, 1989. © 1989. The Burke
      Institute, 800 Broadway, Cincinnati, Ohio, p. 3.01.

100   *One such company is Winnebago . . . each dealer:*
      Ronald W. Post and Randal L. Fingarson, "Quality Service Pro-
      gram," in *Case Studies in Service Quality. When America Does It Right*, ed. Jay
      W. Spechler (Norcross, GA: Industrial Engineering and Management
      Press Institute of Industrial Engineers, 1988), p. 299.

102   *This happened when Pacific Gas & Electric Company . . . with few changes:*
      Stephanie Amsden, "Hitting the Service Excellence Target," in *Case*

Studies in Service Quality. When America Does It Right, ed. Jay W. Spechler (Norcross, GA: Industrial Engineering and Management Press Institute of Industrial Engineers, 1988), p. 552.

103   *In the mid-1980s, focus groups helped Ford . . . for improving customer satisfaction:*
Lee R. Miskowski, "Ford: The Quest for Quality," in *Case Studies in Service Quality. When America Does It Right*, ed. Jay W. Spechler (Norcross, GA: Industrial Engineering and Management Press Institute of Industrial Engineers, 1988), pp. 258–259.

103   *In 1981, Caterpillar Inc. . . . performance:*
James Redpath, Jr., "Delivering Quality Service to the Caterpillar Earthmoving Customer," in *Case Studies in Service Quality. When America Does It Right*, ed. Jay W. Spechler (Norcross, GA: Industrial Engineering and Management Press Institute of Industrial Engineers, 1988), pp. 200–201.

103   *"outstandingly effective . . . activity":*
J. Flanagan, "The Critical Incident Technique," *Psychological Bulletin*, 51 (July 1954), pp. 325–358.

105   *In* Thriving on Chaos, *Tom Peters suggests . . . ". . . rep, etc.":*
Tom Peters, *Thriving On Chaos: Handbook for a Management Revolution* (New York: Alfred A. Knopf, 1987), p. 101.

105   *A food service company . . . airlines:*
The Burke Institute, "Customer Satisfaction Research," seminar given in Cincinnati, Ohio, March 6–7, 1989. © 1989. The Burke Institute, 800 Broadway, Cincinnati, Ohio, p. 4.01.

105   *A manufacturer of office equipment . . . retrieval systems":*
The Burke Institute, "Customer Satisfaction Research," seminar given in Cincinnati, Ohio, March 6–7, 1989. © 1989. The Burke Institute, 800 Broadway, Cincinnati, Ohio, p. 4.02.

105   *The Burke Institute of Cincinnati . . . benchmarking information:*
The Burke Institute, "Customer Satisfaction Research," seminar given in Cincinnati, Ohio, March 6–7, 1989. © 1989. The Burke Institute, 800 Broadway, Cincinnati, Ohio, p. 4.04.

105   *Within the* current customer *category . . . a product:*
J. W. Marr, "Letting the Customer be the Judge of Quality," *Quality Progress* (October 1986), p. 48.

105   *Cantel, the Canadian manufacturer . . . ". . . treating him/her, etc.":*
Stanley A. Brown and Marvin B. Martenfeld, *Creating the Service Culture: Strategies for Canadian Business* (Scarborough, Ont.: Prentice-Hall Canada, 1990), p. 62.

105 *"That's their report card . . . ":*
Stanley A. Brown and Marvin B. Martenfeld, *Creating the Service Culture: Strategies for Canadian Business* (Scarborough, Ont.: Prentice-Hall Canada, 1990), p. 62.

106 *General Motors . . . merchandising programs:*
R. J. Bugno, "General Motors Service Quality," in *Case Studies in Service Quality. When America Does It Right,* ed. Jay W. Spechler (Norcross, GA: Industrial Engineering and Management Press Institute of Industrial Engineers, 1988), pp. 2266–267.

106 *In one case, the customers . . . actual expectations:*
William A. Band, "Customer Satisfaction Studies Changing Marketing Strategies," *Marketing News,* September 12, 1988, p. 14.

107 *Wang Laboratories Inc. . . . are interviewed:*
Joseph Lester III, "Striving for Customer Satisfaction and Quality," in *Case Studies in Service Quality. When America Does It Right,* ed. Jay W. Spechler (Norcross, GA: Industrial Engineering and Management Press Institute of Industrial Engineers, 1988), pp. 345–346.

108 *"Formal surveys . . . third party":*
Tom Peters, *Thriving On Chaos: Handbook for a Management Revolution* (New York: Alfred A. Knopf, 1987), p. 100.

108 *While the formal surveys will give . . . " . . . quality changes":*
J. W. Marr, "Letting the Customer be the Judge of Quality," *Quality Progress* (October 1986), p. 48.

108 *The Burke Institute suggests . . . " . . . measures?":*
The Burke Institute, "Customer Satisfaction Research," seminar given in Cincinnati, Ohio, March 6–7, 1989. © 1989. The Burke Institute, 800 Broadway, Cincinnati, Ohio, p. 4.12.

108 *Xerox Canada . . . two months:*
Stanley A. Brown and Marvin B. Martenfeld, *Creating the Service Culture: Strategies for Canadian Business* (Scarborough, Ont.: Prentice-Hall Canada, 1990), p. 43.

108 *Charles Bultmann . . . " . . . change over time":*
"Satisfying Customers is Easier Said Than Done—But Do It," *Marketing News,* May 8, 1989, p. 22.

108 *The Ford Motor Company . . . to use:*
Lee R. Miskowski, "Ford: The Quest for Quality," in *Case Studies in Service Quality. When America Does It Right,* ed. Jay W. Spechler (Norcross, GA: Industrial Engineering and Management Press Institute of Industrial Engineers, 1988), p. 262.

108   *Amdahl Canada Limited asks for . . . deal with it:*
Stanley A. Brown and Marvin B. Martenfeld, *Creating the Service Culture: Strategies for Canadian Business* (Scarborough, Ont.: Prentice-Hall Canada, 1990), p. 37.

109–110   *The Sheraton Hotel chain uses closed-ended questions . . . :*
Sheraton Hotel brochure.

110   *Closed-ended questions also appear on surveys . . . :*
Stephanie Amsden, "Hitting the Service Excellence Target," in *Case Studies in Service Quality. When America Does It Right*, ed. Jay W. Spechler (Norcross, GA: Industrial Engineering and Management Press Institute of Industrial Engineers, 1988), p. 564.

110   *One major hotel's comment card . . . :*
Sheraton Needham Hotel comment card.

111   *In its quality audit survey, for instance, Herman Miller . . . :*
Ray Pukanic and Dick Holm, "The Herman Miller Quality Audit: A Corporate Report Card," in *Case Studies in Service Quality. When America Does It Right*, ed. Jay W. Spechler (Norcross, GA: Industrial Engineering and Management Press Institute of Industrial Engineers, 1988), p. 182.

111   *Speedy Muffler King uses a rating scale . . . :*
Speedy Muffler King customer comment card.

112   *"the relative . . . these areas":*
J. W. Marr, "Letting the Customer be the Judge of Quality," *Quality Progress* (October 1986), p. 48.

112   *"[m]easuring . . . decisions":*
J. W. Marr, "Letting the Customer be the Judge of Quality," *Quality Progress* (October 1986), p. 48.

113   *A survey undertaken . . . " . . . a drawer?":*
Stanley A. Brown and Marvin B. Martenfeld, *Creating the Service Culture: Strategies for Canadian Business* (Scarborough, Ont.: Prentice-Hall Canada, 1990), p. 56.

113   *Barbara Fraser, the General Manager of P&G's . . . " . . . they're concerned":*
Stanley A. Brown and Marvin B. Martenfeld, *Creating the Service Culture: Strategies for Canadian Business* (Scarborough, Ont.: Prentice-Hall Canada, 1990), p. 50.

113   *Jeffrey Marr suggests . . . results are available:*
J. W. Marr, "Letting the Customer be the Judge of Quality," *Quality Progress* (October 1986), p. 49.

113   *In the 1987 AMA report . . . many companies:*
William A. Band, "The Art of Listening to Customers," *Sales and Marketing Management in Canada* (October 1987), p. 15.

114   *Whatever the context . . . customer behavior:*
Donald B. Berryman, "A New Commitment to the Customer," in *Case Studies in Service Quality. When America Does It Right,* ed. Jay W. Spechler (Norcross, GA: Industrial Engineering and Management Press Institute of Industrial Engineers, 1988), p. 438.

114   *The Burke Institute has identified . . . of analysis:*
The Burke Institute, "Customer Satisfaction Research," seminar given in Cincinnati, Ohio, March 6–7, 1989. © 1989. The Burke Institute, 800 Broadway, Cincinnati, Ohio, p. 7.27.

114   *Ron Zemke points out . . . it's to unlevel it:*
George Dixon, "Keep 'Em Satisfied, *Marketing News,* January 2, 1989, p. 14.

115   *When the Royal Bank . . . " . . . refunded":*
Stanley A. Brown and Marvin B. Martenfeld, *Creating the Service Culture: Strategies for Canadian Business* (Scarborough, Ont.: Prentice-Hall Canada, 1990), p. 59.

115   *For IBM Canada . . . telephone access:*
Stanley A. Brown and Marvin B. Martenfeld, *Creating the Service Culture: Strategies for Canadian Business* (Scarborough, Ont.: Prentice-Hall Canada, 1990), p. 42.

115   *Hewlett-Packard . . . by its clients:*
Phil Carter and Thom Edmonds, "Service Quality at the Hewlett-Packard Company," in *Case Studies in Service Quality. When America Does It Right,* ed. Jay W. Spechler (Norcross, GA: Industrial Engineering and Management Press Institute of Industrial Engineers, 1988), pp. 331–332.

115–16   *In some cases, it may be useful . . . reference points:*
Nessim Hanna and John S. Wagle, "Who is Your Satisfied Customer?" *The Journal of Services Marketing,* Vol. 2, No. 3 (Summer 1988), pp. 5–13.

116   *A few years ago, Vicks . . . market leader:*
Harvey Sknolnick, "Marketing Trivia," *Toronto Star,* September 17, 1989, p. F1.

116   *One marketing research expert . . . line employees:*
J. W. Marr, "Letting the Customer be the Judge of Quality," *Quality Progress* (October 1986), p. 49.

116   *Tom Peters suggests . . . " . . . volume of sales)":*
Tom Peters, *Thriving On Chaos: Handbook for a Management Revolution* (New York: Alfred A. Knopf, 1987), p. 101.

117   *Northern Telecom . . . demand times:*
Roy Merrills, "How Northern Telecom Competes on Time," *Harvard Business Review,* July/August 1989, p. 114.

117   *Through customer research, one major airline . . . round table discussions:*
M. J. Bitner, B. H. Booms, and M. S. Teterault, "Critical Incidents in Service Encounters," paper presented at AMA Services Marketing Conference, Washington, D.C., October 1988. Cited in: The Burke Institute, "Customer Satisfaction Research," seminar given in Cincinnati, Ohio, March 6–7, 1989. © 1989. The Burke Institute, 800 Broadway Cincinnati, Ohio, pp. 8.11 and 8.12.

Chapter 5   Managing Customer Relationships

119   *Building relationships with your customers . . . the product:*
Robert H. Franke, "Sales Management Update: Relationship Selling Must Focus on 'Emotional Bank Accounts,'" *Bank Marketing,* April 1988, p. 12.

119   *Augmenting this type of "bank account" . . . products:*
Robert H. Franke, "Sales Management Update: Relationship Selling Must Focus on 'Emotional Bank Accounts,'" *Bank Marketing,* April 1988, p. 10.

120   *When you continually meet . . . repeat business:*
Theodore Marra, "Calculating the Real Value of Customer Service," speech delivered to the Total Action Plan Conference, Skyline Hotel, Toronto, July 5–6, 1988, p. 2.

120   *"Most customers often . . . received it":*
Karl Hellman, "Don't Just Meet Customer Expectations—Exceed Them," *Marketing News,* March 13, 1989, p. 5.

120   *Telling the customer . . . expectations he set:*
Karl Hellman, "Don't Just Meet Customer Expectations—Exceed Them," *Marketing News,* March 13, 1989, p. 5.

120   *Explaining . . . doing for them:*
Karl Hellman, "Don't Just Meet Customer Expectations—Exceed Them," *Marketing News,* March 13, 1989, p. 5.

120   *In order for relationship marketing . . . subtly:*
Robert H. Franke, "Sales Management Update: Relationship Selling Must Focus on 'Emotional Bank Accounts,'" *Bank Marketing,* April 1988, p. 10.

120   *"Stand in the shoes . . . interest them":*
Karl Hellman, "Don't Just Meet Customer Expectations—Exceed Them," *Marketing News*, March 13, 1989, p. 5.

121   *"establishes you . . . keep them longer":*
Harvey B. Mackay, "Humanize Your Selling Strategy," *Harvard Business Review*, March–April, 1988, p. 2.

121   *"It's continually updated . . . about themselves":*
Harvey B. Mackay, "Humanize Your Selling Strategy," *Harvard Business Review*, March–April, 1988, p. 2.

122   *Value-chain analysis . . . for its customers:*
Michael E. Porter, *Competitive Advantage. Creating and Sustaining Superior Performance* (New York: The Free Press, a division of MacMillan, Inc., 1985).

123   *This approach combines . . . scenes come alive:*
Rob Eil, "Marketing Service Quality to Your Customers," speech delivered to the Institute for International Research Total Service Action Plan Conference, July 5–6, 1988, Skyline Hotel, Toronto. (Achievement Excelerator Systems Inc.)

124   *"Long established customers . . . higher prices":*
Patricia Sellers, "What Customers Really Want," *Fortune*, June 4, 1990, p. 61.

124   *The relationships . . . marriage begins:*
Theodore Levitt, "After The Sale Is Over . . .," *Harvard Business Review*, September/October 1983, p. 92.

124   *These started in the early 1980s . . . repeat purchasers:*
Glenn DeSouza, "Now Service Businesses Must Manage Quality," *The Journal of Business Strategy*, May/June 1989, p. 22.

124–125   *Wink Vogel . . . $30 million in 1988:*
Ian Allaby, "Supersmart Management," *Canadian Business*, May 1990, p. 42.

125   *In one American . . . " . . . feed one another":*
Patricia Sellers, "What Customers Really Want," *Fortune,* June 4, 1990, p. 59.

125   *In its quest . . . richer job content:*
Patricia Sellers, "What Customers Really Want," *Fortune,* June 4, 1990, p. 59.

125   *Other companies, such as Super Valu . . . the same day:*
Patricia Sellers, "What Customers Really Want," *Fortune,* June 4, 1990, p. 60.

126   *Parisian is a well known . . . trading region:*
"Managing, Motivating and Training: Training and Service Ameni-ties are Competitive Distinctions," *The Service Edge Newsletter,* Volume 1, Number 4, May 1988, p. 4.

126   *Like any long-term relationship . . . word of mouth:*
Paul B. Brown, "A Bird in the Hand," *Inc.,* August 1989, p. 114.

126   *Glegg Water Conditioning Inc. . . . " . . . than necessary":*
Ian Allaby, "Supersmart Management," *Canadian Business,* May 1990, p. 37.

127   *For example, Gillette's vice-president . . . major accounts:*
Theodore Levitt, "After The Sale Is Over . . . ," *Harvard Business Review,* September/October 1983, p. 92.

127   *It becomes important for you . . . deteriorating?:*
Theodore Levitt, "After The Sale Is Over . . . ," *Harvard Business Review,* September/October 1983, p. 92.

127–28   *Here are some dos and don'ts . . . shifting the blame:*
William A. Band, "Winning and Keeping Industrial Customers," *Sales and Marketing Management in Canada,* June 1986, p. 8.

128   *Levitt suggests four steps . . . awareness and actions:*
William A. Band, "Winning and Keeping Industrial Customers," *Sales and Marketing Management in Canada,* June 1986, p. 8.

129   *There are at least three dimensions . . . service orientation:*
William A. Band, "How to Develop Customer Retention Strategies," *Sales and Marketing Management in Canada,* October 1986, pp. 30–31.

129   *When considering manufactured goods . . . their selection:*
William A. Band, "How to Develop Customer Retention Strategies," *Sales and Marketing Management in Canada,* October 1986, pp. 30–31.

129–30   *Renowned catalog retailer L.L. Bean . . . in a hurry:*
L.L. Bean. *L.L. Bean Christmas Catalog, 1989.*

130   *Following are some elements . . . component exchange:*
William A. Band, "How to Develop Customer Retention Strategies," *Sales and Marketing Management in Canada,* October 1986, pp. 30–31.

130   *General Electric . . . a service call:*
Leonard Vickers, "Value Leverage and Value Creation," in *Competitive Leverage,* ed. Earl L. Bailey (New York: The Conference Board, Inc., 1985), p. 26.

130–31   *Four Seasons Hotel chain . . . and so on:*
William A. Band, "How to Develop Customer Retention Strategies," *Sales and Marketing Management in Canada,* October 1986, pp. 30–31.

131   *Software manufacturer Microsoft Corporation . . . sophistication:*
Daniel J. Lyons, "Microsoft Beefing up Phone Support," *PC Week,*
October 17, 1988, p. 72.

131   *Management consultant Barbara Bund Jackson . . . vendor support:*
Barbara Bund Jackson, *Winning and Keeping Industrial Customers. The
Dynamics of Customer Relationships* (Lexington, MA: D.C. Heath and
Company, 1985), p. 43.

132   *In his book,* The Customer Is Key, *. . . system problems:*
Milind M. Lele, with Jagdish N. Sheth, *The Customer Is Key* (New York:
John Wiley & Sons, 1987).

132   *Three additional variables . . . risk reduction:*
Milind M. Lele, with Jagdish N. Sheth, *The Customer Is Key* (New York:
John Wiley & Sons, 1987), pp. 196–197.

133   *leading children's toy manufacturer . . . Fisher-Price toy:*
Fisher-Price *. . . Our Company In Brief,* 1988.

133   *Consider AT&T . . . equipment on the spot:*
The AT&T Sourcebook, Summer/Fall 1989. AT&T, *1988 Annual Report.*

133–34   *in how Audi . . . products:*
David Versical, "New Audi Warranty Covers Most Maintenance,"
Automotive News, July 15, 1988, p. 3.

Chapter 6   Delivering on Your Promise: Achieving High-Quality Operational Performance

135   *It is called the Quality and Productivity Center . . . ". . . the first time":*
Thomas A. Stewart, "Westinghouse Gets Respect At Last," *Fortune,* July
3, 1989, p. 94.

135   *"When most . . . the process":*
Thomas A. Stewart, "Westinghouse Gets Respect At Last," *Fortune,* July
3, 1989, p. 94.

135   *The center's job is to improve everything " . . . quality rather than
productivity":*
Thomas A. Stewart, "Westinghouse Gets Respect At Last," *Fortune,* July
3, 1989, p. 94.

136   *More than 100 times a year teams . . . implement improvements:*
Thomas A. Stewart, "Westinghouse Gets Respect At Last," *Fortune,* July
3, 1989, p. 96.

136   *Japanese quality guru Kaoru Ishikawa . . . quality control:*
Kaoru Ishikawa, *What Is Total Quality Control? The Japanese Way,*

translated by David J. Lu (Englewood Cliffs, NJ: Prentice-Hall, 1985), p. 91.

136 *The business journal . . . corporate activities:*
Lawrence P. Sullivan, "The Seven Stages In Company-Wide Quality Control," *Quality Progress*, May 1986, p. 79.

137 *Among them is . . . on the customer:*
David A. Garvin, *Managing Quality* (New York: The Free Press, 1988), pp. 190–192.

137 *Managing quality is not . . . for quality improvement:*
Lawrence P. Sullivan, "The Seven Stages In Company-Wide Quality Control," *Quality Progress*, May 1986, p. 79.

137 *Such was the case . . . finance to shipping:*
Brian Dumaine, "What the Leaders of Tomorrow See," *Fortune,* July 3, 1989, p. 51.

137 *Fuji-Xerox kept this in mind . . . quality in 1980:*
Hidy Kaihatsu, director, International Relations, Fuji-Xerox, from an address at the Second Annual Quality Conference, New York City, May 16–17, 1989.

138 *At General Motors . . . for this effort:*
Alex Taylor III, "The Tasks Facing General Motors," *Fortune*, March 13, 1989, p. 53.

138 *Paul Revere Insurance Companies . . . first year:*
Patrick L. Townsend with Joan E. Gebhardt, *Commit to Quality* (New York: John Wiley & Sons, Inc., 1986), p. xv.

139 *At the BASF Corporation . . . recurring errors:*
Manfred Buller, "Quality Improvement Process at BASF Polymers Group," in *Case Studies in Service Quality. When America Does It Right*, ed. Jay W. Spechler (Norcross, GA: Industrial Engineering and Management Press Institute of Industrial Engineers, 1988), p. 57.

139 *At Winnipeg-based . . . Lorne Evans:*
Ian Allaby, "Supersmart Management," *Canadian Business*, May 1990, p. 32.

139 *This type of thinking was used . . . Japanese competition:*
Patricia Sellers, "Getting the Customers to Love You," *Fortune*, March 13, 1989, pp. 38–39.

140 *With the desire . . . Manufactured Product:*
[No title] *The Economist*, September 23, 1989, [n.p.].

140   *Quality management . . . executives:*
David A. Gavin, *Managing Quality* (New York: The Free Press, 1988),
p. 6.

140   *From statistical quality control . . . operations processes:*
David A. Gavin, *Managing Quality* (New York: The Free Press, 1988),
p. 12.

140   *Then came the concept . . . within a company:*
Armand V. Feigenbaum, *Total Quality Control* (New York: McGraw-
Hill Book Company, 1983) in "Evolution of Quality Improvement,"
unpublished manuscript, Process Management Institute.

140–41   *Recognition . . . "right the first time":*
Philip B. Crosby, *The Eternally Successful Organization. The Art of
Corporate Wellness* (New York: McGraw-Hill Book Company, 1988),
p. 35.

141   *As with corporate-wide quality control . . . personal feedback:*
Philip B. Crosby, *The Eternally Successful Organization. The Art of
Corporate Wellness* (New York: McGraw-Hill Book Company, 1988),
p. 35.

141   *Continuous education . . . necessary:*
Philip B. Crosby, *The Eternally Successful Organization. The Art of
Corporate Wellness* (New York: McGraw-Hill Book Company, 1988), pp.
90–91.

141   *Manufacturing consultant . . . excellence:*
Douglas Cudlip and Benjamin Schlussel, "Managing the Journey to
Total Quality Control," paper presented at Institute for International
Research "Total Quality" conference, Toronto, June 1–2, 1988.

144   *Patricia Sellers . . . end with the sale:*
Patricia Sellers, "Getting the Customers to Love You," *Fortune,* March
13, 1989, pp. 39–49.

146   *"Quality is neither . . . what it is":*
Robert M. Pirsig, *Zen and the Art of Motorcycle Maintenance* (New York:
Bantam Books, 1974), pp. 185, 213.

146   *"It is a condition . . . fraudulent":*
Barbara W. Tuchman, "The Decline of Quality," *New York Times
Magazine,* November 2, 1980, p. 38.

146   *"Differences . . . attribute":*
Lawrence Abbot, *Quality and Competition* (New York: Columbia
University Press, 1955), pp. 126–127.

146 *"Quality . . . attribute":*
Keith B. Leffler, "Ambiguous Changes in Product Quality," *American Economic Review,* December 1982, p. 956.

146 *"Quality . . . wants":*
Corwin E. Edwards, "The Meaning of Quality," *Quality Progress,* October 1968, p. 37.

147 *"In the final analysis . . . consumer preferences":*
Alfred A. Kuehn and Ralph L. Day, "Strategy of Product Quality," *Harvard Business Review,* November–December 1962, p. 101.

147 *"Quality . . . use":*
J. M. Juran, ed., *Quality Control Handbook,* 3rd ed. (New York: McGraw-Hill, 1974), p. 22.

147 *"overall performance and attitude . . . choice of our customers":*
General Electric Company Mission Statement.

147 *"Quality . . . requirements":*
Phillip B. Crosby, *Quality Is Free* (New York: New American Library, 1979), p. 15.

147 *"Quality . . . specification":*
Harold L. Gilmore, "Product Conformance and Cost," *Quality Press,* June 1974, p. 16.

148 *"The degree of excellence . . . cost":*
Robert A. Broh, *Managing Quality for Higher Profits* (New York: McGraw-Hill, 1982), p. 3.

148 *"[what is] best . . . the product":*
Armand V. Feigenbaum, *Total Quality Control* (New York: McGraw-Hill, 1961), p. 1.

149 *Another way to categorize . . . external failure:*
John T. Hagen, ed., *Principles of Quality Costs* (Milwaukee, WI: American Society for Quality Control, 1986).

149–50 *In a manufacturing . . . and personnel:*
Integrated Quality: Cost of Quality (manual) Coopers & Lybrand Manufacturing Services, 1988.

150 *According to cost . . . quality costs:*
Integrated Quality: Cost of Quality (manual) Coopers & Lybrand Manufacturing Services, 1988.

150–151 *Typical appraisal . . . laboratory personnel:*
Integrated Quality: Cost of Quality (manual) Coopers & Lybrand Manufacturing Services, 1988.

151   *Costs associated . . . total COQ:*
Integrated Quality: Cost of Quality (manual) Coopers & Lybrand
Manufacturing Services, 1988.

151   *By designing a control system . . . requirements:*
"The Race To Quality Improvement," Advertisement. *Fortune.*

151–52   *Internal failure . . . efforts:*
K. Theodore Krantz, "How Velcro Got Hooked on Quality," *Harvard Business Review*, September/October 1989, pp. 34–35.

152   *Internal failure costs . . . carrying costs:*
Integrated Quality: Cost of Quality (Manual) Coopers & Lybrand
Manufacturing Services, 1988.

152   *Velcro USA threw away . . . achieved:*
K. Theodore Krantz, "How Velcro Got Hooked on Quality," *Harvard Business Review*, September/October 1989, pp. 34–35.

152   *In 1986, Hyundai . . . their dollar:*
"Why U.S. Car Makers Are Losing Ground," *Fortune*, October 23, 1989, p. 96.

154   *For example, 3M's . . . or higher:*
Roy W. Mayeske, "Improving Service Quality in Transportation," in *Case Studies in Service Quality. When America Does It Right*, ed. Jay W. Spechler (Norcross, GA: Industrial Engineering and Management Press Institute of Industrial Engineers, 1988), p. 409.

155   *Several implementation issues . . . training:*
Integrated Quality: Cost of Quality (manual) Coopers & Lybrand
Manufacturing Services, 1988.

155   *the COQ program . . . at Westinghouse . . . operations:*
George C. Dorman, "Go With the Flow—Measuring Information Worker Quality," in *Total Quality Performance. Highlights of a Conference*, ed. Lawrence Schein and Melissa A. Berman (New York: The Conference Board, Inc., 1988), pp. 29–30.

156   *One group of techniques . . . processes:*
The Memory Jogger, a Pocket Guide of Tools for Continuous Improvement (Massachusetts: Goal/QPC Methuen, 1988).

157   *the Florida Power & Light Company . . . trouble areas:*
Joseph W. Dickey, "Transferring Customer Needs to Nuclear Power Operations: FPL's Policy Deployment Process," in *Total Quality Performance. Highlights of a Conference*, ed. Lawrence Schein and Melissa A. Berman (New York: The Conference Board, Inc., 1988).

158   *The support services group within AT&T . . . time:*
Laurence C. Seifert, "AT&T's Full-Stream Quality Architecture," in *Total Quality Performance. Highlights of a Conference,* ed. Lawrence Schein and Melissa A. Berman (New York: The Conference Board, Inc., 1988), p. 48.

159   *A histogram can also be applied . . . most common:*
Jack Smith, "Quality in Computer Services: Maintenance, Repair, and Support Services," in *Case Studies in Service Quality. When America Does It Right,* ed. Jay W. Spechler (Norcross, GA: Industrial Engineering and Management Press Institute of Industrial Engineers, 1988), p. 135.

159   *Histograms themselves can be further split . . . components:*
John J. Falzon, "Measuring the Quality of Services," in *Total Quality Performance. Highlights of a Conference,* ed. Lawrence Schein and Melissa A. Berman (New York: The Conference Board, Inc., 1988), p. 55.

159   *at the Casting Division of Ford Motor Company . . . improvement:*
Thomas P. Enright, "Customer-Driven Quality," in *Total Quality Performance. Highlights of a Conference,* ed. Lawrence Schein and Melissa A. Berman (New York: The Conference Board, Inc., 1988), p. 70.

160   *The Cummins Engine Company . . . vary over time:*
Marianna Grossman, "Process Improvement in Customer Service: An Example," in *Case Studies in Service Quality. When America Does It Right,* ed. Jay W. Spechler (Norcross, GA: Industrial Engineering and Management Press Institute of Industrial Engineers, 1988), pp. 202–213.

161   *These techniques are . . . presentations:*
Leadership Through Quality, Problem-Solving Process User's Manual (Xerox Corporation, 1985).

162   *at the Casting Division of Ford Motor Company . . . seven items:*
Thomas P. Enright, "Customer-Driven Quality," in *Total Quality Performance. Highlights of a Conference,* ed. Lawrence Schein and Melissa A. Berman (New York: The Conference Board, Inc., 1988), p. 70.

163   *Once the analysis is complete . . . hindering forces?:*
Leadership Through Quality, Problem-Solving Process User's Manual (Xerox Corporation, 1985).

165   *As mentioned earlier, true quality improvement . . . service characteristics:*
William Eureka and Nancy Ryan, *The Customer Driven Company. Managerial Perspectives on QFD* (Dearborn, MI: American Supplier Institute, 1988), p. 2.

165–66   *Such was the case for IBM . . . " . . . in its history":*
Joel Dreyfuss, "Reinventing IBM," *Fortune,* August 14, 1989, pp. 34–35.

166   *General Motors was also jolted . . . in five years:*
Patricia Sellers, "Getting the Customers to Love You," *Fortune*, March 13, 1989, p. 38.

166   *In its broadest applications . . . in your company:*
Sid Ingle and Nima Ingle, *Quality Circles in Service Industries* (Englewood Cliffs, New Jersey: Prentice-Hall Inc., 1983), p. 139.

166   *In their book* The Customer Driven Company *. . . supplier organization:*
William Eureka and Nancy Ryan, *The Customer Driven Company. Managerial Perspectives on QFD* (Dearborn, Michigan: American Supplier Institute, 1988), p. 2.

166   *Quality function deployment is sometimes referred . . . might occur:*
Bob King, *Better Designs in Half the Time. Implementation of QFD, Quality Function Deployment in America* (Methune, Massachusetts: GOAL/QPC, 1987), p. 2–1.

167   *Writing in the newsletter* Customer Focus *. . . :*
Richard Huot, "Meeting Customer Expectations with the 'House of Quality,'" *Customer Focus*, Coopers & Lybrand, Summer 1989, Volume 1, Number 1.

Chapter 7   The Value Creators: People

173   *This scenario cannot last for long . . . " . . . inseparable":*
Robert L. Desatnick, *Managing to Keep the Customer: How to Achieve and Maintain Superior Customer Service Throughout the Organization* (San Francisco: Jossey-Bass Publishers, 1987), p. 15.

174   *According to the Research Institute of America . . . into the 1990s:*
Research Institute of America, "Technical Assistance Research Program," *Money Advisory Newsletter*, June 1985. Cited in Robert L. Desatnick, *Managing to Keep the Customer: How to Achieve and Maintain Superior Customer Service Throughout the Organization* (San Francisco: Jossey-Bass Publishers, 1987), p. 15.

174   *Eighty percent of the opportunity . . . that opportunity:*
Robert L. Desatnick, *Managing to Keep the Customer: How to Achieve and Maintain Superior Customer Service Throughout the Organization* (San Francisco: Jossey-Bass Publishers, 1987), p. 15.

174   *"Your company's real existence . . . its employees":*
Terrence E. Reid and Allan A. Kennedy, *Corporate Cultures: The Rites and Rituals of Corporate Life* (Don Mills, Ontario: Addison-Wesley, 1982), p. 4.

174   *The classic example of this kind . . . early 1980s:*
"The Art of Loving," *INC.*, May 1989, p. 35.

175   *Does your organization care . . . and employees:*
Cass Bettinger, "Use Corporate Culture to Trigger High Performance," *The Journal of Business Strategy*, March/April 1989, pp. 38–42.

175   *This type of attitude change . . . certain products:*
Peter E. Larson, *Winning Strategies. Organizational Effectiveness Through Better Management of People* (Ottawa: The Conference Board of Canada, Report 36-89-E, January 1989), pp. 6–7.

176   *Consultant Ron Zemke proposes . . . " . . . best way possible":*
Ron Zemke, "Questions Readers Ask," *The Service Edge* (November 1989), p. 6.

176–77   *The First National Bank of Chicago . . . customer service strategy:*
E. Neal Trogdon, "Customer Perspective as a Competitive Weapon," in *Total Quality Performance. Highlights of a Conference*, ed. Lawrence Schein and Melissa A. Berman (New York: The Conference Board, Inc., 1988).

177   *Victor Kiam, owner and President of Remington . . . " . . . in its success":*
from brochure for Victor Kiam conference, Massey Hall, Toronto, Ontario, September 19, 1989.

178   Fortune *magazine reports that "visionary leadership" . . . study, however:*
Lester B. Korn, "How the Next CEO Will Be Different," *Fortune*, May 22, 1989, p. 157.

179   *In their book* Leaders *. . . push them:*
Warren Bennis and Burt Nannus, *Leaders: The Strategies for Taking Charge* (New York: Harper & Row, 1985).

179   *Managers, on the other hand . . . today:*
Warren Bennis and Burt Nannus, *Leaders: The Strategies for Taking Charge* (New York: Harper & Row, 1985).

179   *"putting a 'hard edge' on the dream":*
"Vision training. Putting a hard edge on the dream." A case study by Wayne Johnson, Vice-President, Human Resources. Toronto: Gilmore & Associates, 1988.

179   *"having a mental picture . . . for being":*
Leonard L. Berry, David R. Bennett, Carter W. Brown, *Service Quality. A Profit Strategy for Financial Institutions* (Homewood, IL: Dow Jones-Irwin, 1989), p. 83.

179–80   *"Virtually everyone who has studied . . . commitment":*
Walter Kiechiel III, "No Word From On High," *Fortune*, January 6, 1986, pp. 125–126.

180 *"A quality system . . . of management":*
"Quality First," American Society for Quality Control (booklet), Milwaukee, Wisconsin, [N.d.].

180 *Top management must "model" . . . with customers:*
William A. Band, "Work with Your Human Resources Department to Develop Customer-Responsive Employees," *Sales and Marketing Management in Canada*, May 1989, p. 7.

180–81 *"Van Horne was . . . clothesline":*
David Cruise and Alison Griffiths, *Lords of the Line* (Markham, Ontario: Penguin, 1988), pp. 138–139.

181 *An American couple . . . compact disk!:*
John Guaspari, *The Customer Connection* (New York: AMACOM, 1988), pp. 135–136.

181 *At the highly successful University National Bank & Trust Company . . . waiting in line:*
"Case Study: University National Bank," in *Workbook For: "A Passion for Customers"* (Toronto: B/PAA Conference Seminar, September 10, 1988), p. 17.

181 *At Dallas-based Southwest Airlines . . . be with them:*
CBS News—60 Minutes, Volume XXII, Number 5, October 15, 1989, Transcript, p. 65.

182 *One author calls this phenomenon "segmentalism" . . . value delivery process:*
Roseabeth Moss Kanter, *The Change Masters. Innovation for Productivity in the American Corporation* (New York: Simon and Schuster, 1983), p. 28.

182 *Chaparral Steel of Midlothian, Texas . . . quality for customers:*
Tom Peters, *Thriving on Chaos: A Handbook for a Management Revolution* (Toronto: Random House, 1987), p. 169.

182–83 *It was Kaoru Ishikawa . . . to their "enemies":*
Kaoru Ishikawa, *What is Total Quality Control? The Japanese Way*, translated by David J. Lu (Englewood Cliffs, NJ: Prentice-Hall, 1985), p. 108.

183 *If employees consider . . . will be happier too:*
Anne Petite, *The Manager's Guide to Service Excellence. The Fine Art of Customer Service* (Toronto: Summerhill Press Ltd., 1989), p. 55.

183 *Ishikawa recommends that staff groups . . . effectively in the future:*
Kaoru Ishikawa, *What is Total Quality Control? The Japanese Way*, translated by David J. Lu (Englewood Cliffs, NJ: Prentice-Hall, 1985), p. 108.

184   *In 1988, IBM CEO John Akers . . . with their customers:*
Joel Dreyfuss, "Reinventing IBM," *Fortune,* August 14, 1989, pp. 31, 33.

184   *"Organization . . . improvisation":*
Lord Beaverbrook, publisher, sign on his desk in his Fleet Street office in the 1930s, according to Lewis Chester and Jonathan Fenby in *The Fall of the House of Beaverbrook* (1979). Cited in John Robert Colombo, *Colombo's New Canadian Quotations* (Edmonton: Hurtig, 1987), p. 43b.

184–85   *T. D. Rodgers . . . customer satisfaction:*
Brian Dumaine, "What the Leaders of Tomorrow See," *Fortune,* July 3, 1989, p. 58.

185   *For whatever reason . . . nourishment:*
Warren Evans, "Service Management: So What's New?", A.C.M.O. Manager, No. 4, 1987, p. 35.

185–86   *Writing in the newsletter . . . " . . . customer-focused":*
Gregory Lloyd, "Cutting Through Bureaucratic Red Tape," *Customer Focus,* Coopers & Lybrand, Winter 1990, Volume 2, Number 1.

187   *Tom Peters believes . . . levels of management:*
Tom Peters, *Thriving on Chaos: A Handbook for a Management Revolution* (Toronto: Random House, 1987), pp. 355–356.

187   *This is the approach taken at Maritime . . . " . . . marketplace best":*
Ian Allaby, "The Search for Quality," *Canadian Business,* May 1990, p. 34.

188   *As Reginald H. Jones . . . " . . . U.S. business history":*
Walter Guzzardi, "Wisdom from the Giants of Business," *Fortune,* July 3, 1989, p. 84.

188   *As Robert Noyce . . . " . . . they do well":*
Walter Guzzardi, "Wisdom from the Giants of Business," *Fortune,* July 3, 1989, p. 84.

188   *Mike Walsh . . . " . . . middle of the night":*
Brian Dumaine, "What the Leaders of Tomorrow See," *Fortune,* July 3, 1989, p. 51.

188   *A recent* Fortune *article . . . as in the past:*
Brian Dumaine, "What the Leaders of Tomorrow See," *Fortune,* July 3, 1989, p. 51.

188–89   *Federal Express already gives . . . could resume:*
Tom Peters, *Thriving on Chaos: A Handbook for a Management Revolution* (Toronto: Random House, 1987), p. 292.

189 *At Nordstrom Inc. . . . serving customers:*
Tom Peters, *Thriving on Chaos: A Handbook for a Management Revolution* (Toronto: Random House, 1987), p. 378.

189 *"People must not be punished . . . new opportunities":*
Ron Zemke, with Dick Schaaf, *The Service Edge: 101 Companies That Profit From Customer Care* (New York: New American Library, 1989), p. 409.

189 *Unlike the "quality circles" . . . ". . . strategy":*
Brian Dumaine, "Who Needs a Boss?" *Fortune*, May 7, 1990, p. 52.

189 *Some teams, as a 1990 Fortune article pointed out . . . :*
Brian Dumaine, "Who Needs a Boss?" *Fortune*, May 7, 1990, p. 52.

190 *The more complex a problem . . . ". . . entire corporation":*
Brian Dumaine, "Who Needs a Boss?" *Fortune*, May 7, 1990, p. 54.

190 *James Watson . . . ". . . interest in them":*
Brian Dumaine, "Who Needs a Boss?" *Fortune*, May 7, 1990, p. 58.

190 *"People are adjusting . . . rewarding work":*
Brian Dumaine, "Who Needs a Boss?" *Fortune*, May 7, 1990, p. 60.

190 *In 1986, when American Airlines . . . feedback system:*
Ron Zemke, with Dick Schaaf, *The Service Edge: 101 Companies That Profit From Customer Care* (New York: New American Library, 1989), p. 91.

191 *At General Motors . . . $52 million:*
Patricia Sellers, "Getting the Customers to Love You," *Fortune*, March 13, 1989, p. 53.

191 *Now that textile manufacturer Milliken . . . delivery time:*
Tom Peters, *Thriving on Chaos: A Handbook for a Management Revolution* (Toronto: Random House, 1987), p. 112.

192 *"Typically, a team . . . the dissenters":*
Brian Dumaine, "Who Needs a Boss?" *Fortune*, May 7, 1990, p. 60.

192 *Goodmeasure Inc. . . . process:*
Solving Quality and Productivity Problems. Goodmeasure's Guide to Corrective Action (Milwaukee, WI: American Society for Quality Control [ASQC], 1988). Reprinted with the permission of ASQC.

192 *For example, Wal-Mart . . . ". . . on the firing line":*
"Leaders of the Most Admired," *Fortune*, January 29, 1990, p. 46.

194 *The overall purpose of a problem-solving team . . . team members:*
Solving Quality and Productivity Problems. Goodmeasure's Guide to Correc-

tive Action (Milwaukee, WI: American Society for Quality Control [ASQC], 1988). Reprinted with the permission of ASQC.

194   *Individual members . . . active participants:*
Solving Quality and Productivity Problems. Goodmeasure's Guide to Corrective Action (Milwaukee, WI: American Society for Quality Control [ASQC], 1988). Reprinted with the permission of ASQC.

194   *The team leader's role . . . makes clear decisions:*
Solving Quality and Productivity Problems. Goodmeasure's Guide to Corrective Action (Milwaukee, WI: American Society for Quality Control [ASQC], 1988). Reprinted with the permission of ASQC.

194–95   *The more senior managers . . . team members:*
Solving Quality and Productivity Problems. Goodmeasure's Guide to Corrective Action (Milwaukee, WI: American Society for Quality Control [ASQC], 1988). Reprinted with the permission of ASQC.

196   *"In the end . . . the other two":*
Lee Iacocca with William Novak, *Iacocca: An Autobiography* (New York: Bantam Books, 1984), p. 167.

196   *The ability to work in teams . . . a good team member:*
"Winning Strategies," *Canadian Business Review,* Summer 1989, p. 42.

196–197   *A regional vice-president for Nordstrom . . . "friendliness":*
Tom Peters, *Thriving on Chaos: A Handbook for a Management Revolution* (Toronto: Random House, 1987), p. 316.

197   *Retailer Luciano Benetton . . . if not impossible:*
Tom Peters, *Thriving on Chaos* (New York: Alfred A. Knopf, 1987), p. 111.

197   *In* Managing to Keep the Customer *. . . ". . . manager's time":*
Robert L. Desatnick, *Managing to Keep the Customer: How to Achieve and Maintain Superior Customer Service Throughout the Organization* (San Francisco: Jossey-Bass Publishers, 1987), pp. 36–37.

198   *A survey undertaken . . . gross sales:*
Robert L. Desatnick, *Managing to Keep the Customer: How to Achieve and Maintain Superior Customer Service Throughout the Organization* (San Francisco: Jossey-Bass Publishers, 1987), p. 51.

198   *"If you think education . . . ignorance":*
Derek Bok. Quoted in Herbert V. Prochnow and Herbert V. Prochnow, Jr., compilers, *The Toastmaster's Treasure Chest,* 2nd edition (New York: Harper & Row, 1988), no. 612, p. 39.

198   *"To emphasize . . . been achieved":*
Robert L. Desatnick, *Managing to Keep the Customer: How to Achieve*

and Maintain Superior Customer Service Throughout the Organization (San Francisco: Jossey-Bass Publishers, 1987), p. 52.

199   *S&O Copiers Inc. . . . contented customers:*
"S&O Copiers Inc.—Building for the Future," *Toronto Business,* September 1989, p. 8.

199   *The Citicorp survey . . . jobs better:*
Robert L. Desatnick, *Managing to Keep the Customer: How to Achieve and Maintain Superior Customer Service Throughout the Organization* (San Francisco: Jossey-Bass Publishers, 1987), p. 10.

199   *Among the companies . . . John Deere:*
Robert L. Desatnick, *Managing to Keep the Customer: How to Achieve and Maintain Superior Customer Service Throughout the Organization* (San Francisco: Jossey-Bass Publishers, 1987), p. 53.

199–200   *IBM Canada . . . staff members employed:*
Sally R. Luce, *Building Quality Through People* (Ottawa: The Conference Board of Canada, September 1985, Report 03-85), p. 20.

200   *When Canadian Urban Transit Association . . . support of management:*
Canadian Urban Transit Association, "Overcoming Tradition: Transit Drivers in Transition," Seminar given by Michael W. Roschlau, Manager of Training, Canadian Urban Transit Association, at the Total Service Conference, Toronto, Ontario, July 6, 1988, pp. 4–16.

200   *"Selection interviewing . . . Time management":*
Robert L. Desatnick, *Managing to Keep the Customer: How to Achieve and Maintain Superior Customer Service Throughout the Organization* (San Francisco: Jossey-Bass Publishers, 1987), p. 60.

201–2   *Van Horne took this principle . . . " . . . you came from":*
David Cruise and Alison Griffiths, *Lords of the Line* (Markham, Ontario: Penguin, 1988), p. 134.

202   *One supervisor at a Midwestern U.S. Dairy . . . to work:*
Robert L. Desatnick, *Managing to Keep the Customer: How to Achieve and Maintain Superior Customer Service Throughout the Organization* (San Francisco: Jossey-Bass Publishers, 1987), pp. 82–83.

202   *Drew Dimond . . . value to their customers:*
"A Special Report on Developments in Quality Customer Service Practices," *The Service Edge,* Lakewood Publications.

202–3   *Laura Secord . . . Canadian candy market:*
F. C. Van Parys, President and CEO, Laura Secord, "Caring: A Strategy to Win," talk given at "Improved Customer Care Conference," sponsored by Institute for International Research, Toronto, Ontario, April 26–27, 1989.

203   *This is how Emery Apparel . . . two managers:*
Ian Allaby, "The Search for Quality," *Canadian Business,* May 1990,
p. 29.

203   *McDonald's has incorporated . . . McDonald's McBucks:*
Robert L. Desatnick, *Managing to Keep the Customer: How to Achieve
and Maintain Superior Customer Service Throughout the Organization* (San
Francisco: Jossey-Bass Publishers, 1987), pp. 110–111.

204   *"Step 1: Greet the Customer . . . transaction":*
Robert L. Desatnick, *Managing to Keep the Customer: How to Achieve
and Maintain Superior Customer Service Throughout the Organization* (San
Francisco: Jossey-Bass Publishers, 1987), p. 44.

205   *"They rate themselves . . . we talk about it":*
Ian Allaby, "The Search for Quality," *Canadian Business,* May 1990,
p. 32.

Chapter 8   Preparing for Change

211–212   *During the last half of the 1980s . . . not come overnight:*
David Goodhard, "Siemens Revamp Crucial to Future in Electronics
Field," *The Financial Post,* March 20, 1989, p. 25.

213   *Despite the many barriers . . . transition:*
David Goodhard, "Siemens Revamp Crucial to Future in Electronics
Field," *The Financial Post,* March 20, 1989, p. 25.

215   *The transformation of Toronto's* Globe & Mail *. . . business affairs:*
Fraser Michaels, "The Globe Wars," *Saturday Night,* December
1989, p. 49.

215–16   *Perhaps the best-known example . . . leading the change:*
Lee Iacocca with William Novak, *Iacocca: An Autobiography* (New York:
Bantam Books, 1984), p. 223.

216   *. . . executives at Dow Chemical . . . key business goal:*
Personal interview with the author.

217   *Tiffany, once considered the retailer . . . " . . . luxury products":*
Faye Rice, "Tiffany Tries the Cartier Formula," *Fortune,* November
20, 1989, pp. 141–142.

218   *Johnson & Johnson is one company . . . baby products:*
Paula Terry, "Baby Laundry Liquid Finds Niche," *Playback Strategy,*
January 15, 1990, p. 8.

219   *But new research methods . . . traditional market research approaches:*
James Fitzgerald, "New Product Stores Showcases Novel Ideas,"
Playback Strategy, January 15, 1990, p. 28.

220   *If there's one company . . . repeat customers:*
Ian Chadwick, "Dell Computer: From Mail-Order to Market Leader,"
Playback Strategy, January 15, 1990, p. 26.

220   *At the Canadian Imperial Bank of Commerce . . . market-driven organization:*
Jonathan Ferguson, "Here Comes the Commerce: A Stodgy Canadian Bank Uses Teamwork Training and Vision to Chase the Leaders,"
The Toronto Star, Sunday, January 21, 1990, p. F1.

221   *AT&T . . . communications program:*
Peter Coy and Geoff Lewis, "How AT&T Learned to Act Like a
Computer Company," *Business Week,* January 22, 1990, pp. 68–69.

221–22   *The Canadian Imperial Bank of Commerce . . . improvement program:*
Jonathan Ferguson, "Here Comes the Commerce: A Stodgy Cana-
dian Bank Uses Teamwork Training and Vision to Chase the Leaders,"
The Toronto Star, Sunday, January 21, 1990, p. F1.

222   *. . . the Southern California Gas Company . . . $192,000:*
Chris Lee, "Training the Front Line to Train the Front Line,"
Training, March 1987, p. 78.

223   *One company that has devised . . . adopted more quickly:*
David J. Brunnen, "Developing an Enterprise Culture at British
Telecom," *Long Range Planning,* Vol. 22, No. 2, 1989, pp. 27–36.

223   *For example, Dow Chemical . . . why do it?:*
Company pamphlet, *Vision and Strategy For the Nineties,* Dow
Chemical Company.

223–24   *At American Express . . . :*
Cover of *Fortune,* November 20, 1989.

Chapter 9   Developing Your Action Program

227   *Senior executives must not delegate . . . constant leadership:*
Joseph Juran, *Juran on Planning for Quality* (New York: The Free Press,
1988).

230   *Value analysis is a technique . . . at minimal cost:*
Personal interview with the author.

231–32   *Xerox Corporation began . . . Business Excellence:*
Benchmarking for Quality (U.S.A.: Xerox Corporation, 1988), p. 29.

232   *"Xerox's Benchmarking Program . . . more competitive":*
Benchmarking for Quality (U.S.A.: Xerox Corporation, 1988), p. 3.

232   *In Xerox's electronics division . . . improve turnaround time:*
Benchmarking for Quality (U.S.A.: Xerox Corporation, 1988), p. 3.

233   *There are several ways . . . " . . . the first time":*
John M. Groocock, *The Chain of Quality. Market Dominance Through Product Superiority* (New York: John Wiley & Sons, 1986), p. 53.

233   *Surveys by the American Society for Quality Control . . . 20 to 30 percent of revenues:*
Lawrence Schein, "Introduction," in *Total Quality Performance. Highlights of a Conference*, eds. Lawrence Schein and Melissa A. Berman (New York: The Conference Board, Inc., 1988), p. viii.

233   *John M. Groocock reports in* The Chain of Quality *. . . other costs:*
John M. Groocock, *The Chain of Quality. Market Dominance Through Product Superiority* (New York: John Wiley & Sons, 1986), p. 60.

233   *If a typical manufacturer . . . poor quality practices:*
John M. Groocock, *The Chain of Quality. Market Dominance Through Product Superiority* (New York: John Wiley & Sons, 1986), p. 59.

234   *incurring excess overtime . . . :*
A University of Michigan/AIPICS study survey on companies using manufacturing systems. Firms decreased overtime by 85 percent. From a Coopers & Lybrand Consulting Group handout, "Manufacturing Systems: Are You Holding I.O.U.'s?"

234   *Another way of looking at the cost of poor quality . . . complaint management systems:*
Ted Marra, "Calculating the Real Value of Customer Service," speech delivered to the Total Action Plan Conference, Skyline Hotel, Toronto, July 5–6, 1988.

235   *[Ted Marra] indicates the following levels of return . . . 100 percent:*
Ted Marra, "Calculating the Real Value of Customer Service," speech delivered to the Total Action Plan Conference, Skyline Hotel, Toronto, July 5–6, 1988.

235   PIMS Principles, *Robert Buzzell and Bradley Gale . . . customer attrition:*
Robert D. Buzzell and Bradley T. Gale, *The PIMS Principles. Linking Strategy to Performance.* (New York: The Free Press, a division of Macmillan, Inc., 1987), p. 107.

235   *Royal Bank president . . . " . . . drives our bank":*
John Raymond, "Worth Repeating," *Globe and Mail,* April 5, 1989.

235–36   *"Reduced vulnerability . . . build market share":*
Robert D. Buzzell and Bradley T. Gale, *The PIMS Principles. Linking Strategy to Performance* (New York: The Free Press, a division of Macmillan, Inc., 1987), p. 107.

239   *The Maytag Corpiration, which has for years . . . in the marketplace:*
"The Conference Board Management Briefing," *Marketing*, December 1989, January 1990.

240   *As you formulate strategy . . . " . . . explain to the customer?":*
Karl Albrecht, *At America's Service* (Homewood, IL: Dow Jones-Irwin, 1988), p. 173.

241   *. . . on new developments:*
David Clutterbuck, "Developing Customer Care Training Programmes," *MIP*, 7, 1/2, 1989, p. 34–37.

242   *Air Canada has recently launched . . . for better customer service:*
"Special Report on Internal Marketing," *Playback Strategy*, November 20, 1989, p. 31.

242   *Ken Blanchard . . . customer-value-driven company:*
Ken Blanchard, *Inside Guide, Customer Service: Customer Service in the 1990s*, Winter 1989, p. 17.

243   *. . . a nonprofit medical facility in California . . . a review card:*
Gail Collins, "Courtesy Call," *Self*, December 1989, pp. 87–88.

244   *BASF Corporation uses Quality Improvement Teams . . . recurrence of the problem:*
Manfred Buller, "Quality Improvement Process at BASF Polymers Group," in *Case Studies in Service Quality. When America Does It Right*, ed. Jay W. Spechler (Norcross, GA: Industrial Engineering and Management Press Institute of Industrial Engineers, 1988), pp. 55–63.

244–45   *The Metropolitan Life Insurance Company . . . QIT's performance:*
John J. Falzon, "Met Life's Quest for Quality," in *Case Studies in Service Quality. When America Does It Right*, ed. Jay W. Spechler (Norcross, GA: Industrial Engineering and Management Press Institute of Industrial Engineers, 1988), pp. 217–223.

245   *[D]esign quality as a forethought . . . " . . . this service?":*
Leonard L. Berry, David R. Bennett, Carter W. Brown, *Service Quality. A Profit Strategy for Financial Institutions* (Homewood, IL: Dow Jones-Irwin, 1989).

247   *Vincent A. Sarni . . . PPG employees:*
"The Conference Board Management Briefing," *Marketing*, December 1989/January 1990.

248   *Bubbling Bath & Tub Works . . . " . . . been eliminated":*
Paul B. Brown, "For You, Our Valued Customer," *Inc.*, January 1990, pp. 108–109.

248   *IBM uses a rigorous . . . final selection:*
Sally R. Luce, *Building Quality through People* (Ottawa: The Conference Board of Canada, September 1985, Report 03-85), p. 20.

248   *Procter & Gamble . . . company's customers:*
Patricia Sellers, "How to Handle Customers' Gripes," *Fortune*, October 24, 1989, p. 96.

249   *One such series of system-wide audits . . . research data:*
Craig Cina, "Creating an Effective Customer Satisfaction Program," *Journal of Services Marketing*, Winter 1989, p. 12.

249–50   *In* The Service Advantage *. . . waiters will see them, and so on":*
Karl Albrecht, *The Service Advantage. How to Identify and Fulfill Customer Needs* (Homewood, IL: Dow Jones-Irwin, 1990).

250   *IBM, for example, puts out a company publication . . . younger employees:*
Terence E. Deal and Allan A. Kennedy, *Corporate Cultures* (Don Mills, Ontario: Addison-Wesley, 1982), p. 39.

Chapter 10   Tracking Your Performance

253–54   *Masaaki Imai, in his book* Kaizen *. . . performance measurement:*
Masaaki Imai, *Kaizen: The Key to Japan's Competitive Success* (New York: Random House, 1986), p. 3.

254   *The Conference Board . . . consultants' studies:*
The Conference Board Marketing Briefing, September, 1989.

254–55   *Frank A. J. Gonsalves . . . product image among target customers:*
Frank A. J. Gonsalves, "Achieving Customer Satisfaction through Effective Linkages Between Measures of Performance," speech presented to the Manufacturers Institute, November 16, 1989, Miami, Florida.

255   *In* Total Customer Service *. . . satisfaction measures:*
William H. Davidow and Bro Uttal, *Total Customer Service: The Ultimate Weapon* (New York: Harper & Row, 1989), p. 196.

255   *Davidow and Uttal observe . . . " . . . expectations":*
William H. Davidow and Bro Uttal, *Total Customer Service: The Ultimate Weapon* (New York: Harper & Row, 1989), p. 196.

255–56   *. . . the Campbell Soup Company . . . which it later dropped:*
Jared Mitchell, "Where Are They Now," *The Globe and Mail Report on Business Magazine*, December 1989, p. 109.

257   *At the Dow Chemical Company . . . with the product:*
Carl C. Thurman and Sam L. Smolik, "The Management of Product Stewardship," in *Case Studies in Service Quality. When America Does It Right,*

ed. Jay W. Spechler (Norcross, GA: Industrial Engineering and Management Press Institute of Industrial Engineers, 1988), pp. 65–68.

257   *Quality consultant Philip Crosby . . . " . . . goals and objectives":*
Philip Crosby, *Quality is Free* (New York: McGraw-Hill, Inc., 1979), p. 132.

258   *The Amway Grand Plaza Hotel . . . would recommend:*
William H. Davidow and Bro Uttal, *Total Customer Service: The Ultimate Weapon* (New York: Harper & Row, 1989), p. 203.

258   *. . . at Herman Miller . . . level of quality:*
Ray Pukanic and Dick Holm, "The Herman Miller Quality Audit: A Corporate Report Card," in *Case Studies in Service Quality. When America Does It Right,* ed. Jay W. Spechler (Norcross, GA: Industrial Engineering and Management Press Institute of Industrial Engineers, 1988), pp. 175–183.

259   *General Electric has invested millions of dollars . . . " . . . features and preferences":*
John Thackery, "GE's Service Ace," *Across the Board,* September, 1989, p. 37.

260   *According to Dick Berry and Carol Suprenant . . . follow-up procedures:*
Dick Berry and Carol Suprenant, "Defusing the Complaint Time Bomb," *Sales and Marketing Management,* July 11, 1977, p. 40.

260   *Owens-Illinois Glass Container . . . fair to all concerned:*
Bernard L. Keating, "Owens-Illinois: The Best at What We Do," in *Case Studies in Service Quality. When America Does It Right,* ed. Jay W. Spechler (Norcross, GA: Industrial Engineering and Management Press Institute of Industrial Engineers, 1988), pp. 187–192.

206–61   *Armco Steel is one company . . . " . . . are settled":*
Charles R. Day, Jr., "Shouldering Customer Complaints Needn't Turn Knuckles White," *Industry Week,* January 9, 1978, p. 61.

261   *Winnebago Industries . . . to its attention:*
Ronald W. Post and Randal L. Fingarson, "Quality Service Program," in *Case Studies in Service Quality. When America Does It Right,* ed. Jay W. Spechler (Norcross, GA: Industrial Engineering and Management Press Institute of Industrial Engineers, 1988), pp. 294–303.

261–62   *One study undertaken by Sales & Marketing Management . . . will judge you:*
Cited in Dick Berry and Carol Suprenant, "Defusing the Complaint Time Bomb," *Sales & Marketing Management,* July 11, 1977, p. 40.

262   *Strict time standards . . . within five days:*
Donald B. Berryman, "A New Commitment to the Customer," in

Case Studies in Service Quality. When America Does It Right, ed. Jay W. Spechler (Norcross, GA: Industrial Engineering and Management Press Institute of Industrial Engineers, 1988), pp. 436–443.

262–63   *At first our customers . . . our competitors were not:*
Personal interview with author.

263   *. . . IBM, a leader in the use of benchmarking . . . these tasks:*
Robert C. Camp, *Benchmarking: The Search For Industry's Best Practices that Lead to Superior Performance* (Milwaukee: Quality Press, American Society For Quality Control, 1989), pp. 254–264.

263–64   *David T. Kearns . . . value creation process:*
Competitive Benchmarking, What It Can Do For You (pamphlet), Xerox Corporation, 1987, p. 2.

264   *Benchmarking was a vital part of the GTE . . . from suppliers:*
D. Otis Wolkins, "Creating a Culture for Quality Improvement at GTE," in *Case Studies in Service Quality. When America Does It Right,* ed. Jay W. Spechler (Norcross, GA: Industrial Engineering and Management Press Institute of Industrial Engineers, 1988), pp. 535–542.

265   *Lawrence S. Pryor . . . competitive advantage:*
Lawrence S. Pryor, "Benchmarking: A Self-Improvement Strategy," *The Journal of Business Strategy,* November/December, 1989.

265   *. . . some industry observers believe that AT&T . . . withdraw from the market:*
Beating the Competition: A Practical Guide to Benchmarking, Kaiser Associates, Inc., 1988, p. 11.

265–66   *Woodward's, the department store . . . specialty shops:*
Philip Marchand, "Last of the Line," *The Globe and Mail Report on Business Magazine,* June 1989, p. 82.

266   *Business consultant Timothy R. Furey . . . productivity improvements:*
Timothy R. Furey, "Benchmarking: The Key to Developing Competitive Advantage in Mature Markets," *Planning Review,* September/October 1987, pp. 30–31.

267   *One company in the electrical . . . promote its products:*
Beating the Competition: A Practical Guide to Benchmarking, Kaiser Associates, Inc., 1988, pp. 132–135.

267   *When the internal legal group . . . reduced costs:*
Beating the Competition: A Practical Guide to Benchmarking, Kaiser Associates, Inc., 1988, pp. 159–160.

268–69   *Robert C. Camp . . . Recalibrate benchmarks . . . comparison process:*
Robert C. Camp, *Benchmarking: The Search for Industry Best Practices that Lead to Superior Performance,* eds. Jeanine L. Lau and Tammy Griffin

(Milwaukee, WI: American Society for Quality Control [ASQC]).
Reprinted with the permission of ASQC.

270   *Esso Chemical Canada . . . accuracy of documentation:*
Michelle Ramsay, "Esso Chemical Canada—In Search of PD Excellence," *Purchasing,* August 23, 1989, p. 32.

270   *Depending on the nature . . . variables:*
Biff Motley, "Community Bank Strategies, Developing a Customer Service Index," *Bank Marketing,* May 1985, p. 6.

271   *3M's transportation department . . . claims problems:*
Roy W. Mayeske, "Improving Service Quality in Transportation," in *Case Studies in Service Quality. When America Does It Right,* ed. Jay W. Spechler (Norcross, GA: Industrial Engineering and Management Press Institute of Industrial Engineers, 1988), pp. 401–411.

272   *The York Engineering Center . . . fifth year:*
Michael B. Overstreet, "A Service Delivery Measurement and Improvement Program," in *Case Studies in Service Quality. When America Does It Right,* ed. Jay W. Spechler (Norcross, GA: Industrial Engineering and Management Press Institute of Industrial Engineers, 1988), pp. 481–490.

273   *The Financial Products Group . . . staffing attributes, 4.65:*
Biff Motley, "Community Bank Strategies, Developing a Customer Service Index," *Bank Marketing,* May 1985, p. 6.

274   *Sherry Khan . . . around the world:*
Michelle Ramsay, "Esso Chemical Canada—In Search of PD Excellence," *Purchasing,* August 23, 1989, pp. 31–32.

274–75 *Chrysler began a CSI . . . J. D. Power and Associates:*
Chuck Halsig, Dealer Education Manager, Chrysler, "Motivating to Improve Customer Service," speech presented at Customer Satisfaction Measurement Conference, February 26, 1989, Atlanta, Georgia. Cosponsored by American Society for Quality Control and American Marketing Association.

277   *The categories for evaluation . . . customer satisfaction:*
Malcolm Baldrige National Quality Awards Guidelines, 1988, pp. 17–18.

277–78 *Stanley C. Gault . . . "America's Most Admired Corporations":*
"Leaders of the Most Admired," *Fortune,* January 29, 1990, p. 42.

278   *The BASF Corporation . . . recurring errors:*
Manfred Buller, "Quality Improvement at BASF Polymers Group," in *Case Studies in Service Quality. When America Does It Right,* ed. Jay W.

Spechler (Norcross, GA: Industrial Engineering and Management Press Institute of Industrial Engineers, 1988), pp. 55–63.

279 *Telecommunications giant Northern Telecom Canada . . . quality standard:*
Keith Powell, "Quality is Not Free," speech delivered to the Institute for International Research "Total Quality Conference," June 1–2, 1988, p. 1.

280 *In the early 1980s, the Bank of California . . . greatly increased:*
Sid Ingle and Nima Ingle, *Quality Circles in Service Industries* (Englewood Cliffs, NJ: Prentice-Hall, 1983), p. 236.

281 *At Du Pont . . . profitability for Du Pont:*
Patricia Sellers, "Getting the Customers to Love You," *Fortune,* March 13, 1989, pp. 38–40.

281 *AMP Inc., a large producer . . . to 8 percent:*
The Race to Quality Improvement, Advertisement appearing in *Fortune* magazine, [N.d.].

282–83 *"The key to long-term success . . . portfolio managers":*
Quoted in Paul M. Hirsch, "Heroes of the Long Run," *Across the Board,* January/February, 1990, p. 57.

Index